Community Literacy and the Rhetoric of Public Engagement

Community Literacy and the Rhetoric of Public Engagement

Linda Flower

Southern Illinois University Press
Carbondale

13   4 3 2

Library of Congress Cataloging-in-Publication Data
Flower, Linda.
 Community literacy and the rhetoric of public engagement / Linda
Flower.
   p. cm.
Includes bibliographical references and index.
ISBN-13: 978-0-8093-2852-9 (alk. paper)
ISBN-10: 0-8093-2852-6 (alk. paper)
 1. Literacy—Social aspects—Case studies. 2. Literacy—Social aspects—Pennsylvania—Pittsburgh. 3. Literacy programs—Case studies.
4. Literacy programs—Pennsylvania—Pittsburgh. 5. Intercultural
communication—Case studies. 6. Intercultural communication—
Pennsylvania—Pittsburgh. 7. English language—Rhetoric—Study and
teaching—Case studies. 8. English language—Rhetoric—Study and
teaching—Pennsylvania—Pittsburgh. I. Title.

LC149.F56 2008
302.2'244—dc22   2007036746

Printed on recycled paper.♻
The paper used in this publication meets the minimum requirements of
American National Standard for Information Sciences—Permanence of
Paper for Printed Library Materials, ANSI Z39.48-1992. ∞

For Wayne Peck, Joyce Baskins, Tim Flower, Lorraine Higgins,
Elenore Long, and all the Community Literacy Center writers and mentors.

Contents

Acknowledgments

This book is more than anything an acknowledgment of the work of others. I feel privileged to have been a part of the people who made up the Community Literacy Center. It was a source of lasting relationships, joyously exhausting experiences, and intellectual inspiration that became a seedbed for new ideas. This book is deeply and particularly indebted to the vision of Wayne Campbell Peck, Joyce Baskins, Timothy Flower, Lorraine Higgins, and Elenore Long and to the writing and imagination of ten years of teenagers, community neighbors, and college mentors. And it has been shaped as well by valued colleagues like Shirley Brice Heath, Mike Rose, Eli Goldblatt, Glynda Hull, Amanda Young, Ellen Cushman, Tom Deans, Dave Coogan, and others whose own work in building and writing about transformative community relationships has helped me understand what is possible and indeed what we were up to.

As a writer, I am most grateful for the comments various people have made on this manuscript, particularly the good advice of Dave Coogan, Alan Friedman, Lorraine Higgins, Susan Jarratt, Ian Rawson, Mike Rose, and Ira Shor. Elenore Long has been an intellectually and personally generous reader, giving me comments, encouragement, and insight as she completed her own comprehensive look at literacy. And Tim Flower's proofreading marginalia made editing almost fun.

Figure 6.1 from *Problem Solving Strategies for Writing in College and Community* was used with permission from Thomson Learning. A version of chapter 6 previously appeared as "Intercultural Inquiry and the Transformation of Service" in *College English*. Copyright 2002 by the National Council of Teachers of English. Used with permission. A version of chapter 7 previously appeared as "Talking across Difference: Intercultural Rhetoric and the Search for Situated Knowledge" in *College Composition and Communication*. Copyright 2003 by the National Council off Teachers of English. Used with permission.

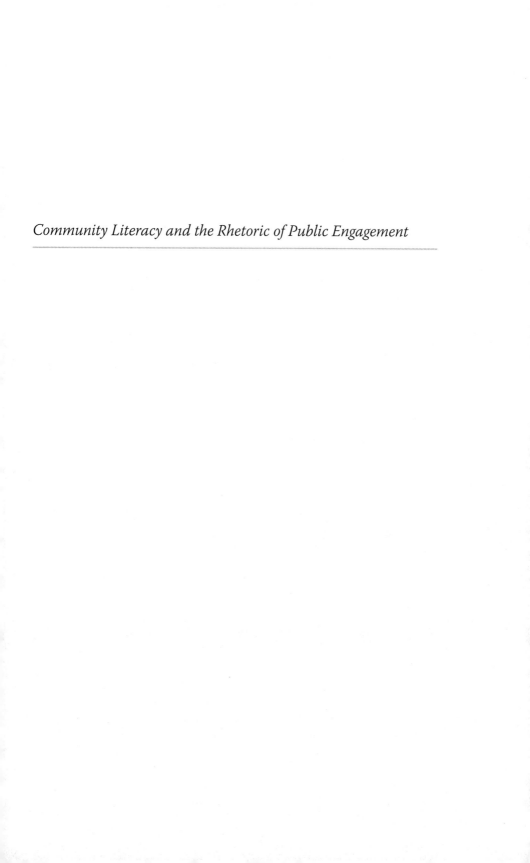

Community Literacy and the Rhetoric of Public Engagement

Prologue: The Rhetoric of Engagement

The call to social, political, and cultural engagement has exerted a magnetic influence on the emerging field of rhetoric and composition, which responded with not one but a family of rhetorics. Since the 1990s, the dominant paradigm within this academically sponsored rhetoric of engagement has been the discourse of cultural critique. However, its roots go back to a powerful historical tradition of engaged rhetors that claimed the Hebrew prophets and Jesus, as well as Karl Marx, Martin Luther King, and Paulo Freire. The work of more contemporary academic writers has modeled a powerful rhetoric of resistance that begins in a profound critique of forces that oppress and dehumanize; of forces that are embedded in the complacent normalcy of the status quo. It is a discourse that is desperately needed.

And the assertive, deconstructive discourse of academic cultural critique has brought socially and politically attuned thinking into classrooms and scholarship—in a way that gentle persuasion would have never achieved. It has created a powerful art, a rhetorical techné of analysis that borrows tools from literary criticism, history, and sociology. Its complex discourses, built around deconstruction and critique, theorizing, antifoundational and counterhegemonic resistance, tend to define themselves in terms of what they stand against—oppression, power, patriarchy, ideology. The situation demands no less. At the same time, the broader, historical tradition of engagement, in which critique is rooted, was *also* marked by an insistent vision of social, political, and spiritual transformation. And that vision demands even more of us.

The effort to discover and describe, to enact and revise what a *transformative more* could be is one of the most energetically exploratory agendas to emerge in our field. Working to integrate theory and practice, this transformative experiment is showing up in critical pedagogy, multicultural studies, service learning, in public rhetoric research, in special interest groups linking theory to local action, and in web sites and list serves drawing students and citizens, public intellectuals and ordinary people into rhetorical democracy (Shor & Pari, 1999; Anzaldua, 1987; Deans, 2000; Weisser, 2002; Cushman, 1999; Roberts-Miller, 2004; Hauser & Grim, 2004). What these experiments seek is a way to conduct a clear-eyed, historically grounded, intellectually rigorous *critique* of others and ourselves and at the same time to imagine and act on a *vision of transformation*. Such a vision would draw us by its rich articulation of possibility, its self-critical negotiation with experience, and its feet-on-the-ground willingness to act, revise, and act again.

The rhetoric of engagement depends on a family of discourses, each able to do certain things uniquely well and each ideally aware of its limitations (Long, in press). The dominant discourses of engagement in composition have indeed taught our students and us how to *speak up* as an expressive practice and how to *speak against* something with the techniques of discourse analysis and critique. But this is not enough, for they do not teach us how to *speak with* others or to *speak for* our commitments in a nonfoundational way. It is here in exploring such a discourse *with* others and *for* a revisable image of transformation that community literacy tries to make its contribution to a new rhetoric of public engagement.

Engaging with Difference

The search for more public forms of engagement has pushed many scholars and students in rhetoric and composition studies into unfamiliar territory. Once one steps beyond academic analysis and critique, perhaps the most significant aspiration and dilemma is how to relate to others—especially to marginalized or culturally diverse "Others"—across chasms of difference. For educators, the problem is not merely theoretical; it means figuring out how to construct a rhetorical space that can support transformative relationships. The work emerging in classrooms, communities, and publics offers different models of this space but some shared insights.

This space must be both political *and* personal—an encounter with the lived reality of others and a caring search for understanding, translated into a commitment to change (Cushman, 1998; Goldblatt, 2005; Schutz & Gere, 1998). To rest in the mere personal puts one on the slippery slope of philanthropy and charity that preserves the status of giver and receiver, expert and client (Flower, 1997a; Gabor, 2006). It allows one to ignore or evade the larger social systems and logics that create a world of "Others" in the first place. So engagement with difference can start in a contact zone where differences are made visible and where assumptions and identities are called into question. Its classroom can be a safe house that nurtures discussion.

But an active engagement with difference also requires a second step that resists easy consensus, confronts conflicts, and accepts the necessity of civil dissensus (Harris, 1989; Trimbur, 1989). It needs a space not only for examining competing values, histories, assumptions, and goals but for actually negotiating a common life—one that accepts, even highlights, rather than avoids differences (Flower, Long, Higgins, 2000; Spellmeyer, 1993).

Going Public

In addition, and in perhaps the greatest break with the modern discipline of English, this engagement is being reimagined within a public space (Coogan, 2006a; Higgins, Flower, Long, 2006; Weisser, 2002). In the language of contemporary rhetoric, one enters into sociability with strangers (Warner, 2005). The process can start in the classroom, which becomes a training ground for intellectual engagement. In the tradition of classical rhetoric, one studies the artful speech that gives persuasive eloquence to values in public affairs and develops a rhetoric of citizenship based on wise judgment (Atwill, 1998; Cooper and Fretz, 2006; Herzberg, 2000; Wells, 1996). For some educators, the classroom is itself this public space of negotiation, drawing students to see their own speaking and writing as a political act as they engage with the authority of assigned texts by exploring competing interpretations or with one another by affirming a contested identity, such as working class, gay, black, feminist, or learning disabled (Spellmeyer, 1993). But for many educators, this search for both a new rhetoric and relationships that are more diverse has led outside the classroom. Here students no longer study public discourse or community writing from arm's length but become writers and researchers with those groups (Adler-Kassner, Crooks, & Watters, 1997; Deans, 2000). Researchers may draw their subjects into a partnership that goes public in policy discussions and statements (Higgins & Brush, 2006). In community-based service learning projects, one uses the role of student, mentor, teacher, researcher, or activist to move beyond the academy and form working relationships across differences of race, class, culture, gender, age, status, or discourse. Many of these community projects then seize the power of publication, art, or multimedia to gain a hearing (Cushman, 2006; Flower, 2003; Heath & McLaughlin, 1993; Heath & Smyth, 1999; Hull & James, 2007; Robinson, 1990; Rousculp, 2006). Still other approaches move more directly to activism and community organizing (Coogan, 2006b; Goldblatt, 2005; 2007).

This emerging rhetoric of public engagement has already discovered some of the challenges to achieving real engagement (Cushman, 2006). For instance, teachers work to locate the public dialogues their students might enter only to find that public spaces are unstable spaces. A public (like a community) is constructed, not found—a symbolic space that comes into being when issues of mutual concern call people into existence as a public, and some people accept the invitation (Grabill, 2001; Warner, 2005). Sometimes that call fails—no one listens. Then rhetoric becomes a mere assignment in the genre of "public writing"—letters to a nonexistent editor or readers, an exercise in convention not conversation (Wells, 1996). But assume the best case: one enters a live controversy in partnership with community partners who have a chair at the table. Even then, communities and public issues have local histories, which well-intended academic partners may ignore to their peril. The public document or the well-designed service learning report may follow the same route to oblivion if it is not preceded by a collaborative investigation into the conversation it is trying to enter (Coogan, 2006b). And the public dialogue itself can be a mere rerun of familiar abstractions, masking divergent understanding and lived realities, unless we can uncover the situated and experiential meanings that support understanding (Flower, 2003). Nevertheless, a growing record of public experiments—like outspoken black women (Royster, 1995), irrepressible activist educators (Kates, 2001), and the new historical pictures of those unsettling Sophists (Jarratt, 1991)—are opening up the road for a new generation of educators.

Engaging around Inquiry

As the rhetoric of engagement moves us out of closed academic conversations, classroom conventions, or service-learning "assignments" and into the unruly dynamics of a live public sphere, the aspiration to combine more profound relationships with genuine transformative power becomes a live option—and our greatest challenge. We discover that familiar academic models of critique, advocacy, and adversarial argument are not the only or even best guides to social change (Roberts-Miller, 2004). To begin, standing in common cause *against* something can produce comrades in arms. But dialogue *with* culturally different others must start in inquiry. It takes an active search for diversely situated knowledges and experiential meanings to understand not only one another but also the social problems we face together. In the spirit of Paulo Freire, the purpose of dialogue is not to achieve a warm *feeling* of mutuality. It is a search for understandings that can transform reality. In this context of posing, interpreting, and acting on problems, speaking *for* commitments becomes a transformative rhetorical act by drawing a public into a new discourse of intercultural inquiry.

Community Literacy

This book has two stories to tell. One is an account of community literacy in action—a documentary of a collaborative, community/university experiment in literate practices that support intercultural inquiry. It is grounded in the experience of the Community Literacy Center (CLC) in its Pittsburgh, Pennsylvania, community, its people, and intercultural relationships; in the writing and insights of its teenagers, mentors, and staff; and in the best-laid educational plans that translated into unexpected outcomes over a decade with this continuing work in progress (chapters 1 and 2). It is the story of college mentors trying to forge identities and new roles in an intercultural partnership (chapter 4) and of educators and students developing and naming community-savvy, problem-solving strategies for intercultural inquiry and building situated knowledge (chapters 6 and 7).

The CLC experience also produced a second, theoretical account of community literacy as a distinctive rhetoric of engagement. It starts in a tension between the dominant images of social engagement and empowerment found in composition studies and the clearly different, strikingly rhetorical action and rhetorical agency we were seeing in urban teenagers, urban residents, and college mentors (chapters 3 and 5). So how does the alternative rhetoric of community literacy actually work? Here we will look closely at how community literacy creates a local public sphere organized around intercultural inquiry and how it uses its capacity as a counterpublic force to transform both understandings and the process of inquiry itself (chapters 1, 8, and 9).

This inquiry into the work of *local* publics has in turn helped shape an observation-based theory of the rhetorical agency of marginalized people and an argument for the role that privileged partners can play in affirming and documenting such agency and its insights (chapter 9).

This account, like the practice of the CLC, has been profoundly influenced by the prophetic pragmatism of John Dewey (1929/1988) and Cornel West (1993)—that is, by its aspiration to transformative personal and public practice married to an insistently experimental attitude that located meaning not in abstractions but outcomes. This work is equally shaped by the performative tradition of rhetoric as a cognitive/interpretive/meaning-making *and* a social/public/dialogic/persuasive act. Even as we felt immersed in the generative chaos and constant reinvention that mark community projects, these frameworks helped us read our experience as an experiment, a set of outcomes, and an argument for what an intercultural rhetoric of engagement could be and do. And for what it requires of us.

In this book, I argue that a prophetic, pragmatic, and intercultural rhetoric of public engagement can teach us two things. First, it reveals the often-unacknowledged rhetorical agency of the voiceless and powerless. That is, it challenges the conventional images of agency focused on either the power and will of charismatic individuals or on the social structures that confer the authority to speak and be heard to a privileged few. Community literacy reveals a contrasting image of rhetorical agency built not on advocacy, authority, or expressiveness but on inquiry. In it, ordinary people justify their place at the table by making two choices. One is a willingness to engage with rival interpretations, attempting to understand a problem rather than advocate an interested position. The other is going public, choosing to stay in dialogue with alternative realities, and working to articulate their own even as they seek a new negotiated understanding.

A rhetoric of public engagement can teach us a second thing: it challenges current images of a media-controlled public sphere with its closely observed accounts of *local counterpublics* that work by circulating ideas and identities (Fraser, 1990; Hauser, 1999; Warner, 2005). In contrast to the large counterpublics of contemporary theory, the *local, inter*cultural publics of community literacy work by circulating new models of dialogue across difference. And such local publics offer university partners a distinctive space for engagement in which we, too, can act as rhetors—not as the experts with answers but as orchestrators and documenters of a more just, generative, and transformative public dialogue.

Part 1

A Community/University Collaboration

A book on community literacy calls out for definitions—just what do you mean by literacy, and what, among the loudly competing images of community, do you have in mind? We, however, start with Mrs. Baskins and a group of college mentors in a van ride touring both an urban neighborhood and its multiple symbolic communities. If we look at how these symbolic constructions do their work (and how university visitors might find a role in them), community literacy emerges as a rhetorical action that calls forth a local public and creates a counterpublic structured around intercultural inquiry.

The notion of literacy here is likewise defined as an action and a practice: a literate action taken to support agency, understanding, and justice; and a rhetorical act built on the social ethic; and a strategic practice of intercultural inquiry. Definitional statements like the one that introduces chapter 2 give us a hypothesis to test and reflect on. The chapter tries to unpack its terms of art by locating them in the unfolding Risk and Stress project. From its start, with an academic, theoretical version of a community problem, the project initiated a dialogue with urban teens who significantly rewrote this representation of urban stress into a story of risk and respect. Along the way, the strategic practices of community literacy (its collaborative planning, story-behind-the-story, rival hypotheses, options, and outcomes) shaped the dialogue. Then the practice of community conversations took these teenage accounts public. In the months that followed, it morphed into a published "Wake Up Call" to adults, a teen-produced CLC video, a training video, and an interactive computer program used to initiate a dialogue about risk and gangs in an urban high school. Over the history of this inquiry, the meanings of risk and stress were transformed as more people entered the dialogue and explored them in new contexts. And we see how the strategic practices of community literacy support inquiry at the same time they reveal the rhetorical agency of both community and university partners.

1　*What Is Community Literacy?*

Mark is a teenage writer at the Community Literacy Center, or, as he would say, a "rap artist waiting to be discovered." Through rap, Mark imagines and sings of a world in which teenagers play powerful roles and have valuable messages to tell. . . . He is a bright and resourceful teenager who, like many African-American males, finds little that interests him in school and is frequently suspended. In his lyrics and his life, Mark flirts with the possibility of joining a gang and finding a group that "cares for him."

—Wayne C. Peck, Linda Flower, and
Lorraine Higgins, "Community Literacy"

The purpose of this rap is to tell what really happens in school between students, teachers, and vice principals, and what causes suspension.

—Mark Howard, introduction, "Communication Breakdown"

The point is that there is a gang problem and until people start to accept it there can't be anything done about it. Instead of denying, . . . try to get them together to find out why they feel they have to join and be a member of a gang.

—Mark Howard, "A Usual Day in Wilkinsburg"

A Space for Dialogue across Difference

This is a book about social engagement and personal agency expressed in an experiment in local public rhetoric. It asks, How does one fashion a rhetoric of making a difference within an intercultural community? Paradoxically, this hope of making a difference collaboratively begins in the inescapable dilemma of difference and the desire to bridge that troubled water. America's rhetoric of change and its call to community is rooted in attempts to confront the divisive and unjust effects of social disparity. The premise of community literacy is that such a rhetoric calls us to speak out *about* and *for* silenced voices. But, in addition, it calls us to talk *with* "others" across gulfs we may not always know how to cross.

Unfortunately, significant talk across cultural difference is considerably more demanding than speaking one's own mind on social issues. And little in our schooling—in rhetoric or composition curricula, in learning to write arguments or to read literature—prepares us to enter such a discourse. There is even less support in our patterns of public life, dominated by the rhetoric of advocacy and interest politics. And in a socially stratified society, superficial or isolated encounters with "others" are not likely to produce significant, change-making conversations. So where does one find the space, and how does one create the kind of "community" that can support a sustained dialogue across difference? The story of community literacy that I have to tell grows out of an experiment in creating such a space and form of literacy within a particular urban community. It began innocently enough by coining a name for its specific focus—*community* literacy. But as we soon discovered, that term was both a source of deeper meanings and a bundle of revealingly contradictory notions.

My inquiry is grounded in the history and practices of Pittsburgh's Community Literacy Center (CLC). Initiated as a community/university project, it found itself already firmly located in three distinctive kinds of community—one was the historic, racial, spatial network of inner-city "community folk." The second was a network of institutions—neighborhood, social, and academic organizations. The third, referred to as the Greater Pittsburgh metropolitan community, was primarily a projection of a political imagination, an entity held together by mutual interests and warm metaphors. It is important to realize that communities like these are not physical but *symbolic* entities, constructed for a complex mix of reasons around affinities rather than visible borders, which means they are notoriously hard to pin down as an identifiable thing, a stable group, or a discourse with explicit defining features. In fact, the most significant feature of a community is not what or where it is (with its shifting features and overlapping boundaries) but how it *functions*. The meaning of a symbolic community is in how it works and the consequences it produces.

This book is about a fourth community that, just like the urban, civic, and organizational entities with which it rubs shoulders, is a symbolic construction. But unlike them, it is drawn together by the practice of community literacy. The chief function of this imagined collective is to create a distinctive kind of rhetorical community—an intercultural, problem-focused, local public sphere designed for talking with others across difference. So on one level, I want to start with the obvious question: just what is the "community" of community literacy? But in doing so and looking at an example of community literacy in practice, I want to pose a more fundamental question: How can such a symbolic community and its kind of literacy actually function? And to what end?

The "Community" Tour

We are standing on the steps of the Community House, a historical and neighborhood landmark. Mrs. Baskins is about to take a group of Carnegie Mellon University students, soon to be mentors at the Community Literacy Center, on their introductory van ride around Pittsburgh's Northside. As the youth coordinator and matriarch of the center, she is called "Queen" by Community House friends (in playful reference to the *African Queen*) and "Msz. B." by the black and white teenagers, who seem magnetically attracted to her imposing presence and her humorous warmth. If you look south, just across the Allegheny River, you can see the expensive new North Shore condominiums, the downtown business towers, and the cultural district inhabited by the "suits." Over there, people use the word *community* to refer to a civic body—a metropolitan area bound by common and competing political, economic, and social interests. But over here, a strong Northside pride of place connects blacks and whites in a more local, familial sense of community.

The Community House, a five-story, 1890 brick building and historic settlement house, stands in the middle of what Northsiders call the Flats. Down by the Allegheny River, a few blocks from where we stand, is the church whose tunnel to the riverbank was a stop on the Underground Railway. From the door of the Community House you can look out across a city park and see a cluster of houses still called Deutschtown, where Germans settled a century ago. Across Cedar Avenue is the deeply faded, red sign of Stedefords, the place to find old jazz, blues, and gospel as well as hip-hop and headphone music. On the corner are the yin and yang of neighborhood bars. On the left side, the rough-looking JR's bar, which visitors might hesitate to enter. On the right, the cheerful cut-glass door of Park House. (When folks said with a wink after choir practice that they were going to the "chapel," you knew where to meet up). Next door are the newsstand and White Tower restaurant, which never look all that appealing, but when police budgets get cut and drug sales rise, the number of brief visits by white college-age males seems to increase.

Looking north across another piece of the park is the great, imposing institutional presence of Allegheny General Hospital, slowly increasing its spread but still unable to displace the Garden Theatre with its adult movies (and white suburban clientele). Homeless people use the park to sleep and hold confabs. When the Community House Church has picnics under these big trees, homeless men who tentatively drop by are welcomed. They stay to help carry the folding tables back into the big gymnasium on the second floor.

On other margins of this large urban park, the mentors will ride past the institutions and areas that link the Northside to its metropolitan setting: the large Allegheny Community College, the Aviary, the Stadium, and the Mexican War streets—a semi-gentrified section of brick row houses with fancy doors, knockers, and lampposts, promoted in the 1980s as a great commute to downtown and as a good investment. Its residents live here with a commitment to urban neighborhoods and with the unkempt or boarded-up sister buildings next door and the next block over. A friendly gay bar, dark wood and fancy glass, is three doors away from a storefront BBQ, pumping out smoke that makes a passerby salivate. When Mrs. Baskins was president of the Central Northside Council in the 1970s, the problems of compatible diversity were always on the agenda.

To a visitor, the Flats seems both vibrant and distressed. Its visible historic, architectural, and institutional identities and its proud urban sense of self are tied to its political, economic fragmentation, where local leaders are more likely to bicker than organize, and small nonprofits struggle for pieces of the same small pie.

As the van rolls north up Federal Street, between the theater and the hospital, climbing up into the steep, narrow, often-cobbled streets on the hill, you are in the neighborhoods. Mrs. B. points out a big-porched Pittsburgh house on her old street. Folks talk about growing up here when every adult was your parent, and if you messed up, you would hear it from a neighbor, and the bad news (for you) would have already reached your folks by the time you got home. Now the streets are a patchwork of safe places and clusters the kids call "bad neighborhoods"—gang territories or hot spots of the underground economy that it is better not to walk down. You just need to know where to go.

Mrs. Baskins rolls down the window—she seems to know half the people on these streets. It is a neighborhood where people give companionable shouts from across the street and lean out of the car to carry on a little business— "How's your mother? . . . Oh, Ok . . . Did you still want to use the Friendship room on Wednesday for your committee meeting?" And when the teenagers make their first appearance at a literacy project, they get placed by Mrs. B. "Right, you're from up on Arch street. I know your Gran" or "Oh sure, I knew your Aunt Flo back in the day, when she was in the Community House summer camps"—and with a lowered chuckle, "She was a pistol!" Everybody seems to be a cousin of somebody you know. Nobody seems to pay much attention to last names that siblings frequently do not share; it is easier to identify teenagers by mother, grandmother, uncle, aunt, or street.

Oliver High School sits at the top of the Federal Street hill. There you are swept into the contrast between the social life carried on its loud jostling halls and the silence, tension, boredom, or restraint of its classrooms. It made the mentors (these usually white, usually suburban college students) begin to feel a little out of their element. Perry Traditional Academy, perched atop an adjoining hill, was the place to go if you want to "do school," but even there further education was more likely to be something talked up rather than planned for.

The tour redefined the term *mentor*—it told you that you were entering someone else's dynamic, intact world that did not feel a particular need for you or your gifts. You would not enter as an authority or celebrity but as an outsider. You would be accepted and valued not by your academic, economic, or middle-class status but by your ability to participate in the common life, the common concerns, and the shared struggle as adults and teenagers saw it.

What this tour of an urban community neighborhood didn't quite prepare you for was the strikingly hybrid community, built around talk, writing, reflection, persuasion, and performance, that would emerge inside the Community House when you and your teenage partner would try to get at the story-behind-the-story of risk, gangs, respect, work, and school in the life of these teenagers. That is, you would enter an inquiry in which most of the expertise lay with your teen. Your expertise would lie in your (still untested) ability to support a process of inquiry, reflection, and argument. Together, you would try to get multiple perspectives on this reality on the table and into words—in a dialogue, a newsletter, a video, a dramatization. These would lay the groundwork for the project's culminating public Community Conversation.

The Community Literacy projects take over the third floor. Everyone meets at the beginning and end of the session around the big table, and in between scatters to work on sofas, in the kitchen, or at the computers with two chairs that dot the walls. The publications lying around from last year's projects give a feel for the distinctly intercultural, *rhetorical* community you are entering.[1] One of them, called *Whassup with Suspension? The Real Scoop*, was published by the ARGUE project—a team of mentors and students (with first-hand experience) who wanted to improve the school suspension practices at Oliver High School. Lorraine Higgins, as a literacy leader, PhD student in rhetoric, and later director of the center, designed the ARGUE projects to turn argument theory into community practice.[2] The twelve-page printed booklet leads off with Mark Howard's rap, "Communication Breakdown," to "tell what really happened."

MISCOMMUNICATION

The purpose of this rap is to tell what *really* happens in school between students, teachers, and vice principals, and what causes suspension.

Communication Breakdown
Mark Howard

It started with two students in the class talking out of place
    The boy starts getting rude and got all up in the girls face
The girl didn't like it so she got up and yelled back
    The teacher told the girl, *Get up and sit down in the back*
She got up with no problem and then sat in the back chair

He had to be a pest so he started to look and stare
    At the girl to test her and try to make her mad
He said, *Respect me girl . . . and treat me like your dad!*
    She stood up and said, *Don't play . . . my dad got shot last year*
The teacher turned around just as the girl broke out in tears

    The teacher kicked her out and said, *Go straight to the VP*
The boy started laughing as the girl said *It wasn't me*
    The teacher didn't listen, even harder the girl cried
When she got to the office she found out the teacher lied

    She talked and talked and tried to tell him what's going on
The VP wouldn't listen but she kept going on and on
    The VP said, *You're lying 'cause that's not what I heard*
The teacher wouldn't lie so I'm going with the teacher's word
    The teacher said you tried to start a fight in the classroom
She said you threatened her then you said you would leave the room
    She also said you tried to pick a fight with another kid
So don't sit there and lie now, tell me what you really did

    She said, *It's hopeless, every time I tell you you say I lied*
The VP didn't listen and slowly the girl cried
    The VP said, *You're going home for about three days*
She shook her head as he said, *You'll learn from your wrong ways*

The point of this story—nobody pays attention
To a student 'cause they're young, now I may mention
   If the teacher would have took one minute and act like she cares
She would have saved a lot of time and a lot of tears
   Teachers prove students right just about every day
They automatically think their way is the right way

Same for the Vice Principal they don't listen too
You're guilty, you're suspended is the only thing they do
   On the other hand the girl was also wrong in her actions
She didn't have to get up and scream for satisfaction
   She could have told the teacher or even the principal
Instead she's in trouble suspended and sitting out of school
   The point of this story is lost communication
Make sure it's always there or you'll be on a vacation

On the page facing Mark's rap is Shay La Burke's "Commentary: Complications between Students, Teachers and Vice Principals" where she offers to "tell you about the different perspectives of the people in Mark's rap." Her prose tries to untangle the feelings of the teacher (who "wasn't sure of what happened," except that "the girl started to scream at everybody and cause more trouble"), the feelings of the female student (who "didn't get a chance to explain" and "now she has an attitude with the teacher and VP because she's missing out on the work she has in her classes"), and the frustrated VP (who "feels the student and teacher should've talked it out"). Shay La concludes with "Five Suggestions," which suggest what is *not* happening now, including the "radical" recommendations that

- The teacher and VP should try to explain why they are sending the student "out" and that perhaps they could
- Write out some plans on what could work out if the problem occurs and what to do to prevent it from getting worse.

Just to show that multiple voices are invited, the booklet includes a rather bad rap written by an English teacher, alongside a student survey in which 106 Oliver students overwhelmingly (91) recommended suspension for fighting—but not for cutting class (only 35 votes for it) or for teacher abuse (25 votes).

What the booklet cannot bring to life is the project's final Community Conversation, which turned text into dialogue. Downstairs in the Community House's filled-to-capacity, one-hundred-chair meeting room, Mark performed his rap to cheers and applause. The authors of a scenario "R.E.S.P.E.C.T. That

Is What It Means to Me" dramatized an encounter with a "screaming" teacher thrusting his finger into the face of a student—who responds this time to the all too-familiar gesture with his own style of physicality. Performances are followed by straight talk from teens who not only reveal rival readings of these problematic events and pose hard questions to adults but also offer options for action. These teen-written, teen-moderated Conversations draw an audience of adults from the community, the schools, the university, and civic organizations into a new kind of dialogue. Instead of defining urban teens as "the problem," they allow teens to pose a problem—as they see it—and draw adults into a discussion about their own adult role in creating and solving problems from suspension to risk, respect, and the effect of gangs *on* the youth of this community.

What Is Community Literacy?

Community literacy is a rhetorical practice for inquiry and social change.[3] Seen in its educational context, it, like other forms of critical literacy, is the heir to John Dewey's vision of progressive education, in which people learn things by a hands-on experiential and strenuously intellectual engagement with the world. We learn, Dewey argued, through active experimentation and reflection—approaching topics from science and technology to language and history as problem posers and problem-solvers. Taking an experimental stance to both received ideas and our own experience, we do not merely acquire knowledge; we make it through the process of inquiry. Dewey's radical call for participatory learning was inseparable from his arguments for participatory democracy, which depends on "communicated experience" (Dewey, 1916/1966, p. 87). He championed humanistic education not as a repository of received knowledge but "because of what it *does* in liberating human intelligence and human sympathy" and for its ability to connect "with the common interests of men as men" and "improve the life we live in common" (1916/1966, pp. 230, 191).

This stance, linking learning, liberation, and community, so controversial in Dewey's own time, has supported the even more politically engaged practice of critical literacy since the 1960s. Under the enormous influence of Paulo Freire's *Pedagogy of the Oppressed* (1962/1985) and his third-world literacy campaigns, critical literacy became associated with dissident politics, bringing our "common interests" with struggling people into college classrooms. At the same time, Freire's liberation theology—his profound respect for the humanity of dehumanized people and his visionary sense of possibility—was helping reshape classroom practice. Like Dewey, he argued that reading and writing should not be used to transmit and "bank" knowledge but as tools for dialogue and critical inquiry. The notable thing about his dialogic "culture circles" is that the learning is mutual; both teacher and student are questioning, envisioning, acting, and reflecting.

In his essay "What Is Critical Literacy?" Ira Shor's definition is succinct: critical literacy "questions the way things are and imagines alternatives"; or to be more precise, it challenges "the unequal status quo" (1999, pp. 24, 7).[4] It's what Patrick J. Finn (1999) calls "literacy with an attitude." However, once one goes beyond this statement, as Shor's essay makes clear, the academically based discourse of "critical literacy" is really a family of quite diverse literate practices. They range from political theorizing about language and education to analyzing the ideology that shapes texts and media, to designing basic writing and English as a Second Language (ESL) instruction around critical consciousness, to initiating community-based creative-writing programs, to organizing students and colleagues to take literate action on live issues from supporting free speech and social criticism in schools, to building a working class network in the academy, to lobbying against the exploitation of part-time college instructors. What holds this family together is an acute sense of social inequities resting on patterns of power and domination—plus a counterfaith in the power of language as symbolic action. That is, critical literacy sees literacy as a way to resist power, challenge injustice, and insist on alternative images of social and self-development.

Where the branches of the family begin to diverge is in the priorities and problems they pose to themselves and literate practices they use to respond to those problems. For example, in the tradition inspired by Marxist cultural analysis, to become critically literate is to become conscious of how one's language and identity have been historically and social constructed within in specific power relations. And this leads, as Shor puts it, to the question "How have we been shaped by the words we use and encounter? If language helps make us, how can we use and teach oppositional discourse so as to remake ourselves and our culture?" (1999, p. 1). In many college classrooms, versions of this question have shaped the practice of critical literacy into multilayered practices of textual and ideological analysis in which resistance is defined as critique.

But a settlement house (with a 3:00 P.M. group of urban teens just liberated from school) is not a classroom. Moreover, resistance that stopped with the critique of texts probably would not engage the hearts and minds of their community, much less remake the culture of teen life, the neighborhood, or the schools. The urban community Mrs. Baskins showed the mentors back at the beginning of our tour is the soul of "community" literacy, its reason for being, and the voice it seeks to amplify. As a result, this *community* branch of critical literacy is more closely identified with the tools of rhetoric and the traditions of African American struggle, where literacy gave a public voice to oppressed people and a tool to reinterpret their shared reality in their own words.

That said, we must also recognize the distinctive imprint of the university in this collaboration. Community literacy could be (but is not) another name for what Barton and Hamilton (1998) call "local literacies"—the diverse, daily forms of reading and writing used by working-class people, often overlooked or dismissed in our preoccupation with the elite literacies of school or business. The community literacy described here values but differs from the literacies of urban street corners, front porches, or churches used by community folk. It actively resists the vocationally oriented, acritical, limited literacy taught in urban working-class schools to community children as well as the bureaucratic language of clients, services, and regulations demanded by social service agencies. And it draws on but deliberately departs from the discourse of advocacy found in many grass-roots organizations.[5]

This community/university collaboration also gives community literacy a distinctive place in service-learning. In Tom Deans's three-panel portrait of community-focused classes, some focus on writing *about* the community, drawing on academic practices of research or critique (2000). Others, shaped by the traditions of volunteer service and of teaching students to write to real audiences, bring their skills to writing *for* the community—producing brochures, newsletters, and histories for civic organizations. Community literacy, Deans's exemplar of a third approach, draws on the traditions of rhetoric, pragmatism, and problem-solving to write *with* the community.

In a revealing comparative analysis of "community literacy studies" more generally, Elenore Long traces common values in these diverse accounts of "ordinary people going public" (in press). However, the theoretical framework she uses to guide this analysis uncovers profound differences (with significant consequences) within five formative elements: (1) the guiding metaphor (e.g., Is the public space imagined as an impromptu theater or a garden, a womb, or an intersection of discourses?); (2) the context that defines a "local" public, shaping what is an effective, even possible performance; (3) the tenor and affective register of the discourse; (4) the literate practices that shape discourse; and, perhaps the most insightful category, (5) the nature of rhetorical invention or the generative process by which people in these accounts respond to exigencies, such as getting around gatekeepers, affirming an identity, or taking a contested agency.

The practice, then, of community literacy (as we named the CLC's community/university experiment in 1990) exists within a network of images and literate practices. It is not simply the language of urban "others." Nor is it primarily an academic (literate) way of talking about others or a professional effort to speak for them, as needed and significant as these projects can be. The community literacy I am hoping to document is an intercultural dialogue *with others* on issues that *they* identify as sites of struggle. Community literacy happens at a busy intersection of multiple literacies and diverse discourses. It begins its work when community folk, urban teens, community supporters, college-student mentors, and university faculty start naming and solving problems *together*. It does its work by widening the circle and constructing an even more public dialogue across differences of culture, class, discourse, race, gender, and power shaped by the explicit goals of discovery and change. In short, in this *rhetorical model*, community literacy is a site for personal and public inquiry and, as Higgins, Long, and Flower (2006) argue, a site for rhetorical theory building as well.

John Dewey (1916/1966) reminds us that meaning resides in actions. The comparisons I have been sketching help us see the work of community literacy as a particular kind of literate *action*, defined by what it is trying to do and its alternatives. We can imagine these actions lying along two axes. One is the continuum from personal writing to public writing in which writers become increasingly engaged with others as collaborators, as audiences, as a community (see fig. 1.1). Writing personal narratives typically sits at the personal end of this *engagement* axis. By contrast, projects such as the CLC's STRUGGLE, the Berkeley/Oakland–based DUSTY, and Chicago's *Journal of*

Fig. 1. 1 Priorities for engagement and transformation

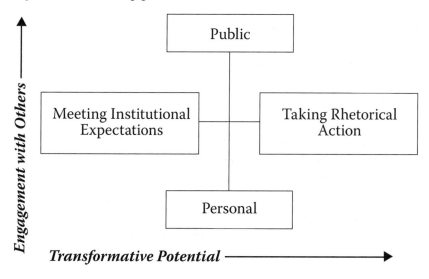

Ordinary People put a high priority on the public end of this continuum. In them, digital storytelling or poetry writing in housing projects is only one step in a process that leads to teen-adult dialogues in response, to neighborhood screenings of teenagers' multimedia stories, or to publication in newsletters and journals. Here personal literate actions draw writers into new levels of engagement with peers, parents, adults, and community.[6]

The second key continuum in figure 1.1 suggests how writers can move from meeting institutional expectations (e.g., writing to learn or fulfill the requirements of school or workplace) to taking rhetorical action (e.g., through community dialogues or community advocacy). This axis helps us think about the *transformative potential* of our literate actions. The stultifying, limited literacies demanded in urban schools, workplace training, and many workplaces (focused only on learning and playing by the rules) clearly pin a writer down on the meeting-institutional-expectations end of this axis with little hope of making a difference in either a personal or public arena. At elite institutions, on the other hand, doing critical analysis lets the writer move down this continuum into thinking about social problems. Yet, the academic work of analysis may still fall short of imagining or taking wider social action through writing or dialogue.

In practice, of course, the ends of these continua are not places to plop down but are descriptions of one's priorities or ends-in-view. As we will see, if community literacy writers are to do their work, they must still understand and negotiate institutional expectations (e.g., write Standard English and respond to authority figures they would persuade)—but not set correctness or compliance as their ultimate goal. And public, collaborative engagement often starts with but does not end with personal inquiry. Community literacy, then, attempts to move writers toward transformative action and collaborative engagement guided by a particular image of public and rhetorical action. These choices can be defined by the ways this symbolic or rhetorical community tries to function.

> *Community literacy is a form of literate action that allows:*
> - everyday people within the urban community to take agency in their lives and for their community;
> - everyday people from places of privilege to participate in this struggle for understanding and social justice.

> *Community literacy depends on the social ethic and strategic practice of intercultural rhetoric to:*
> - draw out the voices of the silenced and the expertise of marginalized people;

- draw people normally separated by difference into new roles as partners in inquiry;
- recognize and use difference in the service of discovery and change, transforming rather than erasing its conflicts and contradictions.

Community literacy is, in short, a working hypothesis about how we might construct a community that supports dialogue across difference. In the Risk and Respect project (chapter 2), we will look at what these aspirations for literate action might actually mean in practice. But before we leave the more tractable realm of theory, one might ask, Why do we need a new space or a different kind of community for such dialogue? Why does it seem to happen so rarely in the available civic, neighborhood, and institutional communities we have already encountered? One reason that we must continually search out spaces for intercultural inquiry lies, I propose, in how these communities function and in the relationships they create.

Some Available Versions of Community

A Civic Body

The metropolitan community of Greater Pittsburgh is a construction of Ohio River Valley geography, of political districting, and of ideology. Bound by a strong pride of place (Pittsburghers don't seem to leave even when the jobs do), by passions for icons, such as, the Pittsburgh Steelers, and by deep neighborhood roots (that can create equally deep divisiveness), this symbolic creation functions to say we are indeed a polity, a single social, economic, political body. The unofficial theme song of the Pirates baseball team (and thus Pittsburgh) at this time was Sister Sledge's hit *We Are Family*.

Pittsburgh's three major family foundations (the Howard Heinz Endowments, the R. K. Mellon Foundation, and the Grable Foundation) plus a collective called the Pittsburgh Foundation gave a face and a material force to the idea of a public body with family ties. They funded the major cultural, educational, and redevelopment initiatives in the city in this period, including the CLC. The educational director of the Heinz Foundation, Joseph Dominic, for example, was a valued longtime partner who not only supported but also challenged and shaped the CLC from his city perspective.

The Work of a Civic Body

In a democracy, this sense of community is so fundamental and valued it can go unquestioned. But for all its necessary political functions, the metropolitan civic body to which Northside urban teenagers or low-wage workers belong offers slim chances for dialogue. It is structured to do its business in response to competing interest groups. In assigning the role of citizen and resident to members, it creates relationships based on rights, services, and return on tax dollars. Far from being the solution, it can be part of the problem the other three communities confront.[7]

Politicians and service organizations often call on this political entity and its fictive unity because it not only justifies philanthropy (after all, we are all in this together) but also the exercise of power that lets those who possess power make decisions about and for those who do not. It papers over the savage inequalities that separate the haves from the have-nots, the urban from suburban, the schools with advanced-placement programs from those with metal detectors. Its unified economic development plans do not seem to distinguish between those families who are buffered against shifting economic winds from those who will be buffeted by every gust. It imagines relationships as cooperative and competitive interest groups. Its public forums are rarely a good place for significant talk with others.

However, this civic community, with its mix of ideals, oppressive fictions, and realities, can be a starting point for community action. It is against the fictions of this ideological construction (the community evoked by civic leaders, philanthropists, educational, medical, and social service institutions) that more concrete communities, described later, often draw together.

A Symbolic Neighborhood

When the Community House/Carnegie Mellon team launched its writing projects in 1990, it chose the term *community literacy* to signal a departure—to teenagers, the neighborhood, and the university—from the limited literacies and authoritarian culture of school. Some funders (spokespersons for the wider civic community) disliked the lowbrow connotations that come with "adult literacy." But the team chose to brandish the name as an argument that we needed to resee literacy as a rhetorical competence that is not based simply on reading and passive reception but on writing, argument, and public dialogue by members of the community—including its youth.

In this setting, the word *community* was loaded with unproblematic meaning for many members of Pittsburgh's large, primarily black, urban neighborhoods. It is an intimate, insider term the inner city, working-class people often apply to themselves and those in their circle of solidarity. *Community folk* is a term of endearment. The companion term *community organizations* is mostly used for grass-roots, neighborhood nonprofits, churches, and local action groups. It would not reference elite organizations like the opera society (in the way a service-learning center might), but it does include institutions like the eighty-year-old Community House. Its historic brick building with tall windows and fireplaces framed with dark wood mantels was built as a settlement house in 1916 like Jane Addams's Hull House in Chicago. It was a place where at different times in its long history, immigrant mothers came for milk, health care, and respite, where mill families could get cheap meals, where kids grew up in its "programs," where young black men played midnight basketball in the gym, where grass-roots groups met in the Community House rooms, and where blue-haired Presbyterian ladies—old Northsiders, too, and longtime members of the adjoined church—felt connected to the neighborhood across class and cultural differences.

In this context, the "community" stands in sharp relief to the "university" arriving with its vanload of white, middle-class, educated outsiders, short on savvy, long on good intentions, and comfortably invested in their own set of elite, academic, literate practices.

The Work of a Symbolic Neighborhood

Arising at the intersection of place, race, and history, the symbolic black neighborhood of community folk offers a sense of identity and bonding that draws on a shared sense of ill-defined oppression, a vibrant cultural style, and an ongoing cultural project of self-definition. It is in the face of the boisterous, assertive, black presence of teenagers that many mentors suddenly come to see themselves as the other, outsiders to a self-conscious, self-styling circle. In the adult world, white folks can be treated as sort of honorary members of this community, usually through church ties, longtime participation in the struggle, or self-identification. One thing that makes this possible is that the available roles and relationships in this community are variations of family built around the relations of real and fictive kinship, brothers and sisters by blood and by choice.

One has the sense in the work of ethnographers and literacy researchers, such as Shirley Brice Heath (1983), Carol Stack (1974), Ralph Cintron (1997), and Ellen Cushman (1999), that they became at times part of this extended family. This openness was indeed part of the ethos of the Community House and Community House Church. But as I have argued elsewhere, this is not a role that most academic activists, much less students, are likely (or maybe even aspire) to achieve in normal projects or the limited time for contact. In the search for a community in which to talk across difference, this is not the opening readily available to most educators and students.

Symbolic Constructions

If *community* works as a comfortable family of meanings on the Northside, it is a much more problematic term in other quarters. For instance, its connotation of warm, happy solidarity has been rightly criticized for masking a habit of silencing minority or dissident voices within its communal grasp. We need to recognize, Jeffrey Grabill argues, that a community is not a physical group of like-minded people but is instead a "symbolic construction" built around affinities that include race, ethnicity, spatiality, or ideas (2001, p. 92). Moreover, he argues, the most interesting thing about communities is that they have to be constructed—and often with some difficulty—around such affinities (p. 101).

As community organizers, such as, Saul D. Alinsky (1989) and John McKnight (1995), have shown so well, the kind of communities that lead to social change must often be strategically "organized," called into being piece by piece, not only with a vision but with persistent and deliberate social skill. Members of an oppressed Republican "silent majority" or Mothers Against Drunk Driving (MADD) are made, not born. For Grabill, the interesting thing that gets constructed is an institution. His careful study of a state-funded adult literacy program, a United Way project, and a neighborhood nonprofit is a compelling analysis of three artfully constructed organizations—entities aspiring to become established institutions, like the United Way itself.

A Local Institution

The CLC is an example of this constructive process; however, the organization it produced will differ in revealing ways from the more corporate model of a United Way agency. An institutional analysis of the Community Literacy Center might start with its parent organization, the Community House, a settlement house endowed by Christina Arbuckle in 1916 as a material protest against the missionary agenda of the mainline Presbyterian church—when the poor and immigrant families at home were in need. Over its history, Community House provided meals, education, visiting nurses, a safe place for women and their children, as it morphed into a provider of summer programs, meeting spaces, and midnight basketball.

In this institutional context, the CLC was set up in the 1990s as a self-supporting nonprofit (or 501(c)3 in community-organizing parlance), which meant it was supported by continual grant writing under the letterheads of its university or community affiliation and under different agendas (depending on the funder). In such proposals, it alternated between being a neighborhood youth project, a recognized innovation in community/university collaboration, a research laboratory, and a working expression of moral visions and commitments. A mixture of personal histories, funding streams, institutional affordances, serendipity, and political climates both allowed and shaped its activity. Unlike the larger United Way and state-funded, state-regulated adult and workplace literacy programs, the CLC represents a style of community center that operates under the radar of many institutional constraints. A chameleon community, it can change color and shape over time, based on its cumulative body of knowledge and growing network of people. And as an institution, it is a kind of symbolic community that newcomers and mentors can find easiest to enter.

The real working structure of an opportunistic organization like this is for all practical purposes located in the structure of personal relationships and shared goals. It began at the CLC with the magnetic, if yet to be defined vision of Wayne Peck that drew a community figure (Joyce Baskins) and an academic researcher-rhetorician (me) into what would be best described as an experimental journey. Coming back to Pittsburgh from divinity studies at Harvard, Wayne Peck had deliberately chosen to be a minister and community house director in this urban neighborhood. Ten years later, he had used a PhD in rhetoric at Carnegie Mellon University to study the rhetoric of community advocacy, looking at the kinds of arguments that lead to action (1991). And he began to develop a new vision of the Community House as a place for learning, talking, and writing, going beyond its then-standard community-center fare of Saturday lunches for the elderly, summer camp for kids, and youth recreation. Inspired by the progressive politics and theology of people like Cornel West, Peck's vision and enthusiasm created an oddly eclectic circle of community, university, and church people, meeting to read Shirley Heath one week and Cornel West the next. It was his infectious sense of possibility that drew me to shift my research agenda from the writing of college and professional writers to the rhetoric of urban adults and teenagers and to a focus on literate problem-solving in a place where it might make a greater difference. And this in turn opened up a sequence of doors to graduate students, who found in the CLC a way to ground their thinking about rhetorical action.[8]

The CLC operated as a formal 501(c)3 for over a decade. From its beginnings in 1990, the practice of community literacy was in constant flux—from community gardens and landlord-tenant projects to videos on dealing with police to interventions in school policy. Sustainability in collaborations like this is not about the continuation of a given incarnation or project but about the development and traveling power of an idea and of a network of support that lets people travel to new locations, to new places in their lives, and toward new responses to possibility. By 2000, new projects, drawing on an expanded network of people, were growing out of this seedbed. One became the Community House Learning Center, where digital storytelling and multimedia technology let teens and parents talk, and kids initiate discussions about bullying in middle schools. The same rhetorical tools are now letting members of the gay-lesbian-bisexual-transsexual (GLBT) community take their stories into local churches, attempting to use narrative in public dialogues where other forms of argument have failed. Another incarnation became the Carnegie Mellon Community Think Tanks, designed to bring low-wage workers and later urban students with learning disabilities into economic and educational decision making. Further afield, community literacy practices turn up in college programs and research projects, like those described in chapter 9. The history of the CLC, like many other Northside enterprises, is opportunistic and experimental, using and depending on institutions but not really becoming one in the enduring sense of the term. What did persist in these new incarnations was a vision and way of doing things, a set of literate practices, and a loose, expanding network of people who cared about each other and liked to work together.

The Work of Organizations and Institutions

The agenda of a community organization may be dictated by philanthropic impulses like the settlement-house movement, by the deliberate tactics of a pressure group like Alinsky's radical political organizers, or by a manager's persistent efforts to listen and respond to local needs (Grabill, 2001; Goldblatt, 2005). This kind of community functions first of all by developing programs, structures, and organizations—ranging from short-lived, one-issue pressure groups to funded centers and projects, such as the CLC, to sustained and sustaining parent institutions like the Community House itself.

There are, of course, other outcomes, as McKnight notes in his trenchant opposition to the social service industry (1995). Looking at the bureaucracies of welfare and housing, at the downtown managerial business of United Ways, at the professionals who run neighborhood agencies, he asks, "Why do the vast majority of social service dollars go to create jobs for white, middle class service 'providers'?" And not to the people in need of both money and jobs?

The role of institutions in community work is a contested one. Some argue that the path to social change lies through institutional structures—through redesigning their practices or priorities (Grabill, 2001, Grabill and Simmons, 1998) or leveraging their power (Goldblatt, 2005). On the other hand, universities, like philanthropies, have a poor track record as reliable partners, entering communities as the "expert" or exiting once their data is collected (Flower and Heath, 2000). So some argue that the path to change lies in a studied avoidance of institutional entanglements. Paula Mathieu's image of the "public turn in English Composition" contrasts the tactics of street journalism and homeless groups with the growing institutionalization of service-learning (2005). Her exposé-styled argument starts with the top-down style of Campus Compact formed by elite college presidents, as she decries the growth of "outreach" programs in the 1990s. Driven by institutional mandates and public-relations agendas, these administrative offices are charged with finding a ballooning number of student "placements." But they often fail to consider the needs of the community clients, much less monitor the value their outreach projects actually had for the community. Teachers find themselves "assigned" to courses with a community component, just as students are to writing projects. Both may enter these supposed partnerships without a personal interest or expertise in creating reciprocity. And "twice-burned" community organizations learn to avoid the phone calls from the local university.

The alternative that Mathieu models depends on informal relationships, growing out of extended personal involvement with a community organization, divorced from departmental or university agendas, and built not around "problems" (e.g., ongoing issues) but around ad hoc "projects" that grow out of the opportunities presenting themselves in a given semester. Mathieu argues for "tactics" rather than "strategies" (identifying strategic thinking with institutional agendas designed to control others through stable, measurable practices) (p. 16). By contrast, she argues, "Tactical power is real, but it is unreliable, unconstrained, and its effects are often unclear" (p. 54). The "tactical discourse" of Chicago street writers captures this responsive rather than proactive style of civic engagement: "Unable to equal or overturn the powerful strategic systems scripting their lives, the group created projects in various polemic and utopian forms—pot shots, poetry, humor, critique and parody—as tactical responses to systems framing their lives" (p. 45). Translated to a college course, Mathieu's tactical stance has little investment in repeating (institutionalizing) a successful project, preferring a creative, responsive gesture. Despite its limited social or measurable impact, tactically driven engagement avoids the danger of being co-opted by institutional agendas.

The CLC operates somewhere between the formal institutions Grabill (2001) describes and the deliberately ephemeral projects Mathieu values. Each new CLC project tried to build on methods and successes from the last. Without any illusions of controlling its environment, it operated *strategically* in response to its longer ends-in-view, in the rhetorical sense of strategic. It took a fairly systematic problem-solving stance to articulating goals, planning an action, and then reflecting on the outcomes, before leaping once again (with what was learned) back into the stream.

One of the enduring sources of controversy in community engagement (and within groups) is this relationship to the problematic power of larger institutions. How does one weigh their tendency to co-opt and control against their potential for wider social change? But this is not the only problem. Analyses of how organizational discourse actually functions reveal troubling barriers to dialogue across difference. Although committed to the necessity for organizational change, Grabill documents the ways service institutions turn an intentionally (?) deaf ear to everyday people. He makes a powerful case for the need to bring clients into the design of even the established, hierarchical, and state-regulated organizations (2001; Grabill & Simmons, 1998). Meanwhile, Mathieu's tactical discourse responds to institutional self-interest by building a protective moat around community actions—if it's from a university, don't return the call. In its own way, the arcane discourse of contemporary social critique within our discipline often enlarges the gulf between the holders of intellectual power and the oppressed.[9] And the practice of theory, based on unassailable certainties about the centrality of power and domination, never bothers with (and has no techne for) seeking the rival perspectives of those about whom it theorizes. Even the realpolitik of Alinsky's influential "rules for radicals"—the bible of impassioned grass-roots organizers—couldn't always afford the luxury of dialogue (1989). In teaching its corps of leaders how to organize people who think they are powerless and how to disrupt the status quo, organizing can be as manipulative of its constituents (for their own good) as it is of its foes.

If we limit community literacy to the discourse of these organizations, the openings for significant dialogue and inquiry across differences are hard to find. The intercultural relationships they create often position community folk as clients, patients, victims, children, immature, or incompetent. Community members typically exist as *participants* in social projects, not as *partners* with expertise who must be respected as agents in their own right.[10] So to the extent that such partnerships are diminished—and people from mainstream and elite circles become experts, leaders, directors, service providers, and tutors—the possibility of a community for inquiry with others, across difference, evaporates.

Is *community* work then best defined as organizational work? Is its transformational potential best realized within institutions? Referring to an understanding of community literacy (as Peck, Higgins, and I first tried to explain it in 1995), Grabill (2001) notes a revealing contradiction: "This definition fails to deal with its most difficult and important term, 'community.' . . . In short, this article, while opening up spaces that make work like mine possible, does not define community in a meaningful way, yet ironically manages to define 'community literacy' within composition" (p. 89).

This ironic outcome—an underdefined yet, for some, defining concept—supports Grabill's own insight: the *community* to which we referred was a symbolic entity, which was and is still and continually under construction.[11] Others "within composition" may use the term *community literacy* because it reflects their need to talk about this hard-to-nail-down sense of a *rhetorically* constructed community—something that is much more like a local public sphere than an institution, community organization, or social group. But perhaps now, more than ten years later, it will be easier to articulate how this symbolic rhetorical space actually works.[12]

A Local Public Sphere

A diverse, urban community like Pittsburgh is more than its institutions and symbolic spaces; it is a polity. A polity consists, as Iris Marion Young puts it, of "people who live together, who are stuck with one another" through proximity and economic interdependence (1996, p. 126). Because my pursuits affect what you can do, we have to deliberate in some public way about how we live together. I will argue that the most significant outcome of community literacy was not its creation of an institutional Center, its projects, or its publications but the creation of a local public sphere. That is, it called into being a deliberative community built around discourse, shared concerns, and different perspectives on change. Such a community did not take action as a group but expected its participants (from mentors and teens to families, public officials, and academics) to return to their own spheres enabled to think and act differently in ways appropriate to their situation. I like to imagine this deliberative space as positioned at a crossroads (under the signpost of community literacy) that identified this space with a search for social justice, an ethic of love and solidarity, and a faith in the power of (or at least willingness to take a chance on) intercultural inquiry. However, people come to such a space for different reasons.

The most important thing about community literacy—as it is described here—is not that it convenes a preexisting community but that the community it creates is a deliberative one, a distinctive local public sphere that was unlikely to exist without it. There are, of course, other local public spheres built around social service, political activism, or philanthropy. What is unusual about community literacy is that without positioning itself in an adversarial or advocacy stance, it reverses some critical patterns of authority (though by no means all) and gives pride of place to the expertise and voice of community folk. From its radical perspective on difference, it defines urban problems as *mutual* problems. The remainder of this chapter places this argument and the practices of community literacy in the context of a vigorous theoretical debate around the nature of the public sphere and the requirements of deliberative democracy.

A Community Called to Intercultural Public Inquiry

The Work of a Public Sphere

Mass media and opinion polls have taught us to think of the "public" as sets of demographically definable groups of people (homeowners, Republicans, the teen market) that can be surveyed or sold to. But such a public, by definition, simply *has* opinions or buying preferences; because it does not discuss or deliberate, it cannot function as a public sphere (Hauser, 1999). The public of rhetorical theory is a very different animal—it is called into being by an issue or concern; it exists in the process of discussion, persuasion, and deliberation about actions. In contrast to the pseudo-dialogues of media-staged politics, working local publics are more likely to be found in the deliberative meetings of school boards and borough councils, in the planning and budget meetings of civic associations, clubs, or workplace organizations, or in the conversations in hair salons, churches, or coffeehouses, where competing visions of the common good are at stake.[13] The public of rhetorical theory is separate from the state (e.g., legislative bodies that can dictate change), but it has considerable power because sooner or later, that state must be validated and must justify its claims to represent its people. On the other hand, there is considerable debate not only over how this public sphere actually works in a democracy but also over whether the ideals (which have shaped humanistic education) are in fact ideal. The following brief look at this controversy is framed by the question this chapter raises: how do we find or create a place to talk deeply and productively across difference?

Our most powerful images of how the public should work are associated with the liberal political theory of the Enlightenment (e.g., of Thomas Jefferson and John Locke). Not to be confused with contemporary "liberal" or left-leaning politics, this rational, individualistic liberal model of the public sphere developed hand-in-hand with the rise of the mercantile middle class and capitalism. Its most influential modern theorist, Jürgen Habermas argues that the bourgeois public sphere began to take shape in the form of discussions in eighteenth-century coffeehouses, salons, and newspapers as the rising middle class found its identity and voice (1962/1989). Public life was a theater for debate and deliberation, separated from the workings of the family, the economic market, and the state. It was the middle class's place for shaping and publicizing its ideas about culture, commerce, and politics. And this public sphere became the middle class's tool for influencing the state to support the needs of capital.

The public sphere of liberal, Enlightenment theory is also an ideal of how public discussion and policymaking should be conducted. Its idealization of universal truth and rational consensus and its deliberate blindness to difference have shaped how we teach humanities and argument writing (Atwill, 1998; Jarratt, 1991b). In this ideal of public discussion (which Patricia Roberts-Miller calls the "traditional-universalist" model), valid arguments are based not on local, particular experience or personal opinion but on universal premises to which all men would agree (as in Jefferson's "We hold these truths to be self-evident: That all men are created equal") (2004, p. 36). This insistence on general principles is tied to a focus on public topics that deal with the general interest or affect the common good.

In practice, this ideal has also had some unhappy consequences. Historically, its public/private split closed off discussion of "private" matters (e.g., domestic violence, child labor, or workplace safety) that it relegated more properly to family life or to economic relations between worker and employer (Fraser, 1990). In recent decades, this same division would define the destructive effects of globalization as purely market-based decisions and would deal with calls for workplace democracy and school reform alike as managerial problems. This narrow version of what is *public* continues to reflect the concerns of a middle-class male business world, shutting out the interests of people marginalized by age, gender, race, class, or status. In the same way, the universal principles or "common sense" on which a public argument should be based tends to reflect the assumptions and traditions of the majority, not the marginalized (Roberts-Miller, 2004, p. 43). For example, the notorious "dead white guys" who make up the canon of liberal education reflect a particular and rather narrow slice of "universal" human experience.

Mark Howard's rap argued that classroom conflicts, dismissed as "personal" examples of bad behavior, were, in fact, a shared problem that cried out for inquiry and communication. We will see many community literacy writers use the CLC's deliberative process to rename issues—from school and city policy to landlord-tenant conflict to growing up in an inner city—as *personal/public* realities for which people share a common responsibility.

A second, long-unquestioned feature of this liberal Enlightenment tradition is an insistence on objectivity and rationality as the basis for argument and on consensus as its goal. The public sphere connoted an ideal of unrestricted rational discussion of public matters. The discussion was to be open and accessible to all; merely private matters were inadmissible; inequalities of status were to be bracketed; and discussants were to deliberate as peers. The result of such discussion would be "public opinion" in the strong sense of a consensus about the common good (Fraser, 1990, p. 59).

These assumptions lie behind composition textbooks in which the "argument" essay is presented as a thesis followed by list of reasons, an optional swipe at possible opponents, and a reiteration of the thesis. The best reasons are facts; that is, statements that are perceived as objective because they are "non-controversial" (Roberts-Miller, 2004, p. 75). But, of course, what is deemed controversial or not depends on who is admitted into our public. The humanist tradition of rational argument has defined its public as an elite, schooled body that wisely dismisses narrative, personal experience, and impassioned argument (even when outrage at injustice might be the rational response). Of course, it also excludes the majority of people not schooled in its distinctive discourse. Critics of these assumptions do not deny the value of reason and education per se but note how the schooled "genre" of this rational argument locks out people who cannot or will not play by its rules, who argue with the tools of other discourses. Roberts-Miller describes this cozily narrowed public as an enclave—an audience that shares our values—and shows how our current enthusiasm for the collaborative classroom allows students to remain sheltered from difference (2004, p. 42). Just as textbooks urge students to write to a neutral audience (one presumably just waiting to be informed), the collaborative classroom pushes students to arrive at a consensus. The discourse moves of elite rationality, normative objectivity, and consensus work to exclude important sources of difference, dismissing different worldviews and experiences (that might see our "objective" assumptions as actually quite controversial). They discourage dissensus and its arguments for change. We will see community literacy wrestle with this problem by trying to create a hybrid discourse, one that expands the repertoire of both the community and university partners and structures a deliberation around the contributions of difference.

A third feature of the public sphere of liberal political theory, admirable in theory but problematic in practice, is its aspiration to focus on the quality of the arguments and ignore differences in the power or status of the speaker. It strategy is to "bracket" such differences, to suspend awareness of status and hierarchy, and to deliberate "as if" all discussants were social equals. Historically, the bourgeois public sphere never *was* diverse or blind to difference (Fraser, 1990). Jefferson's "all men" not only excluded unpropertied men, women, slaves, and the poor (Roberts-Miller, 2004, pp. 47–48), it didn't extend the rights of free speech to white, propertied loyalists). And even in diverse groups, markers of status rarely pass unnoticed. For example, studies of contemporary, mixed, deliberative bodies studies show that women are more frequently interrupted and their interventions ignored (Fraser, 1990).

Even if the injunction to bracket difference by attempting to ignore it were possible, many people argue that it would produce flawed arguments. Because genuine differences are rarely hidden, speakers who wish to play the game must assume a stance of dispassionate neutrality and avoid the evidence of personal experience and any appearance of self-interest. But for disenfranchised groups, denying one's identity as a working-class student, an inner-city African American, or a migrant laborer denies the reality of social difference, of power, and inequality—the very issues these groups want us to see as *public* concerns. When a discourse insists its members suspend, ignore, or neutralize the identities of women, workers, peoples of color, gays, and lesbians, it effectively removes those realities from deliberation.

Students, co-workers, or citizens looking for a space and a way to talk across difference will find their dilemma expressed in Nancy Fraser's words: "Something like Habermas' idea of the public sphere is indispensable to critical social theory and democratic political practice, . . . [but] the specific form in which Habermas [and, I will add, our educational tradition] has elaborated this idea is not wholly satisfactory" (1990, p 57). From the standpoint of community literacy, the injunctions to universalize, bracket difference, and limit discourse to rational argument geared to consensus have two flaws. One is that these notions have been used to authorize a particular style of discourse—what Fraser calls "protocols of style and decorum" (1990, p. 63)—that often exclude whole groups of speakers, their perspectives, and their ways of representing an issue. Good arguments depend on reasoning—on offering reasons and attempting consistency. But when rationality is defined as the conventions and norms of a formal argument or the practices of an elite discourse, other ways of reasoning are excluded. The expressive narrative associated with "women's ways of knowing" (Gilligan, 1982/1993), the complexity and indirection of African-American signifying (Gates, 1988), the personal, experiential assertiveness of Sojourner Truth's "Ain't I a Woman" (Lipscomb, 1995), and even the bold independence and the unflinching descriptions in Ida B. Wells's *Southern Horrors* (Royster, 1995; Logan, 1999) are deemed not just out of bounds but dismissible. And the scope of public inquiry is radically diminished. The public is reduced to an enclave marked by its elite discourse.

A second flaw in this rational discourse is central to service-learning. If we continue to assume that public talk and writing must fit our norms of an elite, educated discourse, where do students learn to move out of this particular enclave (even if it represents a dominant majority) into discussions with others? How do they develop Fraser's multicultural literacy that allows communication across lines of cultural difference (1990, p. 69)? Or when our "collaborative" classrooms bracket difference to reduce the uncomfortable possibility of conflict, where then do students learn to respond to the discursive conflict that is part of dealing with difference?[14]

Alternatives That Engage Difference

The defenders of the liberal bourgeois public sphere acknowledge that it is a utopian model—something to aspire to even if it rarely worked as planned. But many critics, concerned with its suppression of difference, argue that it is not only an inaccurate description but a flawed ideal. Some of the alternatives they propose help us articulate how community literacy could work as a public that engages difference.

One of the most robust alternatives to emerge in theorizing about the public sphere is the notion of deliberative democracy. It is not only skeptical about certain ideals of the traditional-universalist model (e.g., its universalizing rationality, consensus seeking, and the bracketing of difference); it offers a very different story of how the public sphere in an "actually existing late capitalist democracy" operates (Fraser, 1990, p. 57). Although its advocates do not agree on how to do it, deliberative democracy tackles head-on the problem of a productive engagement with difference (Gutman and Thompson, 2004; I. M. Young, 1996). Moreover, it does so not only in theory but in terms of the rhetorical art or techne and the educational practices that would support it (Roberts-Miller, 2004).

So what would a local public attuned to inquiry, justice, and deliberation across difference have to do or include? The debates around deliberative democracy, liberal education, and the public sphere can help to articulate four critical features of such a public (and in the process suggest why such an ideal is no easy walk).

1. *It is open to discovery.* Some models of public discussion assume that people form a public either because they already have common interests (which can lead to an enclave in which one is only preaching to the choir). Alternatively, people go public because their predefined competing self-interests bring them to debate or the bargaining table. The deliberative model, on the other hand, argues that in discussion and exchange we actually *discover* our interests. This process brings our needs to consciousness, lets us clarify vague or poorly understood problems, uncover new ways to frame issues, and discover shared interests. One-way engagement with newspapers, magazines, radio, or TV is no substitute for this process of reflective deliberation. (Hauser, 1999, pp. 18, 26, 53).

2. *It accepts discursive conflict.* Genuinely diverse points of view are essential to understanding a problem, even though the price of difference is tension and substantive conflict. A community that can accommodate *discursive* conflict—without falling into partisan, self-interest advocacy—not only avoids unjust exclusion but also benefits itself by complicating and reducing

the sort of unquestioned consensus enclaves produce (Roberts-Miller, 2004, p. 186). This sort of conflict is different from self-interest advocacy (in which I do not need listen to you) and from expressive argument (in which you cannot challenge me because this is "my opinion"). My personal experience and opinion (which may be in conflict with yours) are allowed here, *but they are also* up for argument because they are interpretations and being used as reasons. And as such they are open to discussion and reinterpretation.

Discursive conflict among ideas—a form of agonistic rhetoric based on tolerance and mutual respect of people—lets people explore and test ideas against the strong contenders. It acknowledges that around issues, such as equality, we may enter areas of deep, irreconcilable disagreement. But the response should not be to avoid, bracket, or silence those uncomfortable differences but to put them on the table *in the spirit of inquiry.*

3. *It reaches for resolution, not consensus.* The traditional-universalist model calls for consensus based on rational warranted assent. That is, the best argument wins the day (e.g., the one that withstands refutation by the rules of the discourse). There is little room for continuing negotiation of difference. A deliberative model, on the other hand, assumes that communal decisions are "always necessarily contingent and cannot be seen as ending the process or permanently answering the question" (Roberts-Miller, 2004, p. 201). The members of a public may continue to hold different opinions about a mutual problem, but as interdependent members of their society, they are willing to seek a resolution (and seek to influence it) through discourse (rather than force, bargaining, or voting).

4. *It requires rhetorical competence.* In Habermas's ideal bourgeois public sphere, public opinion depended on the "critical reflections of a public competent to form its own judgments" (1962/1989, p. 90). Although entry into that competent public was blind to social status (e.g., opening the doors to the middle class), it demanded educated and informed participants who could produce "generalizable arguments that adhere to the norms of ideal speech" (Hauser, 1999, p. 43). In effect, competence could be measured by one's command of the particular conventions of an elite "rational" discourse.

Deliberative models based on justice, on the other hand, assert the competence of marginalized people to interpret reality, to speak for themselves, and to do so out of alternative discourses. They require reasonableness (the need to support claims with reasons), not a particular form of rational discourse, because the goal of participation is to reach a resolution rather than ascertain a generalizable truth.

The "rules of discourse" in deliberation may be even more demanding than schooled rationality.

In a deliberative situation we treat one another with respect, we care enough to disagree, we listen so well we can articulate our oppositions' arguments in terms to which the opposition will assent, we do not try to offend and we try not to take offense, and we try to make arguments using reasons that people who disagree with us think are valid reasons (Roberts-Miller, 2004, p. 207)

And if all this were not enough, Roberts-Miller raises the bar of competence with an additional claim (that challenges the hubris of elite discourses): "In deliberative democracy, one must make one's argument understood in the words *others* use" (p. 213). Talking across difference will demand rhetorical empathy, an attempt not only to listen and understand others but to present our own views in words that speak to them. Young sees such rhetorical empathy in narratives and arguments that speak to people in their own situations. This situatedness "also contributes to political argument," she argues, "by the social knowledge it offers of how social segments view one another's actions and what are the likely effects of policies and actions on people in different social locations" (1996, p. 132).

In community literacy, the search for such situated knowledge operates in the service of inquiry. A social cognitive analysis (see chapter 7) suggests that such inquiry is indeed able to create a distinctive form of knowing. And by unpacking the experiential reality behind abstract claims, it also has the potential to transform understanding in a public deliberation. The catch is that situated deliberative talk requires a rhetorical competency that goes beyond empathetic disposition, assertive advocacy, or rational argument. We must not only create a just representation of complex social meanings and outcomes but be understood and be capable of transforming the understanding of others. The problem of community literacy is the problem of drawing its public into this alternative argumentative practice of inquiry.

Competing Publics and Counterpublics

We need to complete this picture of public talk by returning to the identity of the public itself. Despite the bourgeois public's claim that it *is* the public, Fraser argues that "not only were there always a plurality of competing publics, but the relations between bourgeois publics and other publics were always conflictual." Ranging from elite women's associations to peasant movements and working-class networks, these subaltern counterpublics "contested the norms of the bourgeois public" and asserted alternative styles of political action and public speech (Fraser, 1990, p. 61).

Gerard Hauser's work turns Fraser's "plurality" into an animated network of local publics, linked in the 3-D spider web he calls the "reticulate public sphere" (1999, p. 60). He envisions the members of each local public engaged in the heady rhetorical work of public dialogue, trying to discover their interests, points of difference and convergence, and possibilities for accommodation. Adhering to the standards of tolerance and reasonableness, these publics replace the discourse of rationality with the vernacular language of conversational communication. Then as Hauser's camera zooms back, we see a public sphere made up of all these multiple, nested publics. And we see "a dialogizing rhetorical alternative" to the disillusioning images of a single, hegemonic, bourgeois, media-controlled public (p. 67).

If Hauser's portrait of vernacular voices sets this dialogic web of rhetorical actors abuzz, Michael Warner's accounts of publics and counterpublics describes what goes on in this process and reveals (and revels in) the subversive work of such talk.

Publics, Warner argues, are not found but called into being by discourse. "Public discourse says not only, 'Let a public exist,' but 'Let it have this character, speak this way, see the world this way.' . . . Run it up the flagpole and see who salutes. Put on a show and see who shows up" (2005, p. 114). Although we often use the metaphors of conversation or writer-to-reader communication to describe what goes on in a public, the real activity, he asserts, is "circulation"—the movement and transformation of ideas, language, and attitudes in an ongoing discourse that gives the nod to what went before and anticipates a new response (p. 90). Circulation is an intertextual process that sounds like Bakhtin's dialogic speech acts; that is, I cite Warner, you pick up my words, attach them to yours, and this new version comes back to me, Warner, and others in an ongoing discourse.

So where is the potential for transformation in a network of multiple publics with their own often-closed systems of circulation? One answer lies in the disquieting voices of counterpublics and their ability to elbow their way into other publics, circulating more than good arguments. The tradition of "rational-critical" dialogue might lead us to assume that what circulates are merely arguments, that is, supported claims that can be summarized as logical propositions. But public discourse, Warner claims, is also an intensely performative act of "poetic world making" (2005, p. 114). It attempts to realize a vision of the world through address. One critical part of this vision is its model of what it means *to participate in this relationship among strangers* (because it is this address to strangers that distinguishes a public from a mere group or community). Consider the counterpublic style of Martin Luther King Jr.'s Southern Christian Leadership Council ("caught in an inescapable network of mutuality") versus the Black Panthers separatist stance, or of the Sierra Club's establishment rationality versus Earth First!

sabotage. The particular performative style of a given public helps organize how people interact—it creates a distinctive "consciousness of stranger sociability" (Warner, 2005, p. 108). What circulates in this discourse is not just arguments but models of public meaning-making, listening, responding, argumentation—models that may revise, challenge, or simply thumb their noses at the rational image of speaker-listener (R. Greene, 2002, p. 438). This opening for difference will be particularly significant for the intercultural local publics of community literacy. Modeled around multivoiced problem-solving, such publics define and organize their participants as collaborative partners empowered to exploit the expressive potential of poetic action and to insist on alternative ways of relating across difference.

The counterpublics of contemporary queer culture, feminism, nineteenth-century African American theater, the *Spectator*'s eighteenth-century reading public, and the black public sphere reveal ways difference has made itself heard.[15] Unlike mainstream discourses, which always seem eager to "stand in for *the* public, to frame their address as the universal discussion of the people," counterpublics see themselves as in conflict with the dominant public (Warner, 2005, p. 117). More than just "subalterns with a reform program," they not only assert alternative ideas and policy positions but insist, often with some indecorousness, on alternative public ways of speaking, relating to others, and projecting one's identity. An African American, for example, would be speaking from a counterpublic only if he or she chooses to speak in what is regarded as a racially marked idiom (Warner, 2005, p. 119.)

Another set of subalterns—the Chicago gangs studied by Ralph Cintron—add a problematic dimension to this theoretical discussion. On the one hand, their "language tactics" in graffiti and attire reveal what Cintron calls a "shadow system" that appropriates and reinterprets the topoi of the mainstream or "system world" (such as, nationhood, loyalty, and heart) as a way to demand just what the system refuses to grant—recognition and respect for a marginalized identity (1997, p. 176–77). Painting walls and throwing (hand) signs are performative arguments to both the mainstream public and competing gangs. On the other hand, while these identity and rhetorical actions are "at least, partially determined by the same socioeconomic and power differences that give rise to subaltern counterpublics," they are also linked to a criminality that goes beyond defacing private property to drug dealing and killing. And this, Cintron argues, means that "the public sphere in Angelstown—Fraser's 'actually existing democracy'—is fundamentally closed to gang graffiti writers and street gangs" (Cintron, 1997, p. 186).[16]

So what would it take for gangs to function as a legitimate counterpublic within a deliberative democracy, where the goal of justice must be combined with tolerance and mutual respect? Cintron's carefully hedged "faint hope" suggests the same need for rhetorical structure that we will see in community literacy's Community Conversations and Think Tanks. He would support that hope by "encouraging gang leaders and membership to participate in public forums with majoritarian society, [and] by insisting on careful documentation of the assumptions and beliefs of all parties so that they could later be deconstructed, and by insisting that these forums move toward concrete truces, programs and proposals" (1997, p. 196).

This account of counterpublics let us add two more critical features to our sketch of how the local public called up by community literacy might actually be working.

5. *It builds identities and arguments.* Counterpublics act first as safe houses for withdrawal and regrouping where new representations can be crafted and where identities are formed and transformed. As they expand their network, they can become like the feminist counterpublic that Fraser describes with its "array of journals, bookstores, publishing companies . . . academic programs, conferences, conventions, festivals, and local meeting places" (1990, p. 67). The discourse that circulates there transforms previously silenced concerns (from domestic violence to women's liberation) into public concerns by creating new concepts and language and performing new female/feminine/womanly/womanist identities.

6. *It transforms public interaction.* Counterpublics do more than nurture and circulate the in-talk and agreements of enclaves. Addressing a public is a campaign to extend the frontier, to call others to recognize themselves as members in this discourse, implicated in its concerns. Counterpublics engage the dominant public but not in the familiar form of advocacy, that is, as "interest-bearing strategic actors" arguing particular policies within the existing relationships of power. Counterpublics, Warner insists, exist as a modern form of power by asserting new forms of interaction, new norms of "stranger-relationality" (Greene, 2002, p. 438). "In this way, publics and counterpublics are more than spaces of persuasion: they are poetic-expressive forces that imagine particular worlds of stranger sociability" (p. 438). In practice, they change the rules for talking and listening to one another, for acknowledging the other as a worthy interlocutor. Of course, the more these alternative styles of discourse depart from the norms of critical-rational dialogue, through embodied relationships, emotion, or playfulness, the more tension they create (Warner, 2005, p. 122).[17]

The Local Counterpublic of Community Literacy

At their best, the publics called into being by community literacy enact the six features described above of a public attuned to difference. However, these *local* publics are also of special interest for the ways they differ from larger movements, such as Warner's queer culture counterpublics, Fraser's feminist sub-altern counterpublics, or Hauser's vernacular public of Polish resistance.

To begin, the community of community literacy has a different principle of composition. Unlike a counterpublic called around a shared identity (e.g., having been "othered," as a feminist, African American), this local public is designed around internal difference. From its intentionally diverse identity to its explicit strategies and deliberate search for rival interpretations, community literacy creates a friendly space within its community for *discursive* conflict. Its collaboratively supported style of dissensus often starts around the big table when urban teens and college mentors hear their own voices break the silence in a new kind of public. It moves to the larger public of Community Conversations and publications. But unlike organized advocacy or critique, community literacy treats difference, rival hypotheses, and conflicting realities as a resource for inquiry. Discovery starts with the articulation of difference. It leads to a deliberation (unlike agonistic debate) that enjoins all its participants to act as partners in inquiry, to take on the difficult role of collaborative problem-solvers. That is, to be responsible for understanding the images of others in order to build a new negotiated meaning, workable options, and a resolution marked by justice.

This is not a role any of the partners are typically accustomed to take, especially in standard community/university relations or in the expert-to-advocate dialogues between the privileged and the underprivileged. Intercultural inquiry and collaborative problem-solving calls for a hybrid discourse and for rhetorical competencies that are rarely developed in public schools, college composition classes, political debate, or community organizing. So for community literacy, "going public" does not simply mean publicizing positions and arguments but nurturing and structuring a way to become a diverse, deliberative local public.

In this respect, these local publics act much like the larger counterpublics. The safe collaborative space of the CLC nurtured not only subaltern interpretations of school policies but the rhetorical competence to talk about them, and affirmed the identity of inner-city teenagers as worthy contributors to such public issues. In its newsletters and public presentations, this upstart counterpublic combined tools of rational-critical argument with situated knowledge, personal experience, narrative, and performative rhetoric in music, skits, raps, and dialogue with the audience. Its texts often circulated locally and found their way to web sites. However, the second distinguishing feature of such local publics lies in the arguments they build. I will argue that the most important thing this counterpublic put *in circulation* was not its policy statements on school suspension or its insights on gangs but its model of "stranger sociability"—that is, *its demonstration of a public dialogue that uses difference as a resource for inquiry and decision making.* And I will suggest that its impact is ultimately based on its power to circulate a model of intercultural inquiry.

The test (and, John Dewey would argue, the ultimate meaning) of this claim about community literacy as a local public lies in its outcomes. So it might be helpful to reframe this portrait of a local public as a set of questions focused on visible indicators of impact, of success, or more generally of what actually happened. That is, on the question of outcomes that this book will try to answer. The first (and for many community projects the only) measure of significant action is the safe-house effect. So the first question might be: do students and mentors find value in and grow through this experience? The CLC would add: did they develop more complex interpretations of a shared problem and the ability to test those ideas at the table of rivaling and collaboration? Did they develop a more public expertise in both performative and reasoned argument and the ability to mix the two? Did they see themselves with that counterpublic self-consciousness as creating a new identity as a speaker and writer?

Questions at a second level would ask: what are the indicators that this local public created a widened network of circulation, not just as a media count of one-time spectators but also as an impact on subsequent discussion? How actively did this dialogue (and its style of deliberation) find its way into relations or discussions between teens and peers, parents, teachers? (For example, we will hear from students who report using "rivaling" to get the car keys or avoid a fight; from teachers who suddenly see capabilities in a student like Mark or who criticize the new hubris of CLC boys who now "think they can write"). Does the work of this public find its way into the writing of mentors, graduate students, or scholars? Do its texts and the texts it sponsors circulate? (Indicators of circulation might include *Whassup with Suspension* being used with city school vice principals, *Raising the Curtain on Curfew* being requested by the police academy, scholarly talks being given with the texts, and articles being published, cited, or used in new arguments.)

And on a third level, which I continue to believe is the most significant, we should look at this local counterpublic as a model of public discourse attempting to engage difference. Unlike a community advocacy project targeted on a specific institutional or political change (as necessary as such projects are), the goal of community literacy is to engage its strangers in a public space devoted to foregrounding difference as a resource in inquiry, organized by new norms of discourse that are both modeled and advocated. In its individual projects, Community Conversations, and written documents, community literacy puts its counterpublic style of listening, talking, and interpreting in the foreground. So some appropriate indicators of outcomes would lead us to look for new patterns of dialogue observed among teens, at teen-led public events, and by teens themselves (see chapter 5), in spin-off neighborhood meetings, in inquiry-based educational software, and in projects with other institutions that adapt this mode of dialogue (e.g., dialogues in a women's clinic, children's hospital, nursing home, and city school) as well as in the publications they produced (see chapters 2, 4, and 8). In short, the meaning of a local public lies in the evidence of what it *does*.

So imagine if you will the mentors left back in the van looking for a place to talk across difference. They have before them four robust symbolic communities, to which I have referred for convenience as a civic body, a symbolic neighborhood, a local institution, and a local public. The latter invites them into a disconcertingly diverse space for inquiry and deliberation where the familiar discourse of academic writing will be challenged by alternatives from teen talk to black preaching to political organizing. This cultural intersection and its hybrid discourse acknowledge the contradictions and conflicts that are part of mutual problems at the same time it calls its participants to be partners in creating this space for public dialogue.

The unique ability of the community organizer, nonprofit director, or local leader is to construct a community organization. This book will argue that it is the special prerogative of writers and rhetoricians to create the multicultural, educative, deliberative local public spheres of community literacy. Creating such a space as teachers, researchers, and students is not easy. At the beginning of a literacy project, the idea of participating in this symbolic rhetorical community is something mentors are likely to see as another academic fiction or are at best willing to take on faith. Their education, Kurt Spellmeyer argues, has not prepared them to seek "common ground of understanding" or to participate in "a revitalized public discourse, a conversation open to every person, and to every discipline, dialect, and tradition. . . . [I]n the absence of any visible public dimension, our students correctly surmise that their primary task is accommodation to the established forms of specialized practice" (1993, pp. 15–18).[18]

As it turned out, the mentors we will follow struggled with their roles as partners in learning for many reasons. The college students in Elenore Long's in-depth study of mentoring came with competing if unexamined assumptions about their contributions (1994). If some saw themselves as editors/experts upholding Standard Written English and academic discourse, and some as champions of free expression, others came as cultural critics and emancipators.[19] Few came prepared for collaborative inquiry.

If university students seem perplexed about their role in a public sphere or rhetorical community, many urban teenagers seemed to consider the notion meaningless if not patently absurd. The assumption that adults would listen, much less that these teens' own ideas and writing would matter and might even provoke serious thought or change, fit little in their experience. It often took the experience of the final, public Community Conversation to suddenly give reality to the power of words that many of us take for granted—an experience that the teens later rated as one of the CLC's "highly valuable" features. So, even if such a community offers our best bet for talking with others, it must be constructed not only in fact but also in people's imaginations. And the capacity to be a genuine partner in inquiry is, it appears, something that we learn with difficulty.[20]

The most interesting thing about symbolic communities is what they do in the material world. So let us look now at how community literacy, in the spirit of "build it and they will come," went about creating public spaces for inquiry, understanding, and action across difference—and the unexpected things people did in these spaces.

2 *Taking Literate Action*

The Community Literacy Center mentors we left in the previous chapter stood poised at the beginning of an experiment in civic engagement. Like them, the CLC itself would need to articulate in principle what it was discovering in practice. Standing in the context of other work in composition, critical literacy, and service-learning, it began to shape itself around a distinctive local public rhetoric with position statements like the one below. Such statements are good for thinking with. They force you to articulate what matters most and how those things are related to each other. They stand as a sort of hypothesis that can be constantly challenged by the reality you are trying to describe, which in turn keeps taking you deeper into the mystery and requiring of you a new naming.

> *Community literacy is a form of literate action that allows:*
> - everyday people within the urban community to take rhetorical agency in their lives and for their community;
> - everyday people from places of privilege to participate in the struggle for understanding and social justice.
>
> *Community literacy depends on the social ethic and strategic practice of intercultural rhetoric to:*
> - draw out the voices of the silenced and the expertise of marginalized people;
> - draw people normally separated by difference into new roles as partners in inquiry;
> - recognize and use difference in the service of discovery and change, transforming rather than erasing its conflicts and contradictions.

Definitional statements like these also ask us to unpack their terms of art, which is what this chapter hopes to do. And yet, when you begin to unravel the tangled skein of experiences, meanings, and contradictions that make up such a hypothesis, you begin to feel the limits of formal definition, of theorizing that aspires to a cleanly drawn, internally self-consistent edifice of words and ideas. So in this chapter, I would like to unpack some of the meanings of community literacy in action, not merely by defining terms but by instantiating them. That is, by exploring a complex *instance* of literate action for what it can tell us about three themes of community literacy that figure prominently in its definition and by asking:

What does the *rhetorical agency* of everyday people mean? How does it work?
How does a *strategic practice* shape an intercultural rhetoric?
And if *inquiry* is the goal, what are its outcomes?

This instance comes from early in the history of the Community Literacy Center, initiated by a project called Risk and Stress. The story it tells about the meaning of agency, strategic rhetoric, and inquiry is partial and situated as well as biased by the values and questions I bring to the telling. It is also provocative. And precisely because it is a local, situated account of one way in which literacy does work, it challenges us to take on the work of observation-based theory building.[1]

Risk, Stress, and Respect

The Risk and Stress Project (as it was initially called) was sparked by a conversation with an activist with multiple community identities. Ian Rawson was a gently irreverent deflator of cant and a social visionary with a commitment to service.[2] Despite his academic bent to anthropology, he would have been a great community organizer if he had not already been a vice president for policy at the major tri-state hospital across the park from the Community House. Rawson's outspoken and rather ironic position, given his job as an institutional spokesperson, was that health was not created by hospitals, which only dealt with illness, but by communities.

Posing the Problem in Theory—The Manifesto

Conversations with Rawson and other health-care providers followed by some homework helped us pose this problem in a first-draft manifesto for inquiry. This text, which became material for mentors and a funding proposal, argued that communities are not only sources of health or stress but are also rhetorical forums for understanding what concepts, such as health and stress, actually mean, in practice, if you are an urban teenager. However, when the pilot project and dialogue with the teens began for real, this conceptualization took a new turn. The initial problem statement of our manifesto, excerpted in the appendix with its hands-on logo, contrasted the comfortable middle-class assumptions about growing up in a healthy community with the reality we were recognizing in our own urban neighborhoods. Arguing that urban teenagers need to be drawn into community forums as *expert working partners,* the problem statement sketches three principles for creating such intercultural partnerships (see pp. 71–72).

When setting out on an inquiry, it is good to have a plan or sense of the problem, as long as you aren't too attached to it. As the excerpt from that problem statement (found at the end of this chapter) reveals, there are a number of potential contradictions built into our representation of the situation. First, because institutions like the CLC convene such dialogues (they literally provide and own the table), will marginalized partners be able to get their vision of the problem itself "on the table"? Our small manifesto posed a problem as we—that is, the community and literacy leaders, academics, and health care professionals—saw it. But if problems are only problems *for somebody,* is stress, risk, or health something teens are actually trying to manage? Secondly, if teenagers are not automatically prepared to participate as problem *solvers,* adults are even less ready to listen carefully and collaborate with teens. Can we redirect the impulse to placate anger, the reflex to pet and praise for self-expression and then ignore the substance of what young people say, or the irrepressible urge to give wise advice? Finally, say that some degree of collaboration, reflection, and knowledge-making is achieved; just how does the work of this local rhetorical community make a difference and for whom?

Posing the Problem in Context—The Pilot Project

The working group seated around the CLC table that first day was an unusual mixture. It included Ian Rawson, who brought two health-care colleagues: a trauma psychiatrist and a nurse practitioner (who often dealt with the aftereffects a shooting had on schools, families, and kids). They, like the CLC team, had seen plenty of rap sessions and encounter groups designed to "let the teenagers express themselves" and had done those goodwill gigs in which professionals "show up" in the community. What we wanted instead was a working group who could pose this "health" problem as teens actually experienced it and begin to articulate the hidden story of ongoing stress—if teens even felt their experience in this way. The CLC team at this point included Wayne Peck and Joyce Baskins (introduced in chapter 1); Donald Tucker, an African American in his 40s who, like Joyce Baskins, had grown up in the neighborhood; and me. Most of the six teenagers who joined us at the table as the grounded experts were articulate, confident juniors and seniors, known from past projects as strong working partners. Shirley, however, was only a ninth grader, a slip of a girl, who had been slipped in the group as somebody's cousin to let her have the experience.

That afternoon, Ian launches the inquiry with his surprising assertion: the medical profession, with its hospitals and technology is not the giver of health. Health comes from a community that supplies decent jobs, affordable housing, social support, and a reason for hopeful, health-preserving behavior. His profession needs to learn this. The trauma psychiatrist talks about a similar need but defines the problem as stress. He often deals with stress in its acute form, but he and the nurse practitioner say they feel frustrated when they talk to teachers' groups; they need a way to help teachers see the more hidden but ongoing kinds of stress their students may be facing.

Defining the problem this way, as stress, seems to strike an immediate chord—the six teenagers at the table have a lot to say. They talk about the shock of a drive-by (when shots come crashing through the window as you and your boyfriend watched TV), about how the stigma of poverty produces ailments that allow you to avoid going to school, and about how success itself can place you—in only a month from now—in the intimidating environment of a predominantly white West Virginia college. Shirley, however, seems acutely aware that she is only a ninth grader in this group of assertive, older teens and professionals. She says almost nothing the first hour. At this point, the group breaks out into collaborative planning partnerships: each adult becomes the supporter of a teen writer working to articulate his or her vision of the *story-behind-the-story* of teen stress in a rough text that we will share at the next session. With the support of her partner, Mrs. Baskins, Shirley's story begins to emerge.

The Racist Cop in My Neighborhood: How I Deal with It
By Shirley Lyle

The purpose of this piece is to let people know how the cops are racist in my neighborhood. I want to also tell you how we teens deal with that racism.

Last summer when I was twelve going on thirteen, I noticed a lot of discrimination in Hershel Field, a playground in my community.

That summer was the most heated summer I can remember. Maybe I began to notice because I was becoming a young adult and starting to go out more.

Here's the story. It was a Friday evening. My sister and I went to Hershel Field. It was getting fun up there, and we couldn't wait to go to watch the guys play basketball. We also went to kinda check the guys out.

We were sitting on the bleachers watching the hoop game. About a half and hour into the game, a black Jeep pulled up into the parking lot. The bass from the Jeep stereo was kickin, playing a favorite Reggae tune. We watched from across the court. Three young, well built guys roll out of the Jeep. One had a forty of Blue Bull and the other was drinking from the Arizona size beer can.

They took a sip and sat the beer down by the bleachers and started to hoop. Out of nowhere these two big white cops came up the steps to the hoop court.

Without asking any questions, they grabbed them up and then asked where they got the beer. They put the guys through all kinds of changes, and when they didn't see any more beer, they came over to me and asked if I knew where there was some.

The one cop said to me, "Hey, yo man. You know where the beer is. You can tell me."

I was so mad because they asked me and because I know that at the other field they didn't do that. Hershel Field is where the blacks and whites go but they separate themselves from each other. Blacks play on one side, whites on the other.

The white kids and adults drink beer, smoke pot, but the cops don't hassle the whites or pay much attention to the bad things they do. They just bother the blacks.

I would be so mad and so would the other black kids. We used to just talk among ourselves about it. That didn't solve anything, it just gave us a chance to say how we felt.

The public, police blotter, and news-stringer version of the event Shirley describes is familiar enough: "Police crack down on drinking in the park." A routine check on youths suspected of being likely to drink and cause trouble. Or an alternative adult version might chalk it up as one more incident of police harassment and racist targeting of African American males. But neither tells the story behind the story for a thirteen-year-old in the midst of a belligerent, apparently racist public force routinely sweeping in on you and your friends, violating your developing sense of justice, and pressuring you to turn on your peers. This is instead a story of stress, anger, and vulnerability, coupled with a burning need to respond—to deal with a burden we don't expect thirteen-year-olds to bear. As a working partner in her community's dilemma, Shirley helps us see what another police incident means in the lives of those who watch the adult system of justice work. Her "story behind the story" changes it from a past event to a continuing question in her mind and action.

Bringing More Voices to the Table

At the next meeting, Shirley's text triggers a hot discussion. The intentionally demeaning, apparently racist behavior of the police is a stressful issue
every African American in the room—every teenager and adult—had had
to deal with. It raised a volatile, open question: how do you, as an individual
or group, respond?

Although teenagers offer an inside perspective, they don't have an inside
track on truth or certain knowledge of what should be done. Their ideas
must enter the debate with multiple rival hypotheses in which alternatives
get tested, explored, and conditionalized. Moreover, because teenagers are
accustomed to being marginalized in discussions *about* themselves, they are
likely to bring a rhetoric of complaint and blame to situations that call for
responsible contributions aimed at jointly solving a problem. They need to
develop strategies for entering a public discussion as partners, not just to vent
or state personal opinions. In such a discussion, all the stakeholders—teen
and adult—need to explain their perspective, to offer reasons, to give evidence
and examples—in short, to build a case that is open to evaluation. However,
that is not enough, because *open* questions, the difficult ones that can't be
resolved with single answers, call for more than one perspective. The members of this dialogue must also work collaboratively to build a better, more
inclusive, more complex understanding.

The discussion that surrounded Shirley's text was shaped by the practice
of *rivaling*, or rival hypothesis thinking. (The group had talked through an
example of this strategy as a prologue to this session.) As people read their
drafts and revealed a growing number of stories behind the story, the name
of the game was to bring additional perspectives to the table by generating
rival hypotheses—alternative interpretations, possible solutions—and to
then test those hypothesis by considering possible rivals to them. Rivaling
had become a hallmark strategy of CLC projects because it asks writers not
only to construct strong rival hypotheses about hard questions but also to
rival their *own* ideas.

More than that, rivaling is a strategy for bringing multiple voices to the
table. Creating a mixed group of literal voices at a literal table is good but
not always good enough. Rivaling also asks people to generate perspectives
others might hold, to make that effort of imagination to speak from those
positions, to envision possible rivals from those points of view. Rivaling provides a structure for inquiry that seems essential to community building.
Although it celebrates debate, it takes down the barricades of opposition in
which I fire salvos from my personal opinion at yours. In place of opposition
and entrenchment, the rivaling strategy asks me to step out of my shoes into

yours, to even challenge my own interpretation, to generate a richer definition of the problem and a more inclusive sense of possibility.

The text below is an abbreviated version of the dialogue that followed Shirley's draft. Although based on verbatim comments from a tape of the session,
it is formatted around numbered ideas to highlight the alternative solutions
people proposed and some of the rapid-fire responses they elicited as the group
rivaled each idea, exploring its implications and consequences. To understand
the subtext and tenor of this working partnership, however, imagine laughter,
side conversations around the table, and performative talk as both teens and
adults seize the floor offering rival responses to Shirley's problem.

> LEADER: OK, so what do you think they could do?
> IDEA 1: They could go away and talk about it among themselves.
>
> - Yea, but nothing would change.
> - Everybody would just get angry.
> - Maybe one person doesn't have solution, but together they could
>   come up with something they wouldn't have come up with on
>   our own.
>
> IDEA 2: Listen to my idea. You need to get the older citizens in the
> neighborhood with gun licenses and have them patrol the neighbor-
> hood and carry camcorders. When the cops come, they know someone
> is watching them.
>
> - I agree with going to the older citizens and the camcorder, but
>   when you have guns and carry guns things happen. I'm talking
>   here in the voice of experience. You create problems for yourself
>   when you have a gun. If you just have a camcorder and get angry,
>   that's it, you're just going to use the camcorder, but if you have a
>   camcorder and a gun, then you're going to use the gun.
> - If you got something on tape, they going to take it off of you, that's
>   what I'm saying.
> - I'd rather they take the camcorder than risk the chance of killing
>   somebody and being killed because I have a gun.
>
> IDEA 3: If you had a group with camcorders and guns, you'd get some
> publicity. You'd be talked about.
>
> - Yeah, but what kind? Would it be about these people carrying
>   guns or about people trying to record racism?
> - You all know about biased reporting. The issue that started this
>   would be lost in the shuffle.

- Unless there is a spokesperson, like you, Shirley, [*who says*], "No, I'm gonna tell you what happened."

IDEA 4: OK, now my teacher would say you could talk to the police or write a letter to the police or the mayor.

IDEA 5: I'll tell you how my boys would rival that. They'd say, "I'm gonna confront them right there. I'm just not gonna take it. I'm not taking this stuff."

- Yeah, and they would take you right down to the police station. [*laughter*]

IDEA 6: Could you talk with—not the confront version—with the police person in a way you would avoid the outcome of getting . . .

- If this is on the street, there's no way you're gonna talk to them. When they pull somebody over, have to do with somebody, the first thing they say is, "Shuuut up." Unless they ask you a question, you're not allowed to talk to them.
- Anything you said will be held against you. [*laughter*]
- You said a mouthful.

IDEA 7: I think the gun's the most integral part of the operation, because, look, that's what makes the policeman so confident.

- What channel did you watch last night? [*laughter*]
- OK, say it's me an' you; we're about to fight. I've got a gun, you don't have a gun, you're not going to want to fight me no more. But if we've both got guns, it's the wild wild West. It's even. If they have guns, they're real confident; if you don't have anything, you can't say nothing. Make it fair.
- I'm not saying go out to shoot policemen, but you have to do something to make them a little more hesitant.
- I'm glad you're going away to school. [*laughter*]
- Yeah, I'm glad you're leaving town.
- All I'm saying is violence begets violence.
- You're right about that.

LEADER: OK, Shirley, read us what happened.

Shirley had posed an open question that elicited strong voices and attitudes of cynical despair—including claims that meeting force with force was the only answer. However, what the group hadn't realized was that this account also had a factual ending, which Msz. B. eventually asked Shirley to read.

One day we decided to go up as a group and watch the cops discriminate—hassle the Blacks and not the whites. The second time they came up to the field frisking blacks for no reason, we stood there and stared at them and kept staring at them until they noticed that we were witnesses to what was happening.

When they noticed that we were looking at them, they looked like they were getting kinda scared, because they stopped frisking the kids and let them go.

Me and my friends felt good because we felt that we had did something and that now they were scared of us—like we had some power. After they left, we started cracking up with laughter because they were scared like the kids they mess with might be.

What if . . .

- What if I didn't go to the park?
- What if I didn't notice what was happening?
- What if we had decided not to take some action?
- What if the cops had messed with us for looking at them?
- What if the cops that came to our neighborhood were African American?

When Shirley finished, the pause was palpable. Her story had given a face and a feeling to racism and its effect on children. And our discussion had given a name and presence to rival hypotheses and alternative points of view—including the view of a mere ninth-grader, which took the day.

Meanings as Ideas in Action

Shirley's story offers a situated version of community literacy that lets us ask what some of the features named in that earlier capsule statement might actually mean in action. I want to look at three of those features—rhetorical agency, strategic practice, and inquiry—because they raise both theoretical and practical questions about a rhetorical model of community literacy and the attempt to talk across difference.

To Take Agency in Their Lives and Communities

The young men at the CLC table had no postmodern qualms about the possibility or nature of personal agency. They spoke out of a worldview of free will, in which every man has the right to uncontested freedom of action and the uncompromised power to express his inner self. No one worries that the ideas that seem the natural thing to do (e.g., pack some heat of your own; balance the power) might be the product of ideology, assumptions foisted on you by media, American mythology, or gangsta rap. You are an intellectual free agent. And when barriers arise, they are merely an invitation for the hero to surmount all obstacles and prove himself. Taking agency in this scheme of things means taking independent action, working your will on the world, and influencing its material conditions and other people. Never mind that the realities of urban Northside life offer little support for this ideology; it is the source of solutions and the ideal against which manhood and agency will be measured. (Chapter 8 returns to some alternative notions of agency.)

Neither Shirley nor her actions fit this profile of taking agency. This is the story of a thirteen-year-old, little black girl with a quiet, shy personal style. There is no adult, no father with connections standing behind her, no power. Her response to power acting oppressively was not a counterassertion of her own will to reorchestrate the situation. Her act of agency was an act of witness in both the legal and moral sense of the word: an unflinching stance of observation that could easily make her a part of the problem group and an unmoving sign, a statement of alternative values. Her actions were not dramatic—merely a refusal to participate in an unjust police action and a mute testimony to solidarity with the boys. Moreover, did they change the situation? Did the power of witness, the stare of a line of little black girls actually intimidate the police, push them to leave? It is hard to know.

When philosopher and ethicist Charles Taylor (1985a) tries to define such agency, he places it in a world of intractable material conditions, in situations that do not give way to the assertiveness of the hero, who may him- or herself be far from a free agent, subject like the rest of us to the unquestioned assumptions of his or her culture. Taylor argues that agency is the act of taking an action (even though few avenues of action may be open) based on a "vocabulary of worth" or value. Agency is neither power nor control but reflective action—a value-driven choice, even if refusal and mute testimony seem to be the only tools for witness.

Shirley's actions reveal a related form of agency—not only at the park but also at the CLC table. Among her peers, it was no small thing to resist the boisterous, good-humored, but clearly dominant male tone of the group and its assumption that dealing with racist police is men's work or at least a black male problem. But her action was not simply mute resistance or self-expressive speaking up. Shirley takes what I will call *rhetorical agency*—a move that lies at the heart of community literacy. Shirley's *interpretive* act essentially redefines the problem in a way that shapes the discussion and sparks the next level of *inquiry*. To begin, she draws us away from speculative vigilante-cowboy stories into a very personalized, grounded examination of openings for individual action. She poses the sort of problem that has teeth in it—the kind that exists not in the abstract but *for someone*. And her what-if statements guide the discussion to consider the outcomes not only of individual action but institutional change. Are African American cops, for example, really the answer?

In a second sense, Shirley becomes a rhetorical agent by *going public*, starting with the table at the CLC. In the bigger picture, her problem-posing, interpretive agency actually helped map the future of the entire project, sharpening its focus on the stress everyday kids like Shirley confront living in this risky environment. Her contribution became the basis for a series of new projects. One could, of course, argue with the way Shirley poses the problem, could question her reading of the police retreat, or raise new what-if options, and so on. What I see here, however, is a way to understand agency as a rhetorical action in which a young teenager can act in witness to what she values and in a way that poses problems, redefines assumptions, and opens rather than closes down a path for further inquiry.

The Strategic Practice of Intercultural Rhetoric

The popular notion of how to take agency is pretty uncomplicated: in the face of obstacles, exercise your will, and take action to dominate, control, or alter the situation. The popular notion of how to engage in intercultural dialogue has a similarly self-referential simplicity: in the face of social, economic, racial, and cultural differences, demonstrate your good intentions, concern or desire to help, and develop a person-to-person relationship with the "other" person in order to create empathy and openness. And, indeed, significant intercultural dialogue must be grounded in an ethic of care and solidarity that tries to achieve what Martin Buber called an "I/Thou" rather than an "I/It" relationship between people.

However, in the stories of mentors entering the Community House for a seven-week project, coming armed with goodwill, a friendly smile, and the desire for a personal relationship is often not enough to achieve a genuine dialogue or transformed understanding. What the popular notion of a simple person-to-person encounter fails to see is how such dialogue is already entangled in a history of problematic, one-directional relationships of adult to child, rich to poor, white to black, dominant to oppressed, professional to social service worker, and service provider to client. This history of roles and relationships will not evaporate in the face of goodwill. Nor should it. As Iris Marion Young argues in describing communicative democracy, the goal of communication is not "mutual identification [in which people] have transcended what differentiates and divides them and now have the same meaning or beliefs or principles" (1996, p. 127). Rather, the goal is to figure out how to use difference as a resource.

Another barrier to dialogue is the assumption that empathy, once achieved, will also open the door to free and honest self-expression. But intercultural dialogue often takes place in a contested space. As community organizers like Saul Alinsky and Paulo Freire say, historically silenced and marginalized people may not realize their own expertise, may not have the rhetorical tools to explain and elaborate it, and may not trust the outcome of personal disclosure or speaking out. People of privilege are even more likely to lack the rhetorical skills to listen when expertise comes in unfamiliar discourse packages. Even more to the point, each of us will come to this place of dialogue with a variety of strategies for entering the conversation, presenting our selves, reacting to others, building an argument, and so on. But few of us are really prepared to enter the challenging process of inquiry, much less to be a partner in this literate practice to an "other."

The desire for dialogue cannot escape the pressure of history, social context, political process, psychology of communication, or discourse skills. For all these reasons, community literacy replaces this popular notion of how to achieve dialogue with the more guided, purposeful, and heuristic stance of rhetoric and intercultural rhetoric. Chapter 5 returns to inquiry as an ethic of empowerment. Here I wish to focus on inquiry as a strategic rhetorical practice and on the four tools we see at work in Risk and Stress: collaborative planning, seeking the story-behind-the-story, rivaling, and exploring options and outcomes.

Collaborative Planning

Urban residents, especially teenagers, are so often cast in the role of the client, the done-to, and the uninformed that they are not used to taking the role of the partner, doer, and expert. And professionals—in education, social services, health care, and policy—often have trouble abandoning their accustomed seat of authority and relationships based on giving advice rather than seeking knowledge. Collaborative planning is a problem-solving strategy that helps restructure these relations while drawing out the writer's best work. When Mrs. Baskins, Shirley and the other adult-teen pairs went off to document the meaning of "teen stress," they took the roles of supporter and planner. As planner and writer, Shirley takes authority and the floor, talking out her plan (and in this case her text) for the story. Her adult partner is not an advisor, guide, or teacher but a supporter whose job is to draw out Shirley's expertise and best thinking. The supporter does this by engaged listening and encouragement, on the one hand, and on the other, by posing three questions that challenge and draw writers to more sophisticated and articulate rhetorical thinking: (1) What is your point or purpose? (2) How might your readers respond to this? and (3) What text conventions could you use here to achieve your purpose?

The examples of collaborative planning in action in chapters 5, 6, and 9 show how this strategic rhetorical practice differs from simply talking with a partner—how it tries to reverse the pattern of authority in normal adult/ mentor and teen roles, how demanding this change can be for both partners, and how the supporter's strategic prompting (developed from research with expert writers) can draw out significantly new layers of knowledge for the text and self-awareness for the writer.

The Story-behind-the-Story

Telling the *story-behind-the-story* is a more specific literate strategy that not only calls forth what teenagers know but also acknowledges the significance of their situated, local knowledge. The power of its narrative complements the analytical work of rivaling. In telling the story-behind-the-story and revealing the hidden logics and interpretative reasoning behind their actions, marginalized speakers and writers also reveal their own underacknowledged agency. Shirley's attempt to get at the story-behind-the-story takes her behind the statistics on stress and racism, the abstract definitions of the youth problem. It counters the media generalizations that wash out human distinctions, that make all youth who live amidst violence violent, that make every black male in baggy pants and a hoodie a threat to civilization. Telling the story-behind-the-story not only challenges stereotypes but also replaces abstractions with purposeful individuals, and it conditionalizes overgeneralized claims with situated local knowledge.

These accounts of urban stress also reveal the hidden logic behind why children miss school or avoid teachers, how confrontations escalate into suspension, how poverty and the American dream fuel illegal enterprise. They help explain what is going on when teenagers say X, and others hear Y, and why adult policies and good intentions, out of touch with the street, often fail. They reveal a struggle for respect and strategies for survival. In short, this expert inside knowledge is something teenagers have and adults need.

Seeking Rival Hypotheses

Complex questions do not have single answers. The rival hypothesis stance, valued in science and humanities alike, brings alternative perspectives, interpretations, and claims to the table. It can turn advocacy from fixed positions into inquiry. Intercultural rhetoric depends on what my colleagues and I have called a "strong" rival hypothesis stance: one that actively seeks out rival readings, across differences and discourses (Flower, Long, & Higgins, 2000, p. 50). It was the teenagers who adopted this strategy as way to speak up and yet avoid the touchy suggestion of confrontation who named it "rivaling."

Examining Options and Outcomes

Listening empathetically to the logic of others' stories and to the rivals that may challenge our own assumptions and experience is necessary. But it is not enough. Intercultural inquiry tries to weave rival perspectives into a community-constructed plan for action, first by generating multiple, competing, and complementary options. Secondly, it subjects these options to the test of local knowledge—it uses the expertise of young or marginalized people to play out probable outcomes under real conditions. Action plans are then judged, not by good intentions but by predicted consequences. Chapter 6 explores how this focus on outcomes and situated knowledge is rooted in the vision of philosophical and prophetic pragmatism.

Why Be Strategic?

Jürgen Habermas's influential description of the "public sphere" as a space for democratic social deliberation uses *strategy* as a term of disparagement. He contrasts a "communicative" effort to achieve understanding (that is supposed to lead to consensus) with a "strategic" egocentric calculation to influence an opponent in argument (1981/1984, p. 258). I use the term *strategic* in a different and broader cognitive sense to mean taking a self-conscious, heuristic approach to the process of dialogue itself (rather than to achieving a particular outcome). More important, there are two reasons to question whether the widely cited Habermas model (any more than the empathetic, "just talk" plan) is an adequate tool for community literacy. First, the community of community literacy is not the homogenous, privileged, educated, middle-class (male) set of conversants Habermas (1962/1989) imagines in his public sphere. It is a community defined by strong and potentially divisive differences and a community that is paradoxically attempting to use, rather than set aside, some of those differences in the interest of change.

Secondly, an intercultural inquiry poses a distinctive social and cognitive problem. The social challenge is to somehow realign (or at least unbalance) the deep-seated patterns of power and authoritative discourse that privileged groups bring to the table—as well as the patterns of unproductive resistance and disengagement taken by the marginalized. In this sense, we all already have well-learned if unconscious strategies for engaging with difference, but many of these are unlikely to produce knowledge or change.

Both the Habermas norm of "ideal speech" and the "empathetic, just talk" model ignore this challenge, hoping it will go away. Community literacy by contrast puts difference up on the table as both a resource and an obstacle. It then asks participants to deal with the problem self-consciously and strategically—to play the deeply serious game of an alternative discourse.

In collaborative planning, for instance, the mentor/adult/literacy leader works strategically to support the expertise of the writer/youth/community member. Shirley's story-behind-the-story was one only she could tell. Naming the story-behind-the-story as a strategy (i.e., as a valued language game and a source of insider knowledge) often convinces cautious teens to share their interpretation of an experience. The rival hypothesis stance makes the egalitarian rules of the game even more public. By calling on everyone to explore generative rivals to the "hypothesis on the table"—including to one's own contribution—the strategy undercuts the authority that advocates wrap around themselves to silence others. In practice, we have seen it enfranchise teenagers with a nonadversarial authority to address the media or the mayor. We have seen it formally acknowledge the expertise that minimum-wage nursing aides brought to a dialogue with their supervisors and CEO. And it helped give Shirley a voice and a standing in a men's game of cowboy-vigilante problem solving.

The cognitive challenge of intercultural inquiry is less obvious but no less profound. For instance, you and I may talk about "standing up for yourself" or the need for "respect." It is only after our encounter, if at all, that we realize what you and I meant was worlds apart. We talked in abstractions. Though we used the same words, even as we spoke the meaning of those ideas, embedded in remembered situations and past uses, was playing through our minds—and your scenario is nothing like mine. The meaning of respect, of its denial, or what happens when you try to "stand up for yourself" includes the meaning-in-context embedded in these home videos of the mind. The bid for respect that I am screening in my thoughts is set in the halls of a professional workplace; Shirley, on the other hand, is envisioning a confrontational inner-city playground, young people, and police; and you . . . ? The deep reservoirs of situated knowledge on which you draw may contain options and consequences not dreamed of in my philosophy. And on top of this, I may be blithely imposing my own comfortable middle-class schemas, my it's-a-free-country ideology onto your words or more willfully evading their implications. But even with good intentions, how do I ever know that you and I are envisioning different scripts? How do we give each other access to or at least glimpse of our situated knowledge?

This is not just a matter of interpersonal understanding, although it feels that way when supposed understandings between community and university partners fall apart. The cognitive challenge of intercultural inquiry is to deal with the fact that we are all working with limited but complexly different and valuable interpretations of reality. The rhetorical challenge is to *use* difference to build a more expansive representation of that reality—including its problems, their meanings, and their possibilities.

Attempting to build a strategic rhetoric for community literacy makes this challenge explicit. Assembling and giving names to a small toolkit of strategies make them public property for use in a shared discovery. You need, on the one hand, strategies that draw out narrative, reflective interpretation and reveal situated knowledge and on the other, ones that do the analytical work of proposing and testing hypotheses and options. You need strategies that writers themselves control—that make sense, that can be taken out the door and be used in different home cultures.

My own research with John R. Hayes and others on writing and problem solving had mapped some of this risky cognitive terrain before. We had seen that experienced writers not only knew more about discourse conventions and contexts; they also gave themselves more complex problems to solve. They struggled with their purpose as it developed in response to writing, they projected possible readers' responses, and when they ran into conflicts—as writers often do—they pushed the problem to awareness and brought their meaning under negotiation. They also had and used a larger suitcase of strategies. Youthful decision makers, for example, rarely considered more than a single option. And when experienced writers couldn't draw a ready-made solution from their bag of tricks and conventions, they began a strategic search for options. As educators, we had seen that when less-experienced writers/rhetors were prompted to act like experts—to take on the wider task and its conflicts (supported by a planning partner or a heuristic), even students who were "nonwriters" often rose to the occasion. Community literacy faced the cognitive challenge of inquiry by developing not only a body of literate practices but a body of rhetorical problem solvers.[3]

Inquiry as Literate Action

Inquiry involves a lot of talk—and the pitfall of never going beyond just talk. Inquiry in community literacy differs from community organizing, direct political action, or instruction in that it does not target a specific outcome. And its participants are typically a rhetorical community, not a professional decision-making body or a political-action group. The teenagers, the community members, the health care people, the college students, and faculty engage in a project, at a community conversation, or over a text and then go their separate ways. The fruits of inquiry go with them rather than converge on the passing of a new measure or changing a particular institution. So what are the outcomes of inquiry? Is this public form of inquiry really a tool for literate action? Or is it just talk?

One reading of this question is that until we can see rising test scores, low-ered jobless rates, new legislation, or structural institutional change, nothing indeed has happened. A rival hypothesis is that we need finer-grained ways of seeing. I want to look at some outcomes of this pilot project and Shirley's liter-ate act in particular as examples of ways inquiry works. In the place of direct action or clear cause and effect, the process of inquiry started that summer worked first to open up a distinctive new rhetorical space for dialogue de-voted to discovery and change. Starting with an unlikely mix of psychologists, social workers, administrators, educators, community members, supporters, advocates, and teens, the process created a local public engaged around the issues of risk and stress. By the metaphor of opening a space, I mean that it proceeded to substantially expand the network of partners included in its dialogue. Secondly, with each new project, community conversation, or publication, it transformed our knowledge. That is, it constructed a growing representation of the problem, an expanded set of options for action, and a more compelling portrait of the agency and expertise of the teenagers and their families. Finally, it launched its counterpublic agenda, drawing new people into its strategic process of intercultural inquiry, nurturing the rhe-torical agency, and affirming the expertise of young people like Shirley.[4]

Creating a Local Public

The regular CLC project that Shirley joined in the fall took its lead from the summer's inquiry. The teens working with Carnegie Mellon mentors produced a group document they titled *Listen Up! Teen Stress*. Shirley's contribution to the sixteen-page booklet not only takes us deeper into the personal experience of stress, it asks us to be accountable participants in this inquiry. The text describes how her encounter with police and racism became coupled in her mind with the recent murder of a classmate who found himself "out of his neighborhood" (Lyle, 1994). The images seep into her inner life, fueling her own anxieties and anger. When Shirley finds her-self stranded "in the wrong neighborhood," these events come pounding back into her present as flashbacks, shaping her behavior. In this new text, entitled "A Wake Up Call for Adults," printed below, Shirley moves into direct address and eye-to-eye contact with adults at her imagined commu-nity table that includes teachers, counselors, parents, and adults reluctant to acknowledge pressures they don't see. Shirley has in effect implicated all her readers in this reality.

 **A Wake Up Call for Adults**
By Shirley Lyle

"Hurry up Danette, the bus is leaving." Ten minutes later as I was looking out of the foggy windows, I suddenly realized that we were on the wrong bus. Across the street was a gang of boys sitting on a car beside a corner store. They were smoking weed and very drunk, asking me questions. "Hey girl, where you from? What school you go to?"

FLASHBACK

An announcement on the news pounds through my head from yesterday: "Last night a young 14-year-old boy was shot 9 times while he was out of his neighborhood. He was a freshman student at Oliver." A conversation with a friend runs through my head from yesterday: "Hey, Shirley, I'm not staying after school. They might do a driveby or shoot someone." These thoughts run through my head, like a tape recorder: "HE WAS SHOT NINE TIMES WHILE OUT OF HIS OWN NEIGHBORHOOD! NINE TIMES! OUT OF HIS NEIGHBORHOOD! SHOT WHILE OUT OF HIS NEIGHBORHOD! SOMEONE'S GOING TO GET SHOT!"

INNER THOUGHTS

Here I am standing on this corner wondering what's going to happen to me. If I tell him where I'm from, he might have some beef with my neighborhood and make me a victim of his anger just because I was from the wrong part of town. Some people might say, just ignore them. All you have to do is close your eyes and ears. But he's drunk, so if I don't answer him he may come over and start trouble.

On the other hand, the cops drive around here twenty four seven (all the time), but they probably wouldn't stop for me, because the cops around my neighborhood are racist.

FLASHBACK

I started to remember what happened last week at the park. The cops threw the boys against the fence, hassling them, asking them "Where's your I.D.? You all shouldn't be up here late at night anyway. What you think you grown, drinking beer?" (They said this even though they had I.D.). But I noticed that they didn't hassle the white kids; they never watched them when they played ball. So should I really call the cops, 'cause it's going to start a whole lot of trouble. All they are going to do is hassle the kids that are asking me questions, throw them against the wall, and frisk them, and make them want to fight back. And when that happens, the kids are going to come back for me. I have to decide soon. . . .

COMMENTARY

This story was just an example to show you that kids go through a lot of stressful things. Some kids get angry at the world because some cops have a bad image of kids and take it out on the kids, but it also works both ways. Kids go through a lot of deaths and have to watch where they are going for their sake too. Some kids may kick and throw things and take their anger out on people like parents, faculty and staff. Adults, try not to take it personally because that's the only way some kids know how to handle their problems.

Here are some things I can suggest for kids to do. Just relax. Go to your room and listen to music. Take time out for yourself to think about what is going on. It's not bad to cry. Try to get yourself in order and calm down. If that doesn't work for you, take a walk and talk to yourself. Try to get some balance. Think about how things are going right as well as the things going wrong. Try taking a walk in a park. At the park you can say things louder than you could at home. You can scream if you want to there. If you think about it, it's like talking to the world. You can do almost anything at the park, and you can get your feelings out.

Some people may say why don't you talk to a teacher? Well that can cause you even more stress. Like when my friend told a teacher (whom she trusted) about her problems at home and then later heard the teacher talking and laughing about it in the teacher's room. Other people may say, why don't you tell your friends? I feel when you talk to your friends, you just share some of the same anger. It doesn't lead to anything. What you just shared with them may get out, and then everyone knows all your business and problems. Some people may say that you're scared of your own race then make a big joke out of it, saying you're just as bad as the cops—you're a racist too.

If you decide to share your problems with someone, share them with yourself so that what you're thinking, saying and feeling will be clear, not only for you but for someone else as well.

In November, Shirley's imagined audience became a literal one. The project group chose her text as one of three to dramatize and discuss as part of their public Community Conversation. The mayor, and that meant the media as well, would be there. In the Community House's packed auditorium, the writing and videos of these teenagers ignited a response. In the midst of open discussion, the normally silent Dion, a CLC teenager, stands up at the back of the room. He talks about how "fast-breaking" sensational news coverage of youth and violence seems to implicate any and all inner-city teens, never pausing to record the grief of families, the pain and anxiety of people living in neighborhoods with violence. During the evening news, the local

TV anchor team screens this clip, then pauses to repeat and muse on Dion's words, "I'd rather see it right at 11:00 than wrong at 6:00."

Since July, Shirley has seen her words become a published text, the foundation for a scripted performance, the catalyst for a public discussion, and a wake-up call to a million potential TV-news viewers. Shirley's literate acts were like a pebble cast in a stream. They created a series of ripples that invited not only an increasingly wider public into her concerns but also led to transformations for Shirley herself as an author and working partner in building a better community.

The process her literate act helped set in motion was often cumulative. The next semester a new group of teens transformed the "Wake-Up" text into the script for the CLC's Hands On video production team. Shirley was the director; the other teens were scriptwriters, actors, and producers. By dramatizing a deeply felt and shared difficulty, the *Shirley's Story* video opened another door for exploring the options for dealing with stress.

That summer, the CLC team began an experiment with another way to bring more people into this conversation. Almost a year from Shirley's first tentative foray into social, literate action, these discoveries became the spark for the production of an interactive training video called *Teamwork: Teenagers Working through Community Problems*. It models the strategies of collaborative inquiry and invites viewers to a virtual table for a community-based, problem-solving dialogue about stress.

This growing body of work also became a springboard for Carnegie Mellon PhD students and for discussion outside the Northside. Julia Deems and Amanda Young created two interactive multimedia computer programs, one dealing with risk and respect, another with health and sexuality, which found their way into high school classrooms, Planned-Parenthood counseling, the free clinic of a major children's hospital, and a research program on pregnancy prevention. Another inquiry, which began in the emergency room of Ian Rawson's hospital, led to a research project by Young on patient-doctor relations and to a literacy project started by Lorraine Higgins on women's health care in a low-income neighborhood.[5]

Writing played a central role in this process, as the inquiry moved from talk to text (informal texts, published documents, scripts, and performances) that led back to more talk and further action. However, the text did not exist as an end in itself but as a catalyst for inquiry into people's daily lives. The writing (in text, video, and computer programs) allowed community literacy to create an increasingly articulated problem. And at tables located in Pittsburgh and at conferences on rhetoric, composition, computers, argument, and health care, it brought a growing network of people into a strategic and collaborative search for more and better options.

For funders, these are the outcomes that matter: numbers of people involved, events and objects produced, dissemination, connections made with other institutions, visible impact on something else. But inquiry has other outcomes that deepen this impact, which unfortunately we have not yet found adequate ways to track and validate. One of these is knowledge transformation.

Transforming Understanding

From July to November, Shirley's witness to the realities of her life had undergone some transformation, just as her network had grown. In "Wake-Up Call," a personal-experience story had metamorphosed into a compelling image of an inner life that cannot be disentangled from destructive social forces. In her strongly focused analysis, stress is now envisioned as a physical, psychological, and spiritual problem. Its presentation in artfully crafted flashbacks and commentary reveals the strong rhetorical purpose of a wake-up call.

This transformation is not limited to Shirley's thinking. The discussion initiated by our broad statement on health and stress had turned into an inquiry that went beneath the statistics to the lived experience of risk. It began to capture the attendant effects a stressful environment has on young people on the street, in school, and in their inner lives. But it also showed what the official version rarely includes—the story of personal agency, of decision making, and rhetorical action the young and socially powerless nevertheless take. The documents that followed had names like *Teen's Stress and Survival: A Report on the Risk and Stress of Growing Up in Pittsburgh's Inner City; Are You Ready? The Real Deal about Growing Up;* and *Force: An Everyday Thing.* Taking the fall project booklet as a whole, the problem itself had also morphed: the teenagers had turned the discussion of risk, stress, and violence (issues the adults named) into a reflection on how these flames were often ignited (from their point of view) by the need for respect.

By the time of the *Teamwork* "training video" the next summer, the most striking transformation of the problem appears in the segment in which teens are demonstrating the rivaling strategy, for here Shirley's problem turns into a community's problem, brought to life in multiple representations. The *Teamwork* video introduces the CLC's new media heroes—the Community Problem-Solving Team. As the drama unfolds on camera, the team is on the case, and Jake is putting the video tape of *Shirley's Story* on the VCR for the team (and us) to see. (The video is, of course, the one recently produced by the spring project team, which was based on the wrong-neighborhood episode and Shirley's flashback in "A Wake Up Call for Adults.") As the team responds to Shirley's taped plea for help and advice, we, the viewers, watch the team demonstrate the CLC strategies and see a model of community literacy in action. We see the team talk over the story-behind-the-story, work out rival hypotheses, and mull over Shirley's options and possible outcomes. Occasionally, Yvonne, a playfully conspiratorial narrator, turns to us and the camera to point out the strategies the group is using. At each pause, she asks us to turn off our own VCR and try these strategies, first on Shirley's dilemma and later on problems our own group names. In the excerpt below, the team members have just started their analysis of the initial wrong-neighborhood episode in Shirley's video.[6]

Teamwork Dialogue

Mia: Aw, c'mon. Shirley doesn't even *have* a problem! In that video when those three guys come rolling out, it just gets her imagining things. Those fools are just wannabes. Hell, one of 'em is white!

Yvonne: [*turning to the camera*] Here comes some rivaling. Some people think it's a gang problem, some people don't.

Jake: No way! Look at the way they're dressed, man.

Shaquon: Yeah. And the way they come out of nowhere and get right in her face.

Christy: You *know* they're threatening her.

Jake: Yeah. It's all *gang* stuff.

Mia: Wait a minute. Lemme try this one from the guys' point of view, OK? Look again at Shirley boppin' along the sidewalk. She's fresh, she's good looking, she's alone. Get it? I mean, she's like Little Red Riding Hood! They're just having fun scaring her a bit. It's like flirting, you know?

Jake: Flirting! Look again, sister. Look at all that gangsta graffiti stuff all over the old house where those hood guys were hanging out. And remember the gang graffiti at the beginning? Man, that stuff's no joke! And that house really looks like a crack house. It all adds up.

Joe: How about if we put ourselves in a cop's shoes?

[On the video, the teens camp it up with the Wizard of Oz red-shoe trick. Complete with a magical zing, the camera zooms in on paratrooper boots, and Joe is suddenly transformed into a gruff-speaking impersonator in a policeman's cap; Mom, who speaks next with folded arms and her mouth in a tight line, is wearing fluffy slippers; the Counselor with a pencil in her bun is in sensible shoes, and so on.]

Joe-as-cop: By the time we get there, the people involved already have ten witnesses saying they're somewhere else. There's just nothing we can *do* about it.

Jake: Sure. What about a *bad* cop's shoes?

Jake-as-bad-cop: Hold up, kids, y'all need to get away from there—quit messin' with them nice people. I'm gonna give y'all to "three" to get your punk ass outta there: *three.*

Mia: Well, what if Shirley thinks she can't talk to her mom, right? But, putting ourselves in her mom's shoes . . .

Mia-as-mom: Shirley, it is your fault you're in this situation. I always tell you to pay attention. You wouldn't be missing your bus if you got out of bed on time.

Shaquon: Or maybe a friend could help.

Christy: Yeah, standing in her friend's shoes could help a lot.

Christy-as-friend: I *told* you that was a bad neighborhood. We weren't gonna go there unless we were together.

Mia: You know, a school counselor would have some ideas.

Mia-as-counselor: Shirley's grades have been slipping a lot lately, and I'm afraid stress has been playing a major role in this.

Joe: Or what about somebody who saw the boys threatening Shirley, like the storeowner across the street?

Joe-as-storeowner: These kids have been hanging around here, causing trouble, harassing people. The police should be patrolling this area more often.

Shaquon: I still want to try standing in those three *guys'* shoes.

Shaquon-as-guy: She's kinda cute—I could be tryin' to *talk* to her, instead of tryin' to *get* her. I don't even know why I'm doing this. It's all good; the boys think I'm hard, you know?

Jake: Yeah, we gotta try seeing what was going on in their *minds.*

Jake-as-guy: To tell you the truth, I was afraid of *not* being with those guys.

Yvonne: [*to camera*] Go, Problem Team! OK, do you see how these rivaling strategies are working? Come on and help us out. What shoes do you want to step into? Ready? OK, just shut your VCR off now.

Through rivaling, the CLC team transforms Shirley's inner problem into a shared social problem, one that troubles not only Shirley but also the harassing boys, the cops, and the storeowner. As each player shares his or her perspective, the cumulative representation is more than the sum of its parts. There is a structural social issue here that has led to aimless, jobless boys on street corners, hostility among neighbors, police, and storeowners—a structure in which everyone is implicated. There are individuals caught in the net of its situation who need to rethink the part they play. And there is an opening for new options. And equally important, from the point of view of the video, there is a portrait here of how go about representing such problems—how to intentionally and strategically seek out strong rivals that tell us what this issue means in practice.

And yet, we must be cautious about a claim for knowledge transformation. For many adults this dialogue (its texts and events) was likely to be a source of new knowledge but not necessarily of new understanding. By that, I mean that we do not know if or how this information took root and changed their own representations of the problem or affected their actions. From a cognitive point of view, a change in understanding would mean that this information is no longer someone else's words, images, and ideas but has been integrated into one's own network of knowledge, building new connections between one's ideas, experience, and beliefs expanding and, perhaps, even restructuring a part of that network around new organizing ideas. So it is only in the teenagers' writing that we see actual evidence of this kind of understanding, when they construct a new interpretive framework that connects their own experience, feelings, and those of others.

The Promise of a Counterpublic

From a social point of view, the outcome of this inquiry needs to be a shared understanding. Not because the specific knowledge one can transmit is so crucial but because the process of dialogue—which can affect individual understandings—is. This case study has tracked a series of transformations in talk and text supported by community literacy. At the same time, it keeps posing the question, how does this inquiry produce broader shared understanding, much less change? I end with a note of hope buried in a dilemma. When I piloted Julia Deems's (1996) hypermedia program, "Rivaling about Risk," in an urban school, three young men in braids and Afros, known for frequently missing school, were there for every class, actually leading the rivaling sessions as we looked at the realities of gangs, neighborhood pressures, the necessity to fight. For many students, this was a situation with no real options—you just did what you had to do. (It in fact took the authority of an older student to assert that we really could talk about choices—even within hard constraints.) On the last day, when I taped an interview with the three young men together, I wondered if they thought sustained discussions like this, about the pressures of a gang culture, had any place in school. Two things stand out from that tape. One was my own tone of incredulity after I asked, "This seems so important. Do people talk about these things, outside of school?" and Will replies, "No." "Really?" I ask. Will, with a kind of helpless shrug, just shakes his head "no." Change depends on dialogue—on both the circulation of alternative ideas and the personal understanding that guides action. But Will and his friends appeared to be charting their course through a vast fog of silence. Shirley's solution also depended on isolation: "Try to get your self in order. . . . When you talk to your friends, you just share the same anger. It doesn't lead to anything." At the same time, these young men had been at every writing session and had been spokespersons in the class. As we were about to turn the tape off, Will and Junius volunteered a second critical insight into how inquiry produces change: it creates a counterpublic.

> *Junius*: If everybody do it, not just one person, it might make a differ-
> ence. A group of kids, a group of adults, you understand, talk about
> it, it might bring more people to the group.
> *Will*: Somebody, probably somebody's girlfriend, sitting there talking
> about it and she could go back and tell her boyfriend.

What they envisioned was a local counterpublic, an alternative to the code of tough silence. Chapter 6 looks at this knotty problem in more depth. What are the outcomes of inquiry? How does it lead to networks of people in dialogue and to the transformation of understanding that express themselves in action? As a first step in that question, think back to the mentors in chapter 1, and ask, how does their academic experience in rhetoric and composition prepare them to participate in a rhetoric of making a difference?

Appendix: Initial Problem Statement
for Risk and Stress Project

The Community: A Source of Health, A Site of Stress?

Growing up in a healthy community is a birthright many Americans take for granted. A child is wrapped in a web of support–provided by family, home, neighborhood, by institutions like the school, church, and clubs, by health care, by city services. This healthy community challenges its young with "believable and attainable expectations and standards" for achievement while providing a backdrop of the support and security that encourages growth. A healthy community creates an ecology of mind, body and spirit.

However, many urban centers, like ours, no longer make good on this promise of community. Young people find themselves forced to cope— often beyond their powers to do so—with the overwhelming, everyday stress of troubled homes, violent streets, and struggling schools. Consider these sobering statistics: [Recent youth data on the increase of abuse, STD's suicide, homicide, and depression follow.]

In the 60's a revolution in medical thinking called the "wellness movement" called for the health profession to treat the whole person, their attitudes, their behavior, their inner resources, not just disease. But in the 90's the leaders of that movement began to see that the community you live in is itself a source of health—or its opposite. In fact, one's community may have more influence on even physical disease than anything technomedicine can do. Consider, for instance, most of the major diseases that affect Americans, from hypertension to asthma, diabetes, and heart disease. Say you wished to predict who and how many would get one of these diseases, and whether they were likely to have complications or to die. Would any single predictor—any test, any screening procedure—let the medical profession predict this range of factors—incidence, frequency, morbidity, and mortality? In fact such a factor does exist and it overshadows any test medical technology has devised; it is an even stronger predictor of long-term threat than whether you already have the disease. That predictor is living in poverty. A young person's SES (social economic status) says a lot about what the future holds for them when there is no health-giving community offering regular health care, affordable housing, safe streets, nutrition—offering an image of hope and a future that justifies preventive behavior. The statistics for future physical health are grim.

But what about the lives of individual teenagers, living in the urban community adults have created? The writers that come to the CLC look healthy, full of energy, dressed in baggy pants and sneakers with logos. Normal. Until you begin to hear individual stories: the brother, the cousin who has been shot; the mom on crack; the school suspension; the uncertain future; the poverty lurking beneath the need to save face. A few live in the projects, most come from old Pittsburgh neighborhoods scattered around the city, many belong to an extended network of cousins, aunts and uncles. The L.A. style gang violence in their neighborhoods has come suddenly. The drive-bys and the pointless shootings, the violence triggered by neighborhood identity (rather than adult drug deals) is relatively new to the city—older teenagers date it from the movie, *Boyz in the Hood.*

What does mean to be 14 years old and have friends and schoolmates who have been shot or killed? To grow up watching your own back as you walk home from school? To recognize the police as a "rival gang" trying to rule by intimidation and brutality? To see the streets a few blocks away become a dangerous neighborhood you don't dare to walk through. Your mom is angry because you won't—don't dare to—wear the red coat she paid for last year. Red is the Bloods color and you live in a Crip (blue) neighborhood, and are bussed to a school dominated by LAW (they wear black). And what are the options for what we used to call "getting out"? Getting out to where? Another high school with its own gangs and sets, where you are unknown and less protected? Out into an economy with little promise and less space for you?

The teenagers who come to the CLC are trying to grow up, to become somebody, to spread some wings. But the health-giving community they need to turn to is sometimes a dangerous place, its institutions ineffectual. Teenagers develop personal strategies for survival, and when they see those strategies fail, they see themselves labeled as the Problem by the mainstream political discourse. In place of a health-giving web of support, they face the unholy trinity— stress, and it its backwash, depression, and rage.

Community: A Collaborative Rhetorical Forum

Communities are also political units and rhetorical forums. Many urban centers like ours pride themselves on being sites of struggle and intercultural collaboration. They recognize the truth in the African saying, "It takes a whole village to raise a child." However, as cities and schools try to reinvent their outdated youth policy and as communities struggle to construct better alternatives, teenagers see little place for themselves in this process. Policies in health, education, and social services are often based on models of deficits and disease that turn youth into clients, patients, and problems. They fail to offer teenagers productive roles in the larger community or to position them as responsible agents of change. Moreover, programs that deal with the effects of poverty and crime are seldom informed by teenage perspectives. They ignore the local expertise needed to build a healthier urban community.

Community literacy offers a ground for constructing an alternative forum guided by a model of collaborative problem solving and communication in which urban communities, including their teenagers, work to define themselves as a source of health, wholeness and intercultural shalom.

Community literacy is based on a bold but profoundly simple premise: *Urban teenagers must become working partners in an intercultural collaboration to build healthy communities.*

The success of this collaborative forum is grounded on three principles that change the role of teenagers and adults.

Three Principles for Working Partnerships

• *Working Partners* solve *joint problems*. Institutions must invite teenagers to the table, into the analysis of problems (not as tokens, merely to comment on solutions) and into attempts to explore options and the consequences of decisions that involve youth. Teenagers bring expertise in interpreting the impact of urban stress and in revealing the hidden logic behind those coping behaviors that schools and health providers want to comprehend. In short, teenagers can help generate the new, situated knowledge of the inner city that health professionals and educators are calling for.

• *Working Partners* must *develop the problem-solving skills that lead to understanding and action*. If teenagers are to participate in this public conversation, they must move beyond the discourse of complaint and blame by learning new strategies for planning, collaboration, rival perspective taking, and argument. We as adults must support them in learning new strategies for goal-directed planning and decision-making that support not only discussion but personal change in their own lives.

> • *Working Partners engage in intercultural collaboration and reflection.* Just as mentoring broadens the cultural awareness of college students and teens, adult institutional partners can harness the expertise of urban youth when enter they engage in reflective, intercultural community planning that seeks new knowledge from diversity.

 ## Teenagers as Expert Working Partners

Community literacy—and its vision of working partners—invites people to step out of some of their normal roles and relationships to focus on a problem none can solve alone. This project will explore what we might call "the hidden stories" of stress and health. Drugs, alcohol, pregnancy, and violence make up the public story of teenage health; but what about the stress of living with these problems everyday, of standing in the eye of the hurricane? What are the hidden health stories of kids caught in a health-threatening community?

Part 2

Theoretical Frameworks and Working Theories

The next three chapters are about the multiple theoretical frameworks that stand as challenging and shaping voices behind community literacy. These frameworks were evident in the diverse literate practices, the competing ideas, and unspoken assumptions that mentors, literacy leaders, and teens brought to the CLC. The significant distinctions among these frameworks often reside in the images they offer of what it means for the discipline of rhetoric and composition to be engaged in social concerns, what it means to take the role of a mentor or community partner, and what it could mean to empower oneself and others.

The scaffold for these comparisons is the distinction between a rhetoric of speaking up, of speaking against, of speaking with others, and of speaking for something. Although this frame cannot capture the complexity of actual practice, I use it to foreground a central tendency in mainstream paradigms and to help me articulate the more fully rhetorical and dialogic alternative I believe we need to develop.

This section is framed by academic debates. However, the real story emerging in these chapters resides less in abstract theoretical frameworks and more in the operational working theories that were constructed over time within this history. As John Dewey argues, our theories and ideas will remain a fancy unless they are transformed into working ends-in-view by a realistic inquiry into the conditions and consequences of change. These chapters show academics, mentors, and activists working to construct situated working theories of engagement, collaboration, and empowerment.

3   *Images of Engagement in Composition Studies*

The teenagers, parents, neighbors, teachers, and vice principals who came to the Community Literacy Center events were sometimes perplexed when they tried to place the community-literacy publications and performance in the context of literate practices they knew and expected—the dutiful, correct, personal essay of public schooling, the hip "styling" of teen culture, or the warm fuzzy, recognition discourse of social service/youth programs. Community organizers and neighborhood activists felt a little more at home, but the second word of the CLC's chosen name was *literacy*—and with that came an academic agenda that was as full of multiple meanings and competing stances as the notion of community had been. As the CLC began to build the working definition of community literacy, sketched in chapter 1, it had to negotiate these alternatives. To understand those choices, it helps to reflect on the academic context and the debates surrounding literacy and how it could become what I am calling a *rhetoric of engagement*.

This rhetoric—the art of making a difference through inquiry, deliberation, and literate action in the name of equality and social justice—has been a distinctive voice in American life. And not just in politics but in the more cautious enclaves of our academic and intellectual life. Within the academy, one of the widest bandwidths for this rhetoric of change has been the tradition of American philosophical pragmatism. It has broadcast the powerful voices of Ralph Waldo Emerson (on self-determination in the face of tradition, on abolition, and on moral awareness), William James (on individual consciousness and social consequences), Charles Sanders Peirce (on the communal and revisable nature of our knowledge), John Dewey (on progressive education, social reform, and democracy based on questioning, critical intelligence), W. E. B. DuBois (on the human creative powers of America's subjugated peoples), Reinhold Niebuhr (on walking the tightrope of love and justice in a tragic world), Richard Rorty (on accepting the contingency and instability of our knowledge), and Cornel West (on acting from a prophetic—a critical and committed—stance for love and justice).

I draw this thumbnail sketch from Cornel West's provocative history of philosophical pragmatism and its socially committed, outcome-oriented approach to deep critical thinking. In a book fittingly titled *The American Evasion of Philosophy,* West (1989) talks about how a new focus on the forms of power, "be they rhetorical, economic, or military powers . . . has returned humanistic studies to the primal stuff of human history, that is, structured and circumscribed human agency in all its various manifestations" (p. 4). It is this daring combination that marks West's pragmatism—a vision of individuals committed to being the active moral agents in their own lives even as they work for a clear-sighted recognition of the forces without and within their own minds that deny such action. Moreover, this hard-won spot, this "author's chair" of human agency and reflective action is no longer reserved for the "elite cultural creators" of traditional humanism—the heroes, poets, and leaders. It is occupied by those whom West calls *everyday people*—the young as well as adult, student as well as teacher, and those at the bottom of hierarchies based on class, race, gender, or sexual orientation.

This rhetoric of social awareness and commitment to change, especially on the behalf of others, has taken root in the teaching of writing and the development of rhetoric and composition as a discipline. A rather remarkable achievement for such a publicly owned institution as freshman composition. However, this history is also a site of some disagreement over just what teachers and students should actually *do*, within the world of education, to make a meaningful difference. That discussion, which has involved most of us as teachers or students, formed a critical prologue to the rhetorical choices that shaped community literacy.

Composition Studies: A Response to Social Concerns

From its emergence in the 1960s and 1970s, rhetoric and composition studies has had a history of redefining itself in response to genuine social concerns. Even as it joined the general rush to specialized professionalism found throughout American universities, rhet/comp has been a sort of poster child for the attempt to make a difference through education. In doing so, it also gave itself a tension-filled agenda. For example, rhetoric and composition studies has long held itself accountable to the public and social significance of writing—to the outcry from schools, businesses, and social advocates when "Johnnie" couldn't write in the way they demanded.[1] At the same time, it embraced a potentially contradictory goal of developing personally empowered writers. These individuals would have the capacity to operate in academic, professional, and civic forums by their own lights—which might differ from what the "public," hoping for career or vocational training, had intended. And then—often in tension with both of these agendas—composition saw itself as participating in a broader cultural conversation around issues of social justice in a diverse and economically divided nation. Meanwhile, these agendas were often at odds with the need to achieve the status of a respectable academic discipline. As a result, the problem of the field was not only how to study, teach, and build on rhetorical *theory* (the standard academic agenda) but also how to "do rhetoric" as the art of making a difference. How were we to achieve those broader outcomes—to have the personal, public, and social significance to which the field laid claim? The dominant paradigms of rhet/comp arrived at different ways to manage this tension.

Despite their differences, the writing-process movement and the later turn to social-process theorizing were each success stories of academic engagement—examples of a discipline motivated by a socially responsive effort to make a worldly difference within its own arena. The "process" attempt to redefine composition was a child of the 1960s. It challenged teachers to liberate students from the sterile world of five-paragraph themes and textual conventions by championing individually meaningful writing based on personal exploration and rhetorical invention. It redefined composition as inquiry and expression.

A second major shift in composition studies, associated with the idea of a "social" process, was responding in part to another political reality: a growing number of underprepared working-class and minority students were appearing in mainstream colleges—which were even less prepared for them. Compositionists began to realize that if the current-traditional paradigm of the 1950s (with its focus on correct, conventional texts) had failed these students, the process movement (with its happy neglect of the conventions that conferred social power) was in danger of failing them, too. The nurturing, freewriting, composition classroom with its focus on the individual student could no longer afford to ignore the cultural, social, and institutional expectations and processes that not only marginalized students but also made their teachers blind to and complicit in these social processes.

Meanwhile, the impulse toward liberal, ethical, and compassionate rhetorical action in both of these schools of composition thought coexisted with the need to build a theoretical framework for composition's call to practical action. Even more problematic, such a theory would also have to carve out a professional identity within the field of English studies—a field that has often held itself above practical action.

Rhetoric offered a way to support both the impulse to social action and the call to professional respectability and power. The "new rhetoric" of the 1970s revived a powerful tradition of writing as discovery and change, offering a legitimizing history to composition and a theoretical framework for research in its process.[2] It gave life to the notion of audience. When the field redefined itself as the study of an enlarged "social process," the contribution of rhetoric often metamorphosed into the study of "rhetorics" or discourses of different social groups. We began to reread the Sophists, to recover rhetorica in the work of early and current feminists, to analyze cultural and institutional discourses, and to examine, once again, the definition of academic discourse across the curriculum.[3]

This renewal of rhetorical awareness, however, was not so evident in the composition classroom. When movements of resistance begin to solidify (or ironically, turn into the dominant paradigm themselves), their complex theories turn into "teachable" conventions of discourse and the mini-genres of the composition classroom and textbook.[4] So just as the five-paragraph theme of the 1950s gave way to the equally standardized expectations of freewriting and the personal essay, these soon gave way to the more literary conventions of critical analysis and its ideological critique of social texts. The institutionalized versions of these different educational stances reveal how some of the theoretical voices and practical arts of rhetoric—elements that I believe are central to the rhetoric of engagement—have been buried, marginalized or lost.

Speaking Up, Against, With, or For

The fundamental question to ask about one's composition paradigm is, what is it actually teaching students to do? The expressivist paradigm, for instance, was a rhetoric of personal exploration and empowerment. It transformed students into "writers"—giving them the safe houses and the tools with which to *speak up*—to discover and express themselves, their personal and cultural identities. The social paradigm in composition, on the other hand, drew its rhetoric from literary and cultural studies, which had already developed a highly elaborated practice of deconstructive reading and ideological critique. It offered students a formidable set of literate practices that allowed them to *speak against something*—against the media and ideology, against their own assumptions and inclinations as well as against institutions, oppression, and power. It conferred the certainty of critical consciousness and the authority to resist the status quo. Together the expressive and critical approaches to composition heightened our awareness of the "others" in our society—the people silenced and marginalized by race, culture, gender, class, or poverty.

But what these paradigms—that so strongly influence teaching and scholarship—do not do well is teach how to *speak with* others across the chasms of difference. Although they prompt us to worry about (and repeatedly critique ourselves for) thinking we can speak "for" the powerless, they have little to tell writers about how they might achieve the difficult role of partners in inquiry with those "others." I imagine our students entering the culturally diverse public forums that materialize in dorm rooms, fraternity meetings, or professional courses and later in policy-drafting sessions at the office and decisions at the PTA. And I see rhetors standing up in a sort of splendid isolation, prepared to tell their stories, to assert their feelings, or to critique assumptions and recognize and resist patterns of power. But *speaking up* in self-disclosure or critique does not support the difficult art of dialogue. Where do we learn how to *speak with* others? How could we develop an intercultural rhetoric that supports dialogue, deliberation, and collaborative action across differences?

Our current paradigms also prepare us well to *speak against* forces that diminish and oppress, to deconstruct, critique, and resist. They let us stand without compromise, outside and above. But they often fail us when we face the much more difficult practice of *speaking for something*—in ways that actually make a difference. How do we prepare ourselves to go beyond the safety of critique into the vulnerable stance of reflective, revisable commitment—to speak *for* values or actions even as we acknowledge them to be our current best hypotheses? How do we teach the rhetorical art of ongoing inquiry versus position taking (even when that position is inspired by a liberatory ideology)? And how do we develop the willingness, the acumen, and the literate techne to go beyond questioning the status quo and step toward praxis, toward deliberative and (always) experimental action based on goals and values we are able to articulate (and prepared to revise)?

Lost Voices, Marginalized Practices

In the 1970s, Ken Macrorie taught us that we were "uptaught"—wrapping our students and ourselves in the cotton wool of convention-bound theme writing (1970). I came of age, academically speaking, in that heady atmosphere of change. Writing my dissertation on Charles Dickens had been a genuinely happy interlude, but despite the lure of playing the academic game, I was aware of a nagging pointlessness in the project of publication and in the requirement I felt to create that voice of witty, sophisticated (and middle-aged male) authority, because it was such a voice that often justified a "new reading" of a canonical text.

For me, reading Richard Young and Bill Coles opened a new door on the student as a thinking subject (Young, Becker, Pike, 1970; W. E. Coles, 1978).

Research was liberation into meaningful work. Writing to publish suddenly had the immediacy and significance of sharing discoveries. Teaching mattered as a way to empower students with a new sense of their options as writers and thinkers. Yet, in this early enthusiasm, I vividly remember the CCC Conference conversation with Sonda Perl when I suddenly realized that my beloved but rather specifically rhetorical and cognitive notion of the writing process was not at all what many other people had in mind by the magical word "process."

As the process movement settled into its classroom paradigm, writing became identified with a personal, expressive activity—not a reader-directed rhetorical action. And the process, as Arthur N. Applebee points out, became synonymous with what might be called the "student process," a set of obligatory classroom activities from freewriting to peer review and rewriting (1986). The writer (envisioned as a student) was to be guided though a valued but standardized classroom activity without reference (as Applebee argued) to its effectiveness for a particular task. This domesticated notion of "the writing process" lost contact with the idea of strategic choice I found so central to a more cognitively based rhetoric and to educational research.

Both Aristotle and the Sophists, the early shapers of this rhetorical paradigm, had understood invention (the generative work of writing) as an intensely heuristic act. Strategies had a central but heuristic or probabilistic value: they had to be used as tools. Unlike the student in a "process" classroom, the rhetor was envisioned as a much more self-conscious and strategic agent, making choices, monitoring not only her own thinking but also its outcomes in the resulting text (did it reach her goals or criteria?) and in the response of real and imagined readers. Aristotle's probabilistic "art" of persuasion and cognitive psychology's portrait of expert, strategic problem-solving came to have less and less place in this image of *the* writing process. So if rhetoric initially figured boldly in research, scholarship, and theorizing of the field, the notion of rhetorical action was reduced to a faint strand in the canonized process paradigm.

The social-process movement was in one sense a reawakening of rhetorical consciousness. Its great accomplishment was to bring a commitment to social justice and a heightened consciousness of oppressive powers into composition. One initial impetus to embrace such theorizing was, of course, the continuing struggle to acquire professional authority within literature departments. Doing critical theory conferred status to compositionists, as did doing historical rhetorical scholarship (North, 1987). But as that paradigm began to shape academic practice and crystallize into the classroom genre of cultural critique, it became apparent that the field was losing its hold on some essential elements of rhetoric. Its teaching practice took composition back to the theory-guided analysis of and response to valued texts but its new set of theoretical lenses focused on the play of social power and on the conventions of academic discourse that would let a writer into its prestigious literate clubs. Committed to change but preoccupied with uncovering, naming, analyzing, and rehearsing the presence of oppressive ideological, cultural, social, and institutional forces, this paradigm lost (or denied the significance of) the dilemmas and decisions of the individual writer/rhetor.[5] And it lost its hold on the vision of Cornel West's prophetic pragmatism—the possibility of individual agency working *within* powerful constraints and the possibility of ethical literate action within nonacademic, public forums.

This aspiration to engagement lays down a challenge: How can teachers and students learn not only to speak *up* and *against* but also learn to speak *with* others (by which I mean across differences) and *for* something as a necessary part of literate education? If rhetoric and composition is to achieve the personal, public, and social significance to which the field lays claim, it must recover the practice of "doing" rhetoric in its wider civic and ethical sense. There are many ways to interpretation this goal, but the dominant paradigms of composition studies do not always point us in that direction.

Engagement Based on Intercultural Inquiry and Literate Action

The Community Literacy Center's experiment in a rhetoric of engagement was in part a response to the burst of research and theory in composition. For me, it also shaped (more accurately, insisted on) the questions my own research should pose. Conversation between research and practice takes many forms, but they have a way of crystallizing themselves in memory around decisions and discovery points. I can date an important turn in my own research priorities from a very material moment. I was at the National Reading Conference (NRC) in Tucson, Arizona, with Wayne C. Peck, who was at the time director of Pittsburgh's Community House, but whom I knew primarily as an intriguingly nontraditional PhD candidate in rhetoric with a Harvard University Master's of Divinity and a commitment to the urban neighborhood around his church and community center. We took one of those dawn walks that cold desert air inspires, and he began to lay out his vision of transforming the Community House from a traditional provider of summer camps, midnight basketball, and meeting places to a center for community learning—based on writing. And he did not mean after-school tutoring driven by the limited literacies of the neighborhood schools but the kind of powerful rhetoric of self-definition and socially effective action we were offering to Carnegie Mellon undergraduates. I was becoming aware, as many of us are, that even if the freshman at our elite institutions clearly benefit from our writing instruction, they have the cultural capital to succeed with or without it. That wasn't true of the young people Wayne Peck knew. And if I believed that the results of the writing research we were doing could really make a difference—as I did—then the place to do that would be where it might matter most. Somehow I came in from that walk persuaded to shift my research agenda from the education of freshman and professional writers to the literate empowerment of Community House teenagers and neighbors.

I should perhaps note I was not a "natural" for this job. If Mrs. Joyce Baskins was the African Queen, I was Dorothy from Kansas, more comfortable with horses than hip-hop and inclined to talk research when others wanted to "chill." But my PhD student colleagues Elenore Long and Lorraine Higgins, the undergraduate students who soon joined us, and I were generously guided into inquiry by our Community House colleagues, especially Wayne Peck and Joyce Baskins, and by the urban community we were welcomed into. What we were trying to learn as academics and everyday people was the art of *speaking for something.* Not out of intellectual certainty or political advocacy but by standing with others in the act of inquiry, framing open questions, seeking rival hypotheses, and at the same time trying to articulate what we understood, what we valued, and what we were working for. If that sounds rather optimistically broad and unspecified, it was, but over time, it became clear that speaking with others and speaking for something were at the heart of community literacy.

Speaking with Others

Taking rhetorical action concerned with others begins by learning to listen to and speak with them, especially with those "Others" whose voices are often silenced or marginalized. But simply enfranchising an alternative or a hybrid discourse is rarely enough. As we saw in the research with urban teenagers (as well as college freshmen), the understanding, insights, reasons, and rationales of Others are often hidden to us. When we encounter difference, we assume deficits. Or we assume that our elite discourse, academic literacy, or mainstream language is the gold standard for representing complex meaning. Moreover, genuine dialogue will not simply follow from our goodwill or effort at empathy; talking across differences of race, class, culture, and discourse depends on an active and often strategic search for understanding.

In community literacy, this becomes a commitment to honor the interpretive agency of Others, in an active search for situated knowledge and multiple ways of representing that knowledge across diverse discourses. We described this as the **strong** *rival hypothesis stance*—a rhetorical strategy for actively seeking out meanings (rival interpretations and alternative un-derstandings) and for acknowledging Others as thinkers, problem solvers, and constructive, interpretive agents in their own lives (Flower, Long, & Higgins, 2000, p. 47).

Speaking for Something

The paradox of community literacy is that committed argument and bold assertion are inseparable from inquiry, that is, from an activated response to what you do *not* know. The rhetorical strategies that became the hallmark of community-literacy projects dramatize a deliberate search for new ways of seeing—for eliciting the story-behind-the-story, drawing out rival interpreta-tions, and exploring multiple options and outcomes. Community literacy's rival hypothesis stance, grounded in John Dewey's "experimental way of knowing" and Cornel West's prophetic pragmatism, locates that "something" we would speak for in the midst of an ongoing inquiry with others (Dewey, 1929/1988; West, 1989).

This act of speaking for something, in contrast to the discourse of advo-cacy or critique, is deliberately grounded in the *construction of negotiated meaning*—in an attempt to respond to rival voices, representations, values, goals, and interpretations. A meaning that emerges is our best current hy-pothesis and most responsible response in an inquiry that is exploratory, critical, self-conscious, and ongoing. However, this attempt to forge a revis-able negotiated meaning is also a commitment to go public—to construct thoughtful explicit arguments for something. Such arguments must be bold enough to name problems, clear enough that they dare to be wrong, and wise enough that they can transform, not just polarize.[6] Speaking in this way takes us into the traditional realm of rhetoric.

Engagement through a Rhetoric of Personal and Public Performance

Out of the history I just sketched, an alternative image of engagement began taking shape that combined analysis with both action and dialogue *with* the Others whom social theory would represent. It is grounded in a *rhetoric of personal and public performance* in which writing is not only theorized as a social act; it is an action to be taken. As engagement moves beyond descrip-tion and analysis (alone), researchers, teachers, and students have had to figure out how to take literate action outside the familiar turf of academic discourse. The features of this emerging rhetoric or model of engagement reflect its diverse fields of action.

The attempt to combine analysis with action is vividly demonstrated, for example, in Paulo Freire's call to *praxis* as action/reflection in politically charged literacy work and in the projects of critical educators such as Ira Shor. It appears in Kurt Spellmeyer's redefinition of the humanistic learning as *involvement* in live, lived issues. It enters discussions of *action research, feminist research,* and *critical research* (Stringer, 1996; Kirsch, Maor, Massey, Nickoson-Massey, & Sheridan-Rabideau, 2003; Sullivan & Porter, 1997). It infuses studies of situated pedagogy, which envision teaching as a response to students' personal and social concerns (McComiskey & Ryan, 2003); it calls for bridges between community language practices and academic discourse (Balester, 1993; Moss, 2003). It has entered professional and technical communication as a notion of *critical practice* that aspires to go beyond describing social and material structures of domination "in order to intervene in those relations and initiate change" (Herndl, 2004, pp. 3, 7). Theories of critical practice, Carl Herndl says, work "to *describe* how change and resistance are *possible* in ideologically saturated institutions. . . . [or] to *describe* ways [such a theory] *might* direct research (pp. 6, 7; italics added). Yet, as my italics suggest, building theories of performance often gets academics closer to, though not always actually engaged in a rhetoric of performance outside the world of the classroom or scholarly community.

In community literacy and service-learning, teachers, researchers, and students show up most directly as performers. As Thomas Deans shows, they take action in different ways, writing *about, for,* and *with* the community (2000). Service-learning, Deans argues, makes good on Richard Rorty's forceful call for academics to move from the "spectatorial left" into the "pragmatic, participatory Left" of John Dewey, acting not out of "Truth" but out of "social hope" (2007, p. 11). Using what Paula Mathieu (2005) would call "tactics of hope," Eli Goldblatt (2005) and Stephen Parks (1999) describe community/ university activist collaborations. Activists like Diana George live the work they write about (2002); some, like Michelle Simmons working on local environmental issues, build a record of deep and sustained contribution (Grabill and Simmons, 1998). Articles in new journals (*Reflections* and *Community Literacy*) describe students and teachers moving into prisons and professional settings as well as schools and public-housing projects.

This rhetoric of performance not only takes engagement out of the study and into the street, it invites a wider public into the story. The audience of community literacy not only holds its own interpretations, it often has the power to talk back to ours. Rhetoric can become *literally* dialogic. The significance of performance and production, always at the heart of classical rhetoric, has reappeared in a new wave of revisionist history. These scholars have reexamined both Aristotelian and Sophistic rhetoric, revealing the social relevance of performative concepts, such as *praxis* (which combines theory and action) and *phronesis* (which substitutes situated practical wisdom and contingent judgment for a search for Truth) (cf. Farrell, 1991; Jarratt, 1991b; Poulakos, 1983). And these scholars have helped shape a critical rhetoric that supports deliberative democracy and challenges the oppressive elements of the liberal humanist tradition (cf. Atwill, 1998; McKerrow, 1989; McGee, 1990). In the new field of rhetoric and composition, rhetoric has become understood as an *art* of *discovery* and *change*, focused on knowledge-making and persuasive social action rather than textual analysis (Young, Becker, & Pike, 1970).[7] In this version of engagement, the process of *discovery* calls the writer/rhetor to analyze a rhetorical situation, to name the problem (the stasis or point on which disagreement turns), and finally, through the process of invention, to create interpretations and arguments capable of persuading not only imagined others but the rhetor as analyst. This practice of discovery takes us onto familiar academic ground.

Adding the goal of *change*, however, can dramatically expand this process into a public action with an ethical responsibility. Traditionally, this calls the rhetor not only to understand her audience but also to project and respond to its response and to track and reflect on the outcomes of her actions. The reader, a rhetor, and the public would call into being must now walk into the writer's process as live actors in a dialogic drama. Yet, lest we think performance simply means reviving the nineteenth-century tradition of public speaking, the community-literacy rhetor must, like the cultural critic, also respond to the enormous forces of ideology, power, and money that create and maintain social problems. What if the problem is not only an ill-considered school suspension or city curfew policy but also the systemic marginalization of some of us, which benefits others of us? What if *we* and our increasingly exclusive educational institutions, our service systems, our very ways of talking about Others are also part of the problem? The question then becomes, what form should *local* literate action take within the context of historically, culturally, and socially embedded problems?

It is not surprising then that Aristotle defined such rhetoric as an *art*—as a thoughtfully strategic performance that depends on heuristics or high-probability moves, not conventions or rules. To be strategic, the rhetor must be self-conscious and articulate about her own thinking and choices and able to recognize and respond to outcomes of her action. That is, the writer as rhetor needs a working theory of performance.

The argument I make here (which calls for a *working theory* of how to speak *with* others and *for* something) parallels the arguments Janet Atwill (1998), Thomas P. Miller (2003), and others make for reclaiming the civic tradition in education, for developing what Aristotle called *phronesis* or "practical wisdom." Comparing it to theoretical knowledge, Miller describes the ideal of practical wisdom as "a model for political agency in situations where what needs to be done cannot be known, but must be acted upon"—an ideal that both draws on and criticizes shared beliefs by making differences "a resource for imagining alternatives" (p. 74). Combining commitment and critical cognition, this "intellectual virtue" supports a "holistic understanding of moral action in the uncertain realm of human affairs" (p. 77).

Performative Rhetoric in Practice

Academic projects motivated by a performative sense of rhetoric face important choices. One choice concerns discourse: does one theorize, study, or teach *about* performance, or does one engage more directly in some form of theory-guided rhetorical practice? Another choice concerns audience: how far does one move from the academy (from addressing classmates in assignments or colleagues in scholarly publications) toward a wider, more inclusive public (from community clients or agencies to public dialogue)? The renewed discussion of public intellectuals in composition tends to imagine the public in terms of media exposure, seeing a larger, even national audience as its target. However, it is interesting that the projects most actively engaged in performative rhetoric have often set their sights on building not larger but more *inclusive local* publics. That is, they have attempted to create community-based dialogues in a city, neighborhood, or institution that extend across the borders of race, class, status, power, and discourse. These choices extend a rhetoric of socially engaged performance into a rhetoric of *public* performance.

The CLC's community literacy belongs to the set of influential projects sketched below that cluster around forms of performative rhetoric that aspire to public practice. Committed to marginalized communities, they tend to imagine their audience not as the reader of a given text but as a public in which ideas circulate and where circulation, dialogue, and deliberation can lead, even if indirectly, to individual and social action. The kind of public they envision (and help form) is one in which people speak *with* others, *for* values and ideas. However, each of these projects brings a distinctive theoretical framework and set of rhetorical tools to this task. Looking briefly at these tools, outcomes, and publics suggests some alternative versions of what a rhetoric of performance could mean; that is, in Dewey's sense, what it could do.[8]

Ellen Cushman walks into the bureaucratic world of social service agencies, not only as a researcher but also as an ally of women trying to navigate its oppressive discourse. She uses the tools of critical-discourse analysis to explore their language strategies. By comparing their public discourse with the "hidden" transcripts of talk that happens "off stage," she shows how these marginalized women actively negotiate the barriers thrown up by institutional gatekeepers, documenting both their agency and the rhetorical tools of struggle (1998, p. 68). Cushman's localized practice of "rhetorical activism" leads her to write with and for these women for very specific ends, from getting benefits to getting an apartment (1996, p. 12). Her scholarly writing urges us to revive the tradition of the public intellectual (1998).

Jeffrey Grabill works the other end of the street, bringing the tools of institutional analysis (Sullivan & Porter, 1997) to bear on literacy programs in three United Way agencies. His goal is not "to act in the interest of individuals against the oppressive power of institutions" (a "largely impossible" agenda, he believes) but to find ways "within institutions to design programs which benefit everyone" especially those most in need (2001, p. 58). His research exposes the heavy-handed paternalism of literacy programs that impose their own notions of what adults need to learn and documents an alternative model of "collaborative design and empowerment" in which those labeled "most in need" have "significant decision-making power" (p. 58). Like Cushman, Grabill's more recent work has seized the possibilities of media and technology to design new participatory structures (Cushman, 2006; Simmons & Grabill, 2007).

Three other versions of rhetorical performance most like the CLC move people even more directly into the practice of strategic inquiry, deliberative engagement, reflective decision making, and public action. Although they use different theoretical frameworks to get there, each calls its members to socially engaged performance. Eli Goldblatt draws on the framework of community organizing (and Saul Alinsky's widely influential *Rules for Radicals*) when he describes the work of the New City Writing Institute at Temple University in Philadelphia (2005). Begun in 1998, it has created a wide network of collaboration with Philadelphia schools and community organizations. One might imagine this to be a typical, if unusually vigorous, university-initiated outreach program creating institutional bridges over which students and university expertise can pass. However, the "organizing" process Goldblatt describes turns this pattern upside down. Engaging in what he calls "knowledge activism," an academic partner begins by building relationships and developing the local knowledge of the community that allows him to "listen intelligently." In a Freirean search for mutual benefit, this noninterventionist form of activism does not enter a collaboration to control it but to offer the academic's experience and the academic and institutional resources of the university to help reach the goals set by the community. One good example is the institute's own small press, which allows diverse groups (from Chinatown residents to Mexican farmworkers to the local culture of disability) to reach a wider public with their stories, artwork, and arguments.

David Coogan looks at performance in terms of outcomes. Drawing on the premises of a materialist rhetoric, he interprets the writing of public officials, community groups, and service-learning students alike as a motivated symbolic action intended to produce worldly change. And like Dewey, he is interested in what that change amounts to. For example, his study of the dysfunctional policy discussions within the Chicago Transit Authority (which produced literal train wrecks) uses the tools of materialistic rhetoric to reveal the *ideographs* or loaded public concepts on which competing parties built their arguments. Such concepts turn up in public debate like ideological icebergs, which (the speakers presume) can be used without explanation "to do work explaining, justifying, and or guiding policy in specific situations" (Michael McGee, qtd in Coogan, 2006b, p. 670).

Using this framework to guide participation in live local issues, Coogan's activism takes the form of rhetorical scholarship. He shows how a community campaign to engage low-income parents with their public school failed, in part, because the well-intentioned community group and its university brochure writers had not done their rhetorical homework. They built their arguments around the seemingly persuasive ideograph of <local control>, a notion that turned out to have a troubled history in that neighborhood and that was associated for residents with a discredited agenda. Coogan argues that the path to public action needs to start in inquiry, if we hope not only to intervene in public discourse but also to change institutional practices. More specifically, if we want to produce viable, community arguments, we need to be in the field and library exploring the public vocabulary, placing arguments in a social and historical context, and identifying the competing ideographs, dominant narratives, and the ways people and issues have been characterized—doing rhetorical research with its eye on outcomes. Like Goldblatt's knowledge activism, such engagement enlists our field's analytical skills to *discover* the arguments that already exist in the communities we wish to serve, *analyze* the effectiveness of those arguments, collaboratively *produce* viable alternatives with community partners, and *assess* the impact of our interventions (Coogan, 2006b, p. 668). This version of a performative rhetoric turns critical analysis into literate action in a live public arena where it is judged by its public outcomes.

The community/university partnership that Glynda Hull and Michael A. James call DUSTY (Digital Underground Storytelling for Youth) is a striking example of academic activism that not only takes the public step but also draws its participants into public rhetorical performance as well (2007). Leading up to this venture, Hull had been a powerful voice in educational research, working with colleagues such as Mike Rose (1989), Mark Jury (1997), Katherine Schultz (2001), and James Gee and Colin Lankshear (1996), to build a critical portrait of how literacy is actually learned, used, and valued in out-of-school settings by workers in high-performance manufacturing plants, in vocational training jobs, or in economically devastated communities. Hull's critical assessment of the popular policy discourse around workplace literacy replaced the familiar complaint about workers who "lack basic skills" with closely observed accounts that located workplace problems in social and economic conditions, not literacy deficits (1993). The critical ethnographic studies that followed then flipped the script, revealing how marginalized workers often used the literate tools (demanded by management) to resist management demands, assert agency and identity, and even alter policy.

DUSTY grows out of this social and economic interpretation of literacy work, locating itself in a community center amidst the urban poverty of West Oakland, California, adjacent to its affluent university partner in Berkeley. It takes its spatial, historical, and social location seriously, inviting faculty, students, and residents in the project of "reconstituting images of place and self" (Hull & James, 2007, p. 256). However, like the CLC, the community/university relationship it builds foregrounds the expertise of the West Oakland residents, not the university. The distinctive feature of DUSTY is the multimedia, multimodal composing that goes on in its basement studio and pushes "school-based definitions of *literacy* to include the visual and performative" (p. 270). But the distinctive power of DUSTY as a rhetorical agent of change is that its

> curriculum encourages participants to construct stories that position themselves as agents, as young people and adults able to articulate and act upon their own "wishes, desires, beliefs, and expectancies" (Bruner, 1994, p. 41) and as global and community members able to remake their worlds (Freire, 1970). (p. 259)

The children, teenagers, and young adults (who often return to create a series of stories) use "spoken word performances, written narratives, photo collections, storyboards, musical compositions, animations, or digital stories" to create what Hull and James conceptualize as "identity texts"—representations of "agentive and socially responsible identities" (pp. 259–60).

The first public outcome of DUSTY's principled and strategic design is its creation of a local community of "authors" and mentors through the collaborative construction of these stories. Public screenings in a neighborhood theater expand the circle, not only drawing a crowd but also creating a distinctive new "public"—a body called into being by the circulation of a new set of ideas. In contrast to the din of drugs-crime-and-welfare images of West Oakland residents that circulate on local billboards and media, the DUSTY screenings engage residents in a desperately needed discussion of the actions, options, talents, and future of their youth.

Like the CLC, DUSTY wants to define change in both individual and social terms. Its theoretical commitment to helping youth create agentive selves is complemented by a longitudinal inquiry into if and how that happens. Case studies (with data collected by mentors and faculty) are showing how writers use this literacy work to articulate and reflect on pivotal movements in their lives and how they develop the ability to reposition themselves as agents as they reposition images and texts from other contexts into their own stories for their own purposes (Hull & Katz, 2006).

The Community Literacy Center adds yet another version of performance to this mix by integrating a settlement-house tradition of local activism with the stance of prophetic pragmatism and the tools of cognitive rhetoric and problem solving. It imagines community literacy as rhetoric of individual and collaborative performance designed to support intercultural inquiry and more inclusive public problem-solving dialogues.

Working Theories of Engagement

I have used these thumbnail sketches to suggest that one can engage in a strategic process of discovery and change with different ends-in-view and different theoretical tools in hand. A theory-based rhetoric of performance has many faces. However, we will not understand how theory actually works if we overlook the critical process that translates it into action. Socially engaged critical theories, by their very nature as theories, strive to elaborate abstract, systematic, logically coherent images of action. By the nature of the discourse, such images are logically rather than empirically based, rarely tested, and many times unworkable in practice. The great challenge that faces a rhetoric of performance is moving from "describing what is possible" to building actionable plans, that is, to translating a good *in-principle* theory to a *working* theory.

By *working theory*, I mean something rather different from what Stephen North called the practical "lore" of composition teaching (1987). As a *working* theory, it *works*: that is, it is operational (a tool kit of conditions and strategies); it is situated (adapted to its particular time, place, and people); and it is always under revision (responding to the test of outcomes). At the same time, as a working *theory*, it strives to *articulate* its own goals, values, and assumptions. In doing so, it opens them to reflection, to the test of outcomes, and revision. A working theory provides the bridge that Dewey's philosophical and West's prophetic pragmatist needs to move from theory-guided analysis to theory-guided action. What a working theory lacks in logical coherence and self-consistency, it gains in its sensitivity to context and contingency. It helps one navigate the inconsistent complexity of real institutions, communities, and people. It is odd then that even those academic accounts focused on engagement tend to presume that presenting one's in-principle theory of action on its own is adequate—or accurate.

Understanding the unsung role of working theories is one of the leitmotifs of this book. I argue that the challenging process of constructing and revising a working theory is at the heart of *doing* (rather than just describing) the rhetoric of performance. In the final section of this chapter, I examine one aspect of this process, extended over time, in which the working theory of community literacy responded to practical experience and new research, to competing claims and critiques, and most important to the reflective effort of negotiating these voices and reimagining a more adequate, responsive stance. The experience of the CLC illustrates how the bridge between research/theory and performance allows traffic in both directions. The practice of community literacy changed in various ways over the period I describe, while its developing image of collaborative intercultural inquiry had in turn a profound effect not only on the composition research each of us chose to do but also on the emerging theoretical shape of cognitive rhetoric.

Building a Working Theory of Personal and Public Performance

In the emerging field of rhetoric and composition in the 1970s, cognitive rhetoric grew up in an atmosphere of sibling closeness and competition, first with the dominant expressivist/process and then with the academic discourse/social process paradigms, from which it diverged in some important ways. It took shape as one of the "new rhetorics" that drew on classical traditions of rhetoric in order to replace the formalistic and/or literary discourse of composition with a more robust image of writing as a heuristic thinking process. Influenced by Richard Young, its object was both discovery and change—inquiry as well as persuasion (Young, Becker, & Pike, 1970). This impulse found a natural partner in the research agenda of cognitive psychology and its interest in (and tools for) investigating thinking as a heuristic problem-solving process. Problem solving and cognitive rhetoric, then, shifted the focus from texts and tropes back to classical rhetoric's concern with performance, by asking, How do rhetors (as thinkers) carry out the heuristic art of discovery and change? It wedded this research agenda to the practice of teaching by describing differences in how expert and novice writers—as thinkers and problem-solvers—actually went about working through a variety of academic and professional tasks.

But there was a problem with problem solving. In 1981, J. R. Hayes and I published a theoretical account of writing as problem solving elaborated with an explanatory/exploratory model of key cognitive processes involved in composing (Flower and Hayes). In the early 1980s, the agendas of psychological and educational research and composition in general and of problem solving and our work in particular had a significant limitation, which could be summed up in a sentence: they did not account for—and had not learned how to study—the enormous significance that social and cultural forces have on writing, learning, and thinking. Some compositionists, such as, James A. Berlin, found the entire paradigm of problem solving antithetical to socially engaged teaching.[9] They framed their concerns as a polarizing social cognitive debate in order to advocate a more vigorous agenda of social and cultural engagement in composition (a point on which community literacy would only agree). A second assumption (on which we would part company) was that social engagement called for a discourse of social theorizing, deconstruction, and critique.

The source of contention in this debate was rarely with the actual findings or claims of the problem-solving process research but with its empirical, cognitive, and individually focused perspective. The critiques that polarized cognitive and social processes in composition studies[10] championed an alternative paradigm in which the "social turn" was equated with the study of cultural patterns and language and with the discourse of theorizing and critique, a discourse borrowed from the critical cultural theory in ascendancy in literary studies and English departments. As the paradigm took shape, social engagement became identified with the problems of teaching basic writers, who had flooded universities in the wake of overdue open admissions. This paradigm reinterpreted the needs of marginalized students as ignorance of or exclusion from the discourse conventions and communities of the academy. The social alternative became synonymous for many with the study of the conventions of discourse. Patricia Bizzell's criticism of my work with Hayes puts it well: "Hence, although Flower and Hayes acknowledge the existence of discourse conventions, they fail to see conventions' generative power" (1982, p. 229).

But one could respond that the real problem here was not a theoretical "recognition" of social forces but a need to understand just how those forces actually affected writing and how education and writers should respond. We needed a better *working theory* to guide research, teaching, and performance.

Bizzell's paper offered her own strong answer to these questions. Asking, "What do we need to know about writing?" she takes issue with the generative role of goal setting (1982, p. 213). Hayes and I had described this as a process of recalling familiar (conventional) plans *and* strategically building, testing, and consolidating ideas and inferences to build new task-specific ones, observing that novice writers did much less of this strategic, problem-solving work as they composed than experienced writers did.[11] Bizzell replies, "I think these students' difficulties with goal-setting are better understood in terms of their unfamiliarity with the academic discourse community [and limited awareness] that there is such a thing as a discourse community with conventions to be mastered." The teaching implications follow: "To help poor writers, then, we need to explain that their writing takes place in a community, and to explain what the community's conventions are" (1982, p. 230).

Bizzell's hypothesis was based on interesting arguments going on at the time in sociolinguistics about the theoretical *existence* of discourse communities.[12] But did it follow that once we began to take the shaping, generative force of social context into account, that discourse conventions would be the only or even the best account of "what we needed to know"? Didn't we need a more adequate, accurate, and testable description of what real writers, especially marginalized ones, actually did or needed to do? As Kurt Spellmeyer would say eleven years later, arguing for a more personally and rhetorically engaged pedagogy:

> It is not, as Bizzell maintains, simply ignorance of "conventions" that makes finding something to say a problem for writers, but the inability to discover and exploit revealing contradictions between "ours" and "theirs." By itself a knowledge of "conventions," a knowledge of what has been written in the past and of how it has been written, will not even allow student-writers to repeat the achievements of others—let along accomplish something further—since these achievements were occasioned, after all, by some real-world need, some palpable contradiction, which made them meaningful and worth undertaking in the first place. Without such contradiction, knowledge can have neither a meaning nor a use. (1993, p. 185)

In the midst of this debate over what composition should be about, community literacy was trying to shape a model of literate social engagement built in part on the strategic and problem-focused stance of rhetoric and its alternative approach to social realities. Disappointed with the discourse of academic critique, we felt that a community-based, intercultural rhetoric could not assume the authority of *speaking against* if it has not first learned how to *speak with* the Others it would represent. Moreover, a civic dialogue would demand not only the analytical moves of argument and critical analysis but also the savvy insight into what it takes to *speak with* in a persuasive sense, that is, to actually move readers, to change minds. If you want to do that, "it is not enough," as Gloria Anzaldúa concludes, "to stand on the opposite river bank, shouting questions, challenging patriarchal, white conventions" (1987, p. 100). The rhetoric of making a difference demanded more than critique from academics or conventionally acceptable prose from students; it required an audience-attuned rhetoric, capable of turning critical reflection and personal exploration into rhetorical action.

Recall the aspiring rapper of chapter 1. For Mark Howard, posing, exploring, and dramatizing problems—from the perspective of the ignored, voiceless, or silenced actors—was at the heart of his literate action. To do this, he and Shay La Burke needed what Joe Harris (1997) might call a social and textual *dialogic space* to reflect on the multiple realities and experiences that got named the "suspension" problem. They needed to turn what Alinsky would call merely a "bad situation" into a critical assessment, for example, "The point of this story—nobody pays attention/To a student 'cause they're young." But their problem analysis also had a robust rhetorical purpose. Mark's rap and Shay La's commentary were attempts to bring to light hidden realities (a child shouldering burdens from home, teachers' assumptions, students' quick leap to "attitude"). And they were trying to bring to the table new possibilities that could deal with the underlying problems so inadequately "solved" by suspension. What is most interesting is that Mark's rhetoric takes a critical counterpublic stance—it shows how this local disruption is a thread in a larger fabric of administrative authority. He attempts to speak *with* that authority not by assimilating himself fully to its conventions but by turning rap into an authorized public voice.

Meanwhile, back in the world of research, problem solving saw itself as a fundamentally rhetorical paradigm trying to respond to the critique of competing theories and the grounding experience of the CLC. The problem of problem solving became how to more adequately observe and interpret the play of social forces. And given a goal to understand and teach literate performance, the compelling subject of research had to be the writer—rather than texts, society, history, or theory. What we needed was a more fully envisioned account of thinking, feeling social subjects *doing writing* as a part of their social-cultural contexts and *responding* (in ways we have yet to adequately understand) to those contexts. By context, we meant not only the forces of social ideology, convention, and power but also the demands of individual values and goals, conflicts, and contradictions. Community literacy called us to understand the inseparable individual *and* social nature of literate action.[13]

Rethinking Writing as a Social Cognitive Activity

Attempting to understand writing as an organic social cognitive activity, our research began to focus not on discourse conventions and community norms but on writing as a form of literate *practice*.[14] Of course, any theory of writing is at best only an intellectual map of a still-uncharted territory—reasonable, no doubt, in its general outlines, well specified in various places as far as old borders but inevitably a mixture of grounded hypotheses, interesting speculation, and sheerest fantasy, no doubt, in others. Turning such theories into tested explanatory accounts often depends on persistently and closely observing a segment of human action that contains more than your theory dreamed of—an action that exists as some form of independent data that can talk back in its own resistant terms to your evolving hypotheses.[15] For ten years, my work as codirector of the National Center for the Study of Writing and Literacy at the University of California–Berkeley and Carnegie Mellon (1985–1995) allowed my colleagues and me to study adults, students, mentors, and teenagers writing in both academic and community contexts (creating parallel studies in some cases, such as, the Learning-to-Rival project). This combination of community and university contexts shaped cognitive rhetoric as a social cognitive theory of writing. More to my point here, it helped us develop a *working theory* of community literacy that could support socially engaged, collaborative rhetorical action, on the one hand, and the developing metacognitive, problem-solving awareness of individual writers, on the other.

Out of this research came three insights that had special relevance for a working theory of intercultural inquiry, helping us to see an increasing number of literate differences as choices not deficits, to uncover hidden logics, and to recognize rhetorical agency in others.

The Role of Task Representation

Isn't it a lot to assume that *students*, including "basic" writers, can actually perform as *rhetors*? In a study based on a typical Reading-to-Write assignment, many freshmen seemed unable to do the kind of synthesis and purposeful writing that the college expected—that is, until we examined the transcripts of one section that did think-aloud protocols while writing the paper in their dorm rooms (Flower, Stein, Ackerman, Kantz, McCormick, & Peck, 1990). Focusing our research on literate actions rather than texts alone allowed us to turn student writers into partners in that inquiry and into interpreters of their own thinking.[16] For many students, the failure to create the expected "college-level" synthesis occurred even before they began to write, in the process that cognitive studies calls "task representation." In interpreting this "standard" assignment, these students were giving themselves inaccurate, unworkable, or inappropriate sets of instructions about what was expected, how to do it, and why. And they didn't agree with each other, much less the teacher. Was this merely an ignorance of academic conventions?

It turned out that after key options (such as a dutiful summary or avoiding conflict among authorities) were compared and students were asked to revise, most could actually *do* the harder task in a revision. Differences had not been due to deficits but to interpretations of the task.[17] The knowledge that made the biggest difference in performance was metaknowledge—the awareness of instructors and students that the task writers do is the one they represent to themselves. Moreover, our internal representations of a rhetorical situation (or of one another's intentions) constitute a large, detailed, and complex canvas—that we often fail to share with one another.

At the CLC, it was clear that urban public schools systematically suppressed opportunities for rhetorical awareness in favor of summary and convention. Outspoken teens like Mark were often labeled troublemakers. Others like Tina, who resented the "childish" assignments and simply resisted them, were evaluated as poor writers (but who proved to be astute at projecting a reader's response and adapting to a rhetorical situation in their CLC texts) (Johnson, 1992). For many, the real eye-opener was in the middle of the Community Conversation when they suddenly came to understand their work as rhetorical action. The CLC let them see school writing as a distinctive language game, even as they created a new counterrepresentation of what writing could mean and do.

The Presence of Hidden Logics

The fog of misconception gets even thicker when the writers who miss the mark are basic writers, urban teenagers, returning students, urban residents, or low-wage workers, because we are even more likely to assume the problem is a deficit within their knowledge of content or conventions. But when we inquire into the "logic" of such writers and speakers, we often see that people do things (which we find unexpected or inappropriate) for reasons we never glimpse, guided by an internal, informal rationale. Without denying the enormous shaping force that material conditions, ideology, and discourse have on underprepared or inner-city writers, research that fails to seek out the logic of their performance—as they see it—robs people of even more of their sometimes-fragile opening for agency.

For example, in the Learning to Rival project, Elenore Long, Lorraine Higgins, and I asked student writers to take the demanding rival hypothesis stance to an issue, that is, to treat a discussion about minority students and education as an *open question* by seeking *rival interpretations* and *diverse perspectives* in their writing.[18] We chose a group of minority freshmen (and later urban teens) for the explicit purpose of investigating their process, not as people with problems but as active learners. We wished to track them finding their way in a new and demanding intellectual task, which in this case was writing about a controversial issue from an inquiry-based, rival hypothesis stance. We got more than we bargained for. The textual analysis suggested that some students didn't get it or clung to their old thesis-and-support moves. But the data from collaborative-planning sessions, taped self-interviews, and group discussions told a different story of these students as active agents, trying to deal in meaningful ways with demanding readings on the charged topic of minority students in predominantly white universities. The data showed students who in fact demonstrated the inquiry-based *rivaling* stance in their thinking and planning. But in place of the inquiry structure they were asked to use, their papers only showed the text conventions of a standard argument. Why? Was this a case of *couldn't* or *wouldn't*? Their teachers only saw the mismatch between the papers and the assigned conventions of inquiry. But insight from the planning transcripts into the logic of these learners saw students acting on rhetorical goals that for them superceded the assignment.

For instance, many of these minority student writers were choosing to use this paper for their own deeply felt purposes (a choice some writing instructors dream about!). Some were working through problematic issues of identity. Others were taking the authority of "authors" to speak to the white academics whose articles had built up a composite portrait of black students as people at high risk of failing, as low in personal agency, and as unlikely to beat the odds. These students felt called to challenge those experts to consider the impact their claims had on the object of their analysis—on real students like themselves who read these published articles. A number of students whose texts didn't demonstrate the requested conventions were nevertheless demonstrating what humanistic instruction aspires to—the presence of rhetorical agency.

The next summer a closely parallel study with urban teens at the Community House showed these writers to be even more assertive appropriators of this strategic knowledge. They, too, learned to use the rivaling stance but with a logic or rationale and set of intentions that at times intentionally dismissed the academic expectations of teachers and mentors as rhetorically ineffective. In short, this research said, if you failed to seek a writer's hidden logic, you were likely to misdiagnose problems that were there and most certainly to undervalue the writer's performance and capability.

The Process of Negotiated Meaning-Making

Rethinking writing as a social cognitive activity took us deeper into the way the social and cognitive dimensions of meaning-making interact. As writers enter a rhetorical situation—whether it is a college assignment, a collaborative inquiry, a new discourse, an intercultural dialogue, or the contested ground of speaking for social justice—they entertain a host of "voices" both metaphorical and material that offer the writer language, ideas, and meaning. Writers may feel surrounded by the insistent voices of *multiple* discourse communities and their conventions. If our research gives serious attention to these powerful shaping voices *and* to the interpretive agency of the writer *responding* to them, we see that everyday writers (not just the teachers, intellectuals, and theorists) are actively engaged in constructing negotiated meanings. More specifically,

- First, the activity of writing includes not just hands on the keyboard but acts of self-fashioning and institutional disobedience, of immersion in the conversation of a discourse, response to peers, resisting and appropriating conventions, as well as constructing new meaning. And this activity is a site of unremitting contradiction, contestation, and conflict.
- Secondly, writers will at times rise to an active engagement with these conflicts. And when we have access to these conflicts, these moments of engagement reveal something of the array of potential "voices" or forces actually working to shape writing. Such voices range from discourse conventions to ideological and social demands to interpersonal response to interpretive and rhetorical strategies to personal goals and ideas.
- Finally, out of this engagement with multiple, alternative, and even conflictual voices comes the opportunity to construct a negotiated meaning. By that I mean, the opportunity to acknowledge rather than avoid difference, to embrace its contradictions, and to construct a meaning that is provisional but responsive—a current best effort at a negotiated understanding.

This research-based image of the writer is an intensely rhetorical one. It imagines a meaning-maker working within a contested territory, willing (at least at times) to embrace rather than repress different voices, and move toward a negotiated or responsive meaning.[19] It became a persuasive image of what a rhetoric of intercultural inquiry could be—a space for embracing difference in acts of collaborative meaning-making.[20] The two-way street between the university and community and between research and social action helped shape both a social cognitive theory of writing and a working theory of personal and public performance within a local intercultural public.

The next chapters sketch the practice of community literacy as a series of experiments in *speaking with* others on culturally charged issues and *speaking for* commitments and actions in community, public, and academic forums. The process starts with a close look at the role of educators and college students in this community/university collaboration.

4 *Who Am I? What Am I Doing Here?*

Like many of you reading this, my background has made me a person of privilege, drawn by the hope of making a difference in the larger community and for others. Yet, I recognize that by the standards of identity politics, I have little right to speak on the behalf of a marginalized urban community. Let me be explicit. Where I was born, in Wichita, Kansas, we would occasionally drive through the black section of town—a strange other world where we stayed inside the car and my seven-year-old self wondered why people didn't take care of their lawns like they did around the small frame houses in my neighborhood. I liked, I was curious about, the little black kids in my first grade, but I played with the white ones after school. Before I reached an age of consciousness about social patterns, we moved to a small town that was a county seat in Iowa. The town was named after an Indian "princess," Oskaloosa, and the county after her father, Chief Mahaska. There is a fine bronze statue of him in the city square near the bandstand. There were no longer any Indians in Oskaloosa. In my circle of knowledge, Oskaloosa had one black family (poor) and two Jewish families (plump, flamboyant Anita's father owned the junkyard; good-looking, dark-skinned Lorraine's father was a doctor). I somehow knew this fit a stereotype; but ethnic identities were not discussed.

I made my first black friend in college—a small Midwestern liberal arts college where we went on retreats to discuss difference. I vaguely knew about the confrontations in the South—the *Des Moines Register* didn't cover such things in detail in 1958. Relatively innocent of the deep racial politics and history of my own time, I was proud of my sorority when we bucked the dictates of the national organization to pledge (the only) Hispanic girl on campus. But I didn't know much, except that there was an ethical issue behind racism that called me to acceptance of others, based on a mixture of naïve, potentially sentimental goodwill and on the tougher stuff of an ethical, religious call to do the right thing. Not much I could contribute.

The contrast becomes clear, when I consider my contemporary Franki Williams, who became one of my Pittsburgh friends and speaks at the end of this chapter. In those same turbulent sixties in which I was *discovering* difference, she and her friends were becoming discouraged with the pace of change in Martin Luther King Jr.'s vision, were reading and listening to Malcolm X, were joining the Movement. A Black Panthers group met at her house (where her mother baked cookies for everyone). Franki and her friends were entering adulthood resisting the consequences of difference and literate in the ways of *making* one.

By the time Wayne Peck drew me to the Community House, I had seen that research in writing and problem solving could make one sort of change; that college students found new power and skill as they began to see themselves as thinkers. And it seemed that if I wanted to make a genuine difference, I could do it best by studying and teaching with the staff and urban teenagers at this inspired inner-city settlement house. I was much more politically informed but personally inexperienced with racial difference. Motivated by good will, an ethical call, and the challenge to make a difference—I had good reasons for making a personal and professional choice. But not much of a foundation for achieving that difference. In some ways I was not that far from my college self or from the majority of white college students who would soon be signing up for the community-literacy course. Committed in the abstract, experienced in little. Literate in theory talk, monolingual on the street.

When white, middle-class college students and teachers like me walk into a community organization and become attuned to our status as outsiders, as cultural others, we must face the questions, "Who am I? What am I doing here?" We need to be aware that in walking into an old brick settlement house, the storefront office of a community organization, or a church basement after-school program, we are walking on a path charted by the history of community/university relations, following footsteps, like those painted on the floor to guide you through a maze of corridors. The trouble is the footsteps from this troubled history may lead into roles and into relationships that we cannot or do not want to assume.

Some Available Roles and Relationships

Relationships between town and gown have a checkered history. Especially when the gowns speak for the affluent dominant culture, bent on the self-confident transmission of its cultural tools, its knowledge, its discourse. And when the town speaks for those with far less economic, cultural, or social capital, struggling with problems of poverty, racism, broken schools, unbridled streets.[1]

Consider the typical pattern of literacy programs. When town and gown try to work together, the gowns possess the dominant discourse—and typically assume that their language, concepts, and forms of argument are the most effective for understanding these problems and should be learned and used by everyone else. The gowns deliver expert advice, or they set up tutoring programs in school-based literacy for the children of townfolk. Some gowns, on the other hand, attuned to the oppressive potential of such literate practices may position their work as an act of critique and resistance to academic discourse in the name of supporting diverse communities. Such work however, usually stays within the academy.

In such collaborations between town and gown, then, academics have often chosen among *using* the elite discourse to analyze/advise a community cause, *initiating* at-risk students into that discourse (whether it is computer literacy, math literacy, or Standard Written English), or, more recently, *resisting* and critiquing that discourse. Hard-pressed communities look for help where they can find it but remain wary of the process and wisely skeptical about the effectiveness of much of what they get. The rarer achievement is a relationship in which all of these partners work in the same room—and on the written page—together.

Historians of community/university collaboration locate some of the problems that trouble these relationships in the logic that has motivated them. Describing this history from 1880 to World War I, Harkavy and Puckett note:

> Progressive period academics pedestaled the expert and expert knowledge. . . . [and created a model that] was elitist, hierarchical, and unidimensional, founded on the assumption that the expert's role was to study and assist, but not to learn from the community. (1991, p. 562)

Such arrangements, they argue, not only replicate the status quo on an institutional level but also perpetuate the learned helplessness that poverty and its enabler—the professionally designed welfare system—teaches to urban poor.

Against this historical backdrop, the current enthusiasm for community/ university connections is marked by a more collaborative spirit and multicultural awareness, which have spurred rising student volunteerism, community-service projects, and service-learning additions to the curriculum (Deans, 2000).[2] The justifying principle behind many of these projects is a strong ethic of civic service rooted in the ideals of participatory democracy but balanced by an awareness of the competing demands of the individual and the community (Cooper & Julier, 1995; Cooper & Fretz, 2006). Others are motivated by a long tradition of experiential education, and still others by the urgent call to social justice (Watters & Ford, 1995; Kendall & Associates, 1990; Benson & Harkavy, 1991). However, this growing enthusiasm for and informed commitment to civic service faces two challenges. The first is that such concerns are cyclical with educational trends. Unless this enthusiasm for a community connection is rooted in the intellectual agenda of the university, in academic work, and in the educational system, it will soon fade (Zlotkowski, 1996). Marginal programs, identified with soft money, student enrichment, and institutional obligation, will not compete with disciplinary agendas when they are no longer news. Will colleges and universities be able to turn the principle of experience-based civic education into a robust, academically sophisticated educational practice?

A second, more insidious problem is the danger that well-meaning volunteerism can unwittingly replicate the social structures that are part of the problem. It can end up defining some people as the knowledgeable servers while casting others as the clients, patients, or the educationally deficient—the served (Herzberg, 1994). To succeed, the ethic of service must confront some philosophical and social tensions within the enterprise itself and within the relationships it builds among organizations, among college writers and community contacts, and between tutors and students. To avoid the repetition of history, this ethic needs a spirit of inquiry that cannot only acknowledge some deep-running differences in how people define the problems and goals on which a collaboration is based but can embrace the difficulties of entering a cultural contact zone (Pratt, 1991; Goldblatt, 1994; Long, 1994; Minter, Gere, & Keller-Cohen, 1995). As we try to construct new collaborations in the face of these challenges and our past, it may help to think for a moment about some logics that can motivate service and the relationships shaped by those logics. Consider the logic of cultural mission, of technical expertise, of compassion, and of prophetic pragmatism and problem solving. Because most programs contain some element of all of these logics, my purpose is not to make simplistic distinctions but to consider the roles each logic offers to elite partners and the relationships it tends to promote.

The Logic of Cultural Mission

Historically, community service has often rested on notions of philanthropy, charity, social service, and improvement that identify the community as a recipient, client, or patient, marked by economic, learning, or social deficits.

While "doing good" by the lights of the service provider, this paradigm maintains a strong sense of otherness and distance, of giver and receiver. It makes no demand for mutuality in analyzing or responding to problems; it maintains the social status quo.

Economist William Julius Wilson targets a case in point in the work of those analysts of inner-city poverty who focus "almost exclusively on the interconnection between cultural traditions, family history, and individual character" of the poor. Perceiving an apparent lack of ambition, self-reliance, and a work ethic in the poor, "some even suggest that ghetto underclass individuals have to be rehabilitated culturally before they can advance in society" (Wilson, 1987, p. 13). Calling the logic of this deficit model of cultural repair into question, Wilson shows that the number of single-mother households for young African American women, for instance, is directly connected to the extraordinary and continuing rise of joblessness for inner-city African American males, starting in the economic shifts of the 1960s.[3] If the "culture of poverty" Wilson analyzes is not a self-perpetuating culture but a response to pressing social and economic forces, then the logic of charity is short sighted, and the logic of repairing personal deficits (in attitude, lifestyle, behavior) or demanding mainstream, middle-class habits in the face of chronic economic instability is myopic.

Literacy work waves the cultural missionary banner when it reduces reading and writing to narrow school-based skills (Minter, Gere, & Keller-Cohen, 1995) or concentrates on replacing community languages, such as, Black English Vernacular, with Standard Written English. There is no question that literacy work must help its students recognize the advantages of bidialectalism, where Standard English is the language of power and access in the mainstream community. However, the desire to "help" others be more like oneself often rests on the cheerful arrogance of what Teun van Dijk calls the "elite discourses," which assume that the cultural tools of the white middle-class (the academy, media, business) are the tools to which others do (or should) aspire (1993). How can a literacy program that works with black youth, for instance, balance this presumption with an awareness of the indirect but analytical tradition of African American Vernacular, the logical structures embedded in street talk (Labov, 1972) or the richly expressive literate practices, such as, signifying (Gates, 1988; Lee, 1993), in which white volunteers find they are the illiterate (Flower, 1996b)? Because the logic of cultural transmission valorizes the knowledge and values the *giver* intends to share, it raises questions of mutuality. It can distort the map of community/university relationships by making cultural sharing a one-way street.

The Logic of Technical Expertise

More seemingly benign and disinterested than the stance of the cultural missionary is the logic of technical expertise, which brings needed skills, knowledge, and resources to the problems of struggling communities. Technical expertise allows people to document polluted water, to test for diabetes, to create a sophisticated, computer-based distribution system for food banks, or to create a professionally constructed (fundable) proposal for youth jobs. But we must also recognize that when service is organized by this logic, the relationship is not only hierarchical, it can smother other kinds of expertise.

John McKnight's analysis of medical and social-service policy, for instance, documents the transition from a community ethos based on care to a social-service system based on the professional management of need. The technology and the tools of the expert not only tend to dictate the nature of conceivable solutions, they structure the relationships.

> As *you* are the problem, the assumption is that *I*, the professional servicer, *am the answer. You* are not the answer. *Your peers* are not the answer. *The political, social, and economic environment* is not the answer. (1995, p. 46; italics in original)

Funding for health, education, and welfare supports an enormous middle-class industry designed to deliver services (not jobs) to the poor. But service is not the same as a solution. For instance, the rising technology (and cost) of medicine has had little impact on rates of morbidity or mortality: "The primary cause of physical malady among the modernized poor is distinctly environmental and obviously unchangeable with medical tools. There is no medical prescription to cure poverty, slums, and polluted air, water, and food" (McKnight, 1995, p. 64). Moreover, when this one-way relationship, based on professional expertise and "technological" solutions, is in place, McKnight argues, the citizen is no longer the problem-definer or problem solver, and the power and initiative of the community deteriorates. Service displaces care.

University-based community service has to worry about a naïve complicity in the social structures that put power and prestige on the university side of the ledger while putting passive need and incapacity on the debit, community side. We must be skeptical of this logic, in part because expert, professional, and technological solutions do not have a stellar record of success in meeting urban problems. More than that, the logic of technical expertise can reinforce the power structures and social assumptions that perpetuate problems. It can leave student volunteers with the temporary euphoria of "doing good" for the "less fortunate" but does little to break their sense of distance and otherness or their assumptions that their cultural tools and traditions are necessarily superior. When literacy tutors, for instance, build a relationship based primarily on their educated expertise and the transmission of school-based reading or writing skills, they are not likely to confront larger problems, such as, how to use these cultural tools for intercultural purposes or how to judge when a hybrid discourse, integrating the literate practices of universities and communities, would be more effective.

The Logic of Compassion and Identity

The logic of compassion tends to restructure the relationships of service around the Latin roots of the word—around "feeling with." It turns service from an act of charity or authority into an act of empathy that grasps an essential identity between the one who serves and the one who is in need. Less motivated to blame or reform the victim, compassion is also not afraid to acknowledge the pain, the stress, the sense of dislocation, and even hopelessness that go with poverty, racism, diminished self-esteem, and vulnerability. In our culture, the logic of compassion has its strongest roots in the radical messages of the Torah tradition of Judaism and the transformational tradition of Christianity, both of which depart from the legal, rule-focused sensibility often institutionalized in dominant strands of these and other religions.

In *Jews and Blacks: A Dialogue on Race, Religion, and Culture in America* by Cornel West and Michael Lerner, Lerner argues that the Torah tradition was a revolutionary message in the ancient and medieval world as it is in the modern: "If we are to stay in touch with the God energy within ourselves, we need to be able to recognize the Other's needs as our own needs." In this tradition, he argues, "Jewish identity consists of being a witness to God as the force in the universe that makes possible the transformation of that which is to that which ought to be.... The goal of this transformation is to rectify the oppression of the powerless. *We* were slaves. So now that we are free, our task is to spread that freedom, and to identify with the powerless" (1996, pp. 8–9). Lerner contrasts this tradition of compassion to the cynicism of contemporary intellectuals that led "to a kind of lonely 'see through everything, believe in nothing' world view that they thought was revolutionary, but actually fit very well into the needs of the dominant society" (1996, p. 39).

Marcus J. Borg, a member of the revisionist social-history scholars known as the Jesus Seminar, places compassion at the center of an equally radical tradition in Christianity. Although this tradition was shaped by its historical, social, and religious struggle against first-century Roman oppression, it is also at the center of an ongoing conflict between the politics of holiness (focused on correct conduct and shaped by the legalism of enculturated religion and its conventional wisdom) and the politics of compassion (guided by a conviction that culture can be transformed by the power of the Spirit) (1987, pp. 155, 196). Borg places the message of Jesus in the tradition of Jewish charismatics who advocated and modeled an alternative consciousness, in which "God and the world of Spirit are all around us, including within us. . . . We live in Spirit, even though we are typically unaware of this reality" (1987, p. 28). And at the center of this alternative consciousness (and in contrast to the vision of religious legalism) was acceptance—a "vivid sense that reality was ultimately gracious and compassionate" (1987, p. 100). For Paulo Freire, this alternative, compassionate consciousness becomes the foundation for genuine dialogue. Dialogue, he argues, "requires an intense faith in man, faith in his power to make and remake, to create and re-create, faith in his vocation to be more fully human (which is not the privilege of an elite, but the birthright of all men. . . . Founding itself upon love, humility, and faith, dialogue becomes a horizontal relationship of which mutual trust between dialoguers is the logical consequence" (1970/1985, pp. 79–80).

The logic of compassion and identity, grounded in an alternative consciousness and shaped by these religious traditions, works to reorient relationships away from cultural imposition, commodified service delivery, or expert, technology-driven knowledge transmission toward ones that replace power relations with greater mutuality.

But its strength also poses a problem. How do we translate this intensely individual, experiential consciousness into public action—into literate practices, educational agendas, and institutional initiatives? I ask this question not because there are no ready answers but because there are so many competing answers. Can we claim that any given literate practice or educational agenda has a corner on compassionate or democratic collaboration as we plan and argue for a course of action? Let me put our dilemma as educators and program developers another way. Given that our moral and ethical commitments are inevitably culturally inflected, given that our best interpretation of what it means to enact service, compassion, or mutuality is itself a hypothesis to be tested and inevitably revised, how do we find the grounds for action? If the business of the intellectual is skepticism, is there a legitimate alternative to the ironic stance of those who "see through everything, believe in nothing"?

When universities ask the questions "Why are we here? What are we doing?" the answers supplied by the logics of mission, expertise, and compassion challenge us to look thoughtfully at the relationships and the practices to which they lead. The next approach tries to build on the strengths of these other logics but to do so in a way that grounds action on and transforms relationships into a form of collaborative inquiry.

The Logic of Prophetic Pragmatism and Collaborative Problem Solving

The logic of this fourth approach points to collaborative social action. Community outreach built on problem solving alone could easily turn into a hierarchical association between people who are "the problems" and those who are "the solvers," unless it is wedded to a compelling vision of mutual inquiry. A logic for this alternative can be found in the prophetic pragmatism of African American cultural theorist Cornel West and in the work of John Dewey, who has influenced many current experiments in service-learning. This pragmatism offers one answer to the questions posed above: how does one take moral social action without the crutch of dogmatism or even the certain confidence about how one *should* act?

The logic of philosophical pragmatism is the logic of inquiry. In its vision, communities and universities embark on Dewey's experimental way of knowing, which begins by repudiating the "quest for certainty" that has traditionally undergirded the quest for knowledge in science and philosophy (1929/1988). He challenges us to recognize the unsettling alternative that all our knowledge is hypothetical. It is a hypothesis (even though it is based on the best evidence we can muster) that we use to guide our steps. What, for instance, is the appropriate response to the terrible decay of neighborhoods in the inner city if you are a policy maker? What is the response to risk and stress on those streets if you are an inner-city teenager? What is the right way to interpret or engage with the life of that teenager if you are a college-student mentor? These questions people must and do answer, but how should we regard or evaluate those answers?

Dewey, looking at both academic theories and personal conclusions, urges what amounts to a courageous vulnerability to the reality of our own uncertainty: "All general conceptions (ideas, theories, thought) are hypothetical." Even when they liberate us, these conceptions are "conditional: they have to be tested by the consequences of the operations they define and direct." In giving up the quest for certainty, we must recognize that the final value of our theories, policies, and beliefs is not determined by the normal tests that confer academic comfort and certainty, such as, the internal elaboration and consistency of a theory. Rather, value is determined "by the consequences they effect in existence as that is perceptibly experienced" (1929/1988, p. 132).

Dewey's pragmatic stance recognizes that standard assumptions, best ideas, and even deeply held beliefs are always and only guiding hypotheses about outcomes, built on stronger or weaker bodies of evidence—that is, some hypotheses are much more reliable predictors than others. This stance translates *knowledge* (including the expert knowledge the academy would offer the community) from a stable object into an *act of knowing*, that is, into an urgently ongoing attempt to improve hypotheses by an intentional effort to reveal new connections and relations. Dewey puts it concretely: "To grasp an unfamiliar object of the mind, we discover its qualities by uncovering its relationships: We turn it over, bring it into a better light, rattle and shake it, thump, push and press . . . for the purpose of disclosing relations not apparent otherwise" (1929/1988, p. 70). The knower is an interpretive seeker, and knowing is an act of inquiry.

However, the radical premise of Dewey's philosophical pragmatism is not just that knowledge is interpretation but that the meaning and value of ideas lie in their enabling *conditions* and their *outcomes* (1922/1964). The meaning of an urban policy lies in the conditions required for that policy (with its unpacked baggage of assumptions) to work and in the world it would produce as a result if it were enacted. The meaning of a street-savvy teenage strategy for dealing with stress (and a mentor's response to that strategy) lies in the conditions under which it exists (e.g., the street conditions under which a strategy, e.g., acting "hard" or even aggressive, may seem the best proactive defense). And meaning lies ultimately in outcomes: the pragmatic meaning of mentoring (like the meaning of adult "advice") is not in its "truth" or "wisdom" but in its outcome for that teenager and for the relationship it creates between the teen and mentor.

This connection among conditional knowledge, continued inquiry, and ethical action seems central to a new model of community/university relations. American philosopher C. I. Lewis describes it.

> Pragmatism could be characterized as the doctrine that all problems are at bottom problems of conduct, that all judgments are, implicitly, judgments of value, and that, as there can be ultimately no valid distinction of theoretical and practical, so there can be no final separation of questions of truth of any kind from questions of the justifiable ends of action. (qtd. in West, 1993, p. 109)

Thomas Deans's closely observed, theoretically grounded study of contemporary "writing partnerships" has shown how Dewey's "pragmatic experimentalism" and the tradition of progressive education laid the foundations of service-learning. This legacy, he argues, affirms "the radical interconnectedness of individual cognition and social context" in which the end-in-view of education is civic participation (2000, p. 33). However, as Deans (1999) points out, Dewey's communitarian view never fully grappled with diversity and conflict.

The Logic of Intercultural Inquiry

If community/university relations are to be based on the logic of inquiry, the first issue to put on the table is the problem and potential of cultural difference. Difference exists not just in simple distinctions, such as, town/gown, rich/poor, black/white, but also in the alternative discourses, literate practices, goals, and values brought to an inquiry. When the people doing this hypothesis making, testing, and judging live much of their lives in different worlds, talking different languages, they may indeed struggle to be understood at times. But when they come to the table as collaborative equals (where everyone's discourse, practices, and goals are recognized), those differences can produce an explosion of knowledge. Consider Dewey's (1922/1964) insistence that the *meaning* of ideas (e.g., of social concepts about youth or urban policies about work) is found in the continuing examination of the situated conditions for and the outcomes of those concepts and policies. It follows that no one group can lay claim to omniscience about all those conditions and outcomes. No one can pretend to take a God's eye view of how those concepts and policies play out in the daily lives, psyches, and social histories of the people affected or how those hypotheses need to be revised in light of that reality. Intercultural collaboration extends the reach of our knowledge.

Cornel West, who speaks as a cultural critic and professor of both Afro-African American studies and the philosophy of religion at Harvard, then Princeton University, extends the reach of inquiry yet further with the intellectual stance he calls *prophetic pragmatism*. The first thing to understand about the addition of "prophetic" is that it does not carry the popular suggestion of predicting the future (Brueggemann, 1978). Rather, it "harkens back to the rich, though flawed, traditions of Judaism and Christianity that promote courageous resistance against, and relentless critiques of, injustice and social misery." To be more operational, it is a stance that "analyzes the social causes of unnecessary forms of social misery, promotes moral outrage against them, organizes different constituencies to alleviate them, yet does so with an openness to its own blindnesses and shortcomings" (West, 1993, p. 139).

West shares with Paulo Freire and other radical educators an intense awareness of both social oppression and our role in persistent resistance and critique.[4] Freire calls for a combination of problem posing and problem solving that begins in inquiry, in "naming the world" in a way that makes its problems newly alive to us—and then calls us to both new understanding and action (1970/1985, p. 76). However, it is West's sense of the rigorous demands of inquiry that I want to emphasize here. In the spirit of Dewey and the tradition of American pragmatism, the critical temper of prophetic pragmatism "highlights the provisional, tentative and revisable character of our visions, analyses and actions." But unlike the distanced, disillusioned, or ironic stance of much cultural criticism, it provides a logic for mutuality in community/university and intercultural relations. That logic is based on what West calls democratic faith—"a Pascalian wager (hence underdetermined by the evidence) on the abilities and capacities of ordinary people to participate in decision-making procedures of institutions that fundamentally regulate their lives" (1993, pp. 139–40).

In building relationships across class and race, democratic "faith" in ordinary, fallible people is probably too weak a word for what West has in mind—which is really a politics of representation. His bolder argument calls for a representation of difference that insistently foregrounds not the deficits but "the agency, capacity and ability of human beings who have been culturally degraded, politically oppressed and economically exploited by bourgeois liberal and communist illiberal status quos" (1993, p. 29). The challenge to universities, then, is not to deny their own power, expertise, or agendas. Their technical tools, specialized discourses, and intellectual goals are needed. The challenge is to construct a mutual representation of the intentionality, the communal wisdom, and the evaluative competence of the community partners. The question is not whether such agency is there but whether institutional partners can organize themselves to uncover and acknowledge it.

In short, the logic of pragmatism calls for a rigorous openness to inquiry and the consequences of our actions. Prophetic pragmatism shapes a compassionate commitment to such inquiry in the midst of social and cultural struggles in which "we are forced to choose, in a rational and critical manner, some set of transient social practices, contingent cultural descriptions, and revisable scientific theories by which to live" (West, 1993, p. 134).

The community literacy project sketched in chapter 2 is grounded in the logic of prophetic pragmatism and intercultural inquiry that resists the problematic role of cultural missions and expert transmission. However, it certainly cannot hope simply to avoid those problems, since its literate practices are focused on education, grounded in research, and trying to employ the technological capability of the university. The challenge of *doing* community literacy is how to turn this notion of an inquiry-based community/university relationship into actual practice. So it is natural that students and teachers turn to the rhetorical roles and genres offered by academic practice.

Borrowing Roles and Relationships from Academic Practice

If we turn to current academic debates as a model for available roles, the dominant rhetoric of engagement is the rhetoric of resistance. This academic discourse often achieves its focus and power by avoiding the complications of naming a working alternative. A recent volume called *Alt Dis: Alternative Discourses and the Academy* illustrates the problem of moving beyond resistance to a working model of what community literacy would call a "hybrid, multi-vocal" discourse.[5] One of its most revealing moments is in Patricia Bizzell's analysis of a traditional historiographer who, coming to grips with his own racial and gender blindness, had published a personal essay to this effect in a traditional scholarly journal (2002). For some members of his academic audience (primarily other white males), this move against the grain was highly valuable, indeed needed, but many black and female scholars dismissed the significance of, what was to them, a belated and hardly original gesture. As the ensuing fracas made clear, *this* personal narrative was the wrong discourse in the wrong place.

Is resistance—that is, opposing mainstream, dominant, or expected conventions—good in itself? Is it enough? Does it give the worried editor of that history journal an articulated notion as to what a valued "alternative" would be? The stance of *Alt Dis* texts, built on the rhetoric of resistance, gives us few ways to decide which "alternatives" we want to stand for and which forms of "alt dis" are merely out of place, idiosyncratic for the sake of transgression, or even self-indulgent.

A less-nuanced example of resistance talk appears in Sidney J. Dobrin's argument against this whole enterprise: even "to discuss hybrid discourses is to enact a meta-discourse, [that functions to label] "'alternative' discourses not as equivalent to academic discourse. . . . We may be enacting a kind of silencing . . . To be blunt about it, I'm not sure I agree with discussions of alternative, hybrid discourses" (2002, pp. 45–46, 54). This is familiar language of resistance. It urges us to resist not only the concept of alternative, hybrid, or mixed discourses but also the discussion itself and to retreat from "creating such a conversation" (p. 54). Setting aside whether it is even remotely possible to stop an academic discussion, it leaves us wondering what a better discussion might be; what the author and his readers might stand for—in the full knowledge that making such a claim is a far riskier stance to take. When you stand for something, unlike engaging in critique, you are certain to have gotten (at least a part of) it wrong. But you usually learn most when you attempt, fail, regroup, revise, and essay again.

Community partners will find a more productive model in Helen Fox's forthright attempt to stride into her dilemma. How can you, as a writing-center instructor, be an *ally* in graduate students' search for mainstream success and—at the same time—a progressive *idealist/critic* of oppressive discourses? As she puts it, "If I want to be an ally I have be more than wistful.

I have to figure out what I'm going to do with my dilemma. If I want to be an ally, I do have to teach my craft rigorously, both because students want to learn it, and because like all cultural forms, it is powerful and pleasing if practiced well" (2002, p. 64).

If Bizzell left us wondering where to stand after we agree that *some* alternative discourses *can sometimes* be valuable, Fox sets her course right into the wind of her dilemma. In choosing both to teach *and* to raise questions about white privilege in classrooms and faculty meetings and to recognize the shifting and blurred boundaries of all discourses, she seeks to negotiate the problem her competing commitments raise, imagining actionable agendas. Nevertheless, she concludes in the discourse of academic resistance with a series of problematic assumptions and responses.

> Should we teach them . . . ? (Paternalism stands tall and kindly behind this question. Or maternalism, reflective, deeply concerned: Should we teach them academic discourse at all? Should we teach them in their own dialects: Should we allow both? Should we? Should we?)

> How should we teach them . . . ? (The inevitability of acculturation lurking behind this ordinary, everyday question.) (2002, p. 66)

Although I agree with Fox's claims, for me (as it might be for a new teacher in this dilemma), this concluding discourse move is not a fully adequate basis for reflective action.[6] It retreats to a kind of academic theorizing we do so well—be aware of the bear in the bushes. Yes, but just what shall I do when the dark shape appears? Should I have bought the $2.25 bear whistle I saw at a mountain shop last summer; or shall I follow my instincts to stalk up for a better look, or as an old *Field and Stream* editor says, "When the bear advances, get down, protect your head and kiss your ass good-bye." You're going to have to make some compromised choices.

The Stance of Resistance in Community Collaboration

When the rhetoric of resistance moves out of academic debates and into community engagement, it can create a problematic relationship with others and in the ways we are led to represent them. Postmodern theory has tended to dismiss personal agency, especially I would add, the agency of poor, less-educated, or marginalized people. As Ellen Cushman argues in *The Struggle and the Tools* (1999), if such people don't talk the official talk of resistance and cultural critique or engage in collective action, our theory accuses them of false consciousness—of complicity in their own domination because they failed to resist in the way we find appropriate.

When we use the powerful lens of resistance and theory to look at others, it seems (to shift metaphors) to block out our ability to hear what they are themselves saying. The voices of the subaltern—the Native American, the urban teen, the welfare parent—drop to insignificance. We are the central—and at times the only—consciousness on the airwaves. Stuart Gilbert Brown's fine account of his experience as an Athabascan bush teacher in *Words in the Wilderness* is a compelling story that begins with a richly humanized account of coping with his own expectations in the face of cultural difference. Yet, when his thoughtfully "theorized narrative" gives way to the critical-theory version of the same story, with its "repeated calls for a 'radical red subjectivity' or for 'alter/native narratives of resistance,'" his reviewer Scott R. Lyons (an Ojibwe-Dakota and scholar of American Indian rhetoric) gently questions "the implicit heroism of such rhetoric" with its suggestion of "barricades that might go up at any minute" (2000, December, p. 308). We become like the students whom Joe Harris (1992) describes as the professional critics who, unlike "other readers," the other "dumber viewers," are not taken in by the media we analyze.

Identifying a social consciousness with resistance has also had some distancing effects on our relationship with students. John Trimbur (2000) puts it succinctly:

> While we and others working in the cultural studies vein were quite aware of the danger of representing students as cultural dupes, with no defenses against interpellation into an Althusserian ideological state apparatus, the tendency nonetheless was to identify students mainly as readers, consumers, viewers, and spectators in need of training to resist the onslaughts of mass culture. (p. 198)

Why then did this stance—this preoccupation with holding the world at arm's length, remaining the safely distant critical reader, the unduped viewer—become a norm in academic articles? Why does it seem to dominate the way cultural and social concerns enters the classrooms—even if it erects a "barricade" between teachers and students, between social critics and the people they wish to speak for? Trimbur suggests that it has a lot to do with the academic genres we already felt comfortable writing and assigning.

> In the hope of fortifying student resistance to the dominant culture, such assignments [e.g., the ideological critique and interpretive essay demystifying mass culture and denaturalizing everyday "common sense"] actually smuggled in and restored unwittingly the close text-based readings of the specialist critic as the privileged practice of the writing classroom. (p. 198–99)

Digging out and resisting the implicit cultural assumptions of "other readers" was an old, familiar, new-critical way of reading text and events applied to new topics of culture. A tested and powerful method.

Another irony attends the stance of resistance. Within what Trimbur calls cultural theory's "restricted coterie of cothinkers," critique appears to have had "a limited social usefulness for wider audiences. There seems, that is, to be a radical disconnect between the desire of academic leftists to make their work relevant to ordinary people and the way it actually circulates through normal academic channels" (2000, p. 212).

West criticizes Michel Foucault, whose "reification of discourses, disciplines, and techniques" (West, 1993, p. 225) has made him so compatible with what Trimbur calls the "literary legacy of cultural studies and its residual textualism" (Trimbur, 2000, p. 203).

> Foucault tends to reduce left ethics to a bold and defiant Great Refusal addressed to the dominant powers that be. Yet by failing to articulate and elaborate ideals of democracy, equality, and freedom, Foucault provides solely negative conceptions of critique and resistance. . . . Like Foucault, prophetic pragmatists criticize and resist forms of subjection, as well as types of economic exploitation, state repression, and bureaucratic domination. But these critiques and resistances, unlike his, are unashamedly guided by moral ideals of creative democracy and individuality. (West, 1993, p. 226)

Finally, I would argue that there is an unavoidable poverty in an identity built around resistance. It enables us to relate to Others in an urban community as victims or at best as comrades in arms—united in a theorized battle plan (that academic intellectuals supposedly understand better than do the victims). What is even more problematic for our capacity to create a collaborative working plan is that the focus of our attention and energy is on the immovable, impersonal forces of power and ideology. These forces cannot be ignored; they demand the constant renewing of our awareness; we must reflect and resist. Yet, is it enough to build an identity based on a baroquely elaborated analysis of what we choose to stand *against*—and to leave our image of what we stand *for* and stand *with* a weakly asserted, undeveloped abstraction? Consider the complex literate practice of critique and the extended analyses of oppressive ideology that define cultural studies. Where is the parallel and equally articulated statement of the better alternative? Should we be satisfied with generalized assertions of social justice and democracy? Such underdeveloped arguments sound like a monosyllable hurled at the problem when what we need is a complexly persuasive invitation to Martin Luther King Jr.'s beloved community. Are we preparing students and ourselves to stand with others and for commitments with the same level of thoughtfully developed, reflective, experimental skepticism that we bring to standing against?

My premise is a simple one: representations of what we are working toward, like identities, must be constructed and articulated. I mean *articulated* in both a cognitive sense—that is, a named, elaborated, qualified, and connected representation—and in Stuart Hall's sense—that is, a socially constructed and therefore alterable set of connections (1986, p. 53). An impoverished, unreflective, under-elaborated representation is an inadequate guide to action.

Working Theories of Partnership

If, as prophetic pragmatists, teachers, and students engaged in community literacy, we want a role beyond resistance and an identity based on partnership in inquiry and transformation, we need to construct just such a guide. Saul Alinsky called his no-holds-barred guide for leftist community organizing *Rules for Radicals* (1989). Literary cultural theory has given what we might call "rules for resistance"—a complex conceptual toolkit for theorizing structures of domination and for naming (as Trimbur puts it) "the performative rules that code the production of media messages" (2000, p. 203). So what does a reflective, self-critical, outcome-oriented, revisable articulation of our ideals or commitments look like when it is embodied in literate practice and everyday action? At one level, the account of a community/university collaboration in chapters 1 and 2 and the description of its rhetorical tools in chapters 6 through 10 describe one extended attempt to construct such an articulation.

However, in practice every student and teacher must construct a working theory of that role and identity for him- or herself. Coming to grips with what a partnership in inquiry and transformation means in action is an ongoing process of writing, sharing, and rethinking one's own rules for engagement. The kind of writing this requires is not an expressive personal essay, espousing general ideals, that is, an identity statement that vigorously asserts an uncontested endorsement of liberal values—diversity, democracy, apple pie. Instead, this identity calls for a local, situated, operational statement of what one is working toward.

Dewey calls this an *end-in-view*. In his repeated criticism of our quest for certainty, he points to our attempt to justify our goals by equating them with abstract, idealized, eternal, or "fixed ends" (1929/1988). Dewey argues that ends "arise and function within action" (1922/1964, pp. 70–80). They are not "terminals" but merely "turning points *in* activity," not an end-in-themselves but an end-in-view. "The great trouble" he says, "with what passes for moral ends and ideals is that they do not get beyond the stage of fancy of something agreeable and desirable based upon an emotional wish (p. 79). *Meaning well* becomes *the* goal. Worse yet, this focus on fixed ends diverts attention from where it needs to be—on the "examination of consequences and the intelligent creation of purpose" (p. 77). The transformation of an ideal to an end or aim (a terminal of deliberation) depends on what Dewey calls a realistic study of the actual conditions that would give an idea substance—"to give it, in short, practicality and constitute it as a working end" (p. 79).

As suggested in chapter 3, a *working* theory of partnership is a guide to acting that, as a *theory,* invites us to test and revise our understanding and beliefs. Trying to articulate a working theory of our role in inquiry is undoubtedly more difficult than taking on the available roles of a critic of social structures or of "other readers," but it is central to the work of prophetic pragmatism. So I conclude the current chapter with a closer look at some college students trying to answer the questions, Who am I? What am I doing here? The intensely personal issues they confront about role and identity are, it turns out, not unique but have direct parallels in disciplinary debates surrounding literacy and social action, intercultural research, the role of expertise, and the efficacy of inquiry. *The paradox is that if these socially shared questions are general, the answers are not. They are instead deeply situated, personally constructed in response to conflict, and designed not as "terminal" truths but as "turning points" and plans for action.*

Negotiating Identity

The closely observed picture of college mentors in Long (2000) shows students not only trying to construct their own situated guides to action but also trying to answer for themselves the same question posed in disciplinary debate: What is the (appropriate) link between literacy and social action? Like the published writers, the students' answers cluster around a set of what Long calls four "contested practices." For some, their role is to emphasize grammatical correctness and Standard English as tool for entry into mainstream society. For some, it is to invite free expression, helping teenagers take authority as writers. Others see their role as supporting emancipation, stimulating a Freirean critical consciousness. And still others would develop rhetorical skill.

Liz's plan for mentoring fourteen-year-old Chaz is "helping him to develop a consciousness that might not have been there. He wants to be a professional football player. I challenge that. He's a little guy, you know. I ask him to analyze this cultural thing—football, which I don't think is too much to ask of some-one at this age level (2000, p. 292). Keith, on the other hand, sees his role as supporting action-oriented problem solving. Keith wants Chanda to be heard by people in authority: "I keep asking tough questions like, 'What would you propose as a change' and 'How can you get adults to take you seriously?'" (p. 293). Meanwhile, Paula had been trying to create social equality by avoiding *any* explicit instruction or suggestion—until the day that circumstances made her the group leader with only one session left to complete and rehearse the skit for the public Community Conversation. Should she railroad the kids, write it herself, or just have a great day with little concern for productivity? Or, could she find a way to negotiate her conflicting goals and roles? In practice, the tacit assumptions and chosen identities students bring to mentoring are often vigorous sites of conflict, challenged by the competing claims of other mentors, the literacy leaders, the agenda of the CLC—and, most important, by the boisterous realities of this interpersonal, intercultural, historically located community/university relationship.[7]

College students found their role as a researcher under negotiation as well.[8] Flipping through copies of *Ebony* and *Jet* magazines at the CLC, Rachel had been perplexed by the ads she just "didn't get" as well as the ones "seducing African American teenagers into buying malt liquor, fast cars, or $200 tennis shoes" (Long, 2000, p. 301). Rachel framed her course project as an inquiry with teens into the everyday cultural knowledge they bring to reading and critiquing such ads. But enter William Labov (an authoritative, admired linguist we were reading) with his devastating critique of adult white researchers whose inability to create a genuine dialogue with African American youth led them to conclude the children lacked verbal skills. Labov made it clear: if you wanted to study what kids thought and how they talked, you needed a researcher who shared the culture. In the face of this conclu-sion (which leaves most mentors out in the cold), Rachel must negotiate her own identity, as she did in her final paper.

> But, Labov, I don't want to try and find an African American inter-viewer to conduct my inquiry. I'm a Jewish American 20-year-old, and I want to have the conversation. I want to see what I can learn firsthand. What this project is all about is finding a strategy for instigating inter-cultural conversations here at the CLC. (Long, 2000, p. 302)

Expert versus Learner

Jon's class was helping organize a Community Think Tank on "Healthcare: The Dilemma of Teamwork, Time, and Turnover" by documenting rival readings of problems and options, with management, nurses, *and* nursing aides in local nursing homes, including Lemington, a local African American nursing home.[9] We wanted the think tank's public, intercultural problem-solving dialogue to foreground the plight and the often-overlooked, situated knowledge of the nursing aides, who work on the bottom level of the medical world's hierarchy. Jon arrived assuming he should somehow play the expert—and was unnerved that he clearly couldn't. It was a role built on good intentions, not hubris, and a sense that his academic expertise was all he had to contribute. Yet, here he was, he felt, talking to women twice his age with ten times his experience in adversity—an "advice" giver, with nothing to say: "How was I, someone who had never been involved with a community-based project and had never even worked in this particular sphere, going to offer any useful advice that could possibly change the working conditions for nursing assistants?" By the time he wrote this final reflection, what Jon had discovered led to a radical change in how he saw his role in inquiry.

> But as we worked with the [nursing home] employees I saw that my inexperience with such endeavors really didn't matter. So when you ask me what I found, I can tell you what I truly believe to be more important—that the mere act of taking interest in someone's life can help you break through any barriers that block communication, even those created by differences of race and culture.—Jon

Like Jon, Nick found he had to start by giving up some assumptions about what he *did* know.

> *I believe the most important thing I learned about the inquiry process was that I knew nothing about the problem.* . . . I took for granted that the C.N.A. [certified nursing aide] I interviewed would be unhappy. I assumed that problems of low-pay, high turnover and a lack of teamwork would affect their job satisfaction. *Having envisioned interviewing a dissatisfied employee, I was both shocked and somewhat unprepared to find myself conversing with someone who loved their job.* It seemed incomprehensible to me that someone who worked for slightly more than minimum wage would openly declare that they love their job. Yet, this C.N.A. repeatedly declared that love.—Nick (italics added)

These two students tried to redefine their roles in different ways. Jon, I would say, tried to avoid his dilemma by moving into a caring person-to-person relationship. But Nick seemed to be working on a new role (and set of literate practices) for himself as a listener and learner.

It would be both politically and educationally naïve to conclude that a change of heart (even one more rigorous than Jon's "mere act of taking interest") will let students rewrite the problematic role of expert. The challenge in being a partner in inquiry is using whatever expertise one does have in a context in which neither disengaged academic analysis or resistance is going to be enough. As Joanna concludes, don't underestimate how difficult it is to "apply" what you do know to "a real life situation."

> When I first began this class, I vividly remember being intrigued by the "hands-on element" of learning to rhetorically make a difference. I think at the same time, I underestimated how difficult and often frustrating it is to really get at the root of this concept, to in some way invoke change in whatever it is that you believe in. But what this course was able to accomplish that no other class has ever taught me, is the process of applying what you read, what you know, and what you think about to a real life situation.

Activism and Inquiry

Over this term project, Jon, Nick, and Joanna—undergraduates new to community contexts—were writing, testing out, and rewriting internal rules of engagement for themselves. One of the master's students, a quiet leader in the class, was working from a very different place: Franki, an African American activist, knew about the civil rights actions of the 1960s—she had been part of both the nonviolent protests of King and the Black Power stance of Malcolm X. It is in that context that she ends up defining inquiry as an act of "mutual regard."

> The point of intercultural inquiry is to provide intellectual, emotional, and in this case chronological space in which to examine a notion . . . [in] an atmosphere of abiding (even though it may be transient) mutual regard. For a few moments the playing field is leveled and most masks are removed. Participants begin to offer contributions of exploration and helpfulness rather than accusations and blame. . . .

> Mutual regard is the fundamental element missing from other actions we might take as writers/speakers. Self-renewal by definition gives little place for the values and perceptions of another person. Speaking out suggests that we have something to say, to teach. Nowhere in the concept of "speaking out" is there apparent room for receptivity. Volunteers bestow benevolence. Whether in the form of food, time, or dry socks in winter, these are acts of outreach and outpouring. Political activism

and community organizing might give a tiny space to mutual regard but only if the activist/organizer can suspend his/her agenda long enough to recognize a human being rather than a pawn. It is because we have so little mutual regard that we cannot hear one another or see one another much less cooperate together.

Alan was the most dedicated skeptic in this group—a Berkeley graduate turned professional writer for the university, with a personal history of (and a whole family known for) political activism. He had no illusions about the outcomes of expert advice or resistance, much less the "mere act of taking interest." Against the backdrop of his own informed commitments, the problem of the class was indeed a problem of identity, which forced him to ask, Who am I? What am I doing here?—especially in the mild-mannered stance of an inquirer. Here is a part of his reflection as he designed it.

> "I just feel like there isn't much hope," I said to Jen, my wife.
> "Well, I think you should change your attitude," was her reply.
> "Start small. Try cleaning the bathroom."
> As I sat down to write this reflection, I was brimming with cynicism. What good is activism, I thought, when all the righteous indignation in the world doesn't do a damn bit of good? What good is grassroots activity if the whims of a few people in positions of great power carry so much more weight than the assembled voice of a majority? In this climate, could even Martin Luther King ignite a revolutionary fire across the country? I highly doubt it. Too few people have the energy for outrage anymore. Angry or not, most American activists are too comfortable to take to the streets.
> But leave it to your spouse to put things back in perspective. "I just don't feel like there's much hope," I said, face-to-face with a blank computer screen, thinking out loud about the value of intercultural inquiry. And this is what Jen meant by her response: Maybe there isn't much of a place these days for transformational, revolutionary action. But progress isn't out of the question. It *can* occur—in small, incremental steps; like those we took by visiting Lemington; like that I might take yet by cleaning the bathroom. . . .
> I don't foresee any fundamental changes in health-care policy occurring any time soon. Nor do I see any CNAs making overnight fortunes. But *approximations* of successes, such as securing higher pay and better training, can be realized through a long process of incremental advances. Intercultural inquiry, in other words, doesn't have the power to reinvent a workplace on its own. Nor does any one strategy

or tactic, I imagine. Bringing about significant changes—in, say, the working conditions of thousands of health-care workers—depends on the aggregate of several approaches: Lobbying, consciousness-raising, shrewd bottom-line appeals to executives and administrators, and empowerment from within. It's this last item on the list that intercultural inquiry engenders.

Our experience at Lemington also reinforced the value of bringing a diversity of opinions and perspectives to bear on a problem. I was reminded that some measure of humility does a problem-solver a world of good. Having admirable intentions doesn't necessarily equate with being well informed. I may have the occasional good idea, but I can be much more productive as a *facilitator* than as an isolated actor.

If the paradox of a working theory is that socially shared, broadly significant questions have personally constructed, locally situated answers, the paradox of identity was that it, too, seemed to be made, not found. Community/university projects offer a variety of ready-made identities, from the service provider, technical expert, organizer and advocate to the cultural critic, role model, or buddy. However, these may lead to roles and relationships we do not want to claim, especially if they blind us to the agency and expertise of others. So the question of What am I doing here? can take on a special urgency and feel very much like a problem of identity. Yet, these reflections by mentors and writers suggest that, first of all, identity in this partnership is not something you bring with you; it is not about who or what *you* are. Identity is defined by *the relationships you create*. It is built around the shared goal of inquiry and literate action and your role in that partnership. Secondly, identity as a rhetor who can speak *for* something is not based on a quirk of personality as some students assume. That was not what gave thirteen-year-old Shirley the authority to speak about risk to a table of white professionals and assertive, fast-talking male peers. This identity, shared by people as different as Nick and Alan, appears to be constructed through collaboration and over time in an effort to confront competing voices, to explore alternatives, and to imagine for oneself a committed, revisable stance. The challenge for educators is to scaffold a constructive process around such shared questions that each of us must answer for ourselves.

5 *Images of Empowerment*

The rhetoric of making a difference is the work of empowered people. But empowerment, like the notion of community, can mean a set of very different things in practice. It all depends on how you answer three key questions: Who is being empowered? To what end? By what means? To build a working theory of empowerment, the Community Literacy Center had to recognize competing images that leaders and mentors alike brought to this work if we hoped to build a negotiated meaning that would be persuasive and workable for the whole group.

The first question to ask is, who is being empowered by whom? For instance:

- Are the poor, excluded, marginalized, and oppressed, themselves *wresting* power from the rich, the privileged, the powerful?
- Or are the normally silenced and excluded being *given* membership and agency by someone (e.g., community organizations, educators, social services, philanthropies, and the like)?
- Or are the privileged *developing* their own capacity to resist, serve, and act on the behalf of others?
- Or are excluded and privileged people *achieving together* the moral and/or material power of solidarity?

If you are a minority student, a mentor, or a college teacher looking for your place in one of these scripts of empowerment, it matters a great deal who the principal players are imagined to be and how (or whether) they are expected to relate to one another. For instance, the scripts of identity politics, on one extreme, and charity, on the other, often build strong ideological walls between the players who regularly exclude outsiders or Others from the role of agent.

In scripts for educational and rhetorical empowerment, the plot is also shaped by how you name your end-in-view. That is, what are the newly empowered being empowered to do? Are they empowered to

- participate, gain discourse membership, or cultural competence within the dominant group?
- speak up for one's self or culture with a "special" personal voice?
- speak against forces of marginalization with a newly aroused critical or cultural consciousness?
- speak with others in a dialogue of intercultural inquiry?
- speak for values, commitments, and change out of solidarity with others?

Finally, the meaning of empowerment cannot be separated in practice from the means you use to translate ideas into outcomes. Here, the critical question becomes, what kind of scaffold are you building to support the process of empowerment you envision?

This chapter considers some ways these scripts of empowerment play themselves out in rhetoric, composition, and communication studies and in the scaffolds we build to support different scripts. All of these forms of empowerment (and others of a more political style as well) play a necessary role in the larger drama of social action. Empowerment depends on speaking appropriately, speaking up, and speaking against as well as speaking with. None has a corner on the rhetoric of making a difference, but each may call for decisive choices, and we need to be more self-conscious about the outcomes and trade-offs. In particular, I want to ask why our dominant educational paradigms have so much trouble supporting an *intercultural* empowerment—one focused on solidarity, speaking with others, and speaking for values. I want also to raise the educational and moral dilemmas that the enterprise of literate empowerment presents, not to engage in critique for its own sake but to explore the committed, inevitably fallible ways we can try to negotiate decision, such as:

- Can I presume to participate in the empowerment of anyone else? (On the other hand, can I presume that my choice to ignore or evade the question is really neutral if it preserves a status quo that disempowers someone else?)
- How can the privileged—in particular—actually support the empowerment of cultural others?
- How can educators (who by their actions cannot avoid the question) help scaffold a process of empowerment for students and community partners?

Scripts for Empowerment

Speaking Appropriately—Empowerment
through Communicative Competence

In the script of intercultural communication (a well-defined subfield of communication studies), the players in need of help are designated as strangers—the immigrant, the exchange student, the business associate in a foreign culture. In *Communicating with Strangers*, communications scholars William Gudykunst and Young Kim lay out the dilemma (1997). Strangers trying to carry on their public or professional lives in a strange land are exchanging messages or signs or codes that come with culturally loaded meanings. These messages are either unrecognized by the other party or are more or less incomprehensible. The research in this field (primarily on Asian–Western European contact) locates the barriers to communication within the underlying habits of mind associated with different cultural groups. Without making deterministic arguments, these scholars seem to agree on a set of key cultural variables or differences that are predictable disrupters of intercultural communication:

- an individualistic versus a collective emphasis in the culture
- a strong or weak investment in hierarchies that maintain social distance and power
- a strong or weak need to reduce uncertainty and anxiety within social interactions by creating rules and codes
- an emphasis on "masculine," materialistic success versus "feminine" nurturance

The goal of empowerment in this script is adaptive competence. We learn to participate in a coordinated management of meaning—to recognize the rules, roles, rituals, and relationships that go with the social meanings of strangers. And we learn to manage our own anxiety, uncertainty, and need for in-group identity (Gudykunst, 1983). Speaking more broadly, Gudykunst and Kim imagine their ideal as the "intercultural person" who lives on the boundary, with a "tolerant sensibility and behavioral repertoire . . . equipped with the capacity to function in more than one culture effectively" (1997, p. 253). That said, when we look in the research and the handbooks for how this will happen, the "behavioral repertoire" or the literate tools designed to create this sensibility seem surprisingly limited to cultural analysis. Students are aided to recognize the features noted above in themselves and in their target culture and are then encouraged to adapt—to acculturate, assimilate, and cope with the stress of social participation.

As seen in chapter 3, composition has a variation on this script of assimilation (minus the social science). The stranger, who must be initiated into academic discourse, is defined more narrowly in terms of written performance as the basic writer or underprepared student. The goal is limited to joining the community of academic discourse. There is little talk of developing "an intercultural person" because the focus is usually on linguistic and genre-based competence.

Speaking Up—Empowerment through Self-Expression

Nurturing a Personal Voice and Identity

The expressivist tradition in composition has long used the notion of "voice" to value writing as a way to express identity and to support personal development.[1] This shows up in intercultural discourse as code-switching or the use of dialect, in-group argots, or tropes that may be intentionally obscure to outsiders. However, for a writer like Gloria Anzaldúa, such a voice communicates the mixed, mestiza consciousness of a border crosser and allows her to work out the tangled web of her own identity (1987). It gives textual form to the double consciousness of being an Other in mainstream America. Such a voice asserts, like the motto of Chicago's *Journal of Ordinary People*, that "Every person is a philosopher."[2]

Building Self-Understanding

The empowerment script written for mainstream students in outreach and service-learning projects uses writing quite differently, starting with entry into the contact zone of intercultural discourse—through reading and volunteer work—before moving into the essential work of writing and reflection.[3] Writing turns "service" into "service-learning," letting mainstream students translate the experience of difference (and the anxiety and uncertainty communication scholars describe) into personal growth and articulated understanding. Much of this new understanding grows out of the frustration and satisfaction of collaborating.[4]

Unfortunately (as college instructors, student mentors, community/university partners, bush teachers, and VISTA workers can testify), a meaningful dialogue across difference does not just happen through goodwill. One needs a social scaffold and a shared literate practice that can manage conflicts and set priorities for what counts as meaningful talk. But differences between the scaffold a communication scholar would build and one that an expressive writing instructor might construct point to contradictory notions of what a "discourse of empowerment" should attempt to do or to empower. Is it the creation of a unique, literate voice; or is it the broader construction of a personal, racial, political identity, perhaps one armed with the cutting edge of critical consciousness? Or perhaps this discourse should be designed to empower disruptive social critique? Or to nurture a border-crossing collaborative understanding? Should (could?) all of these goals apply to young people in a Community Conversation?

Speaking Against—Empowerment through Resistance

Our boldest, most comprehensive vision of empowerment is without doubt Paulo Freire's liberatory education. Locating learning in the immediate context of the student's life and the larger context of society, liberatory education transforms uncritical perceptions of experience to critical understanding through a process of problem posing, democratic dialogue, and action (cf. Shor, 1987, pp. 2–3). Problem posing, the first of these three key moves, produces a rhetoric of resistance in which students "problematize all subjects of study, . . . to understand existing knowledge as a historical product deeply invested with the values of those who developed such knowledge" (p. 24).

In English departments, where literary and cultural theory has been a major instigator of a new political discourse, this initial problematizing move has merged into the practice of theory-guided critique (although in the process, it has often become detached from Freire's additional expectations for dialogue and action). Literacy studies have created a library of empowerment scripts based on resistance, in which writers achieve identity, recognition, and critical consciousness by speaking against the forces that disempower people. This rhetoric of critical analysis can take many forms.

Enfranchising Local Literacies

Literacy researchers who come to the work of empowerment as ethnographers document and celebrate local literacies, following a path broken by Shirley Brice Heath's *Ways with Words* (1983). More recently, researchers who are more politically explicit seek out the everyday practices of writing and speaking found at kitchen tables, in the doctor's office, on the factory floor, and in union groups and neighborhood organizations (Barton & Hamilton, 1998). They are not interested in teaching anybody to speak appropriately (much less to adapt to high literacy) but in showing how intelligent, effective, complex, and appropriate these local literacies are to their context. These studies set out to challenge the assumptions of elite discourses that only see error in these local discourses and to redefine literacy as a set of social and discursive practices that get the job of living done. In fact, when people in a community can trade off skills, most do not even use high literacy.[5]

Empowering Marginalized Discourses

This script works in the hands of the teacher who allows (or invites) alternative discourses into his or her class. Coming out of cultural theory, this stance interprets the personal voice of a marginalized writer as itself a political act of resistance against the dominant culture. The individual speaker becomes a stand-in for a silenced race, class, gender, or sexual orientation and for the non-elite, native, local, or nonstandard discourses he or she represents. This basically passive stance empowers a speaker by allowing and encouraging the speaker to resist the authority and the limitations of mainstream society and its dominant discourses by speaking his or her own language. On the other hand, minority educators like Lisa Delpit (1988) vigorously oppose both this choice and its expressive counterpart for their failure to teach students what such educators argue is really necessary—the language of power.

Developing a Vocal Critical Consciousness

Feminist pedagogies like Susan Jarratt's script resistance in more active terms by bringing mainstream students and their teachers into the practice of intercultural rhetoric. Like bell hooks's pedagogy grounded in an "oppositional world view," this script pushes students into "serious and rigorous critical exchange" quite unlike the nurturing and nonconflictual style of the expressivist classroom (Jarratt, 1991, p. 120). Subjecting their personal experience to social analysis, students must see their writing as a public activity.

Stuart Gilbert Brown's work as a "bush teacher" with the decidedly disempowered argues for a "pedagogy as agonistic in practice as it is in theory" (2000, p. 117). Because intercultural relations are always in danger of slipping into patterns of dominance and oppression, he puts emotional and intellectual resistance at the heart of his curriculum for the native students in Alaska's Atabas reservation. He abandoned the Foxfire pedagogy (which recovers local artifacts and lore) when it turned native artifacts into commodities and collectables and when the local knowledge of the elders produced a portrait of an "authentic" native past—which was unconnected to current social or political realities (p. 145). The road to empowerment, Brown concluded, was not to recover the past but to aggressively critique the present.

> The borderland students must become the active subjects of the knowledge-making process, and the objectification of their own oppression must become the first text that they "read" and "write," for this truth is as emancipatory when objectified as it is oppressive if left unexamined. It is indeed a truth, which when named and possessed, can set the native free. (p. 117)

Note that in both Brown and Jarratt, the social script is not about dia-logue with an Other but about the practice of analysis, critique, and public argument, which examines the self and social patterns within the pressure cooker of difference and in the challenging presence of Others.

Creating a Special Voice

The empowerment script of critical-race theory shows how to turn the tools of expressivism into yet another form of resistance. Its goal, Catherine Pren-dergast argues, is to validate a "special voice"—the distinctive expression of a postcolonial double consciousness that "embodies contradiction, ambigu-ity, and even irrationality as it reflects the experience of discrimination in a society which professes to be colorblind" (1998, p. 40). Celebrated in the transgressive and digressive textual practices of legal writers, such as, Derrick Bell and Patricia Williams, this voice gains its power as a tool of critique by choosing to "deliberately distort, embellish, and evade the discourse of their discipline in order to address the subject of racism" (p. 38).

Gloria Anzaldúa's work is a stylistic and linguistic argument for a special voice that expresses identity wrapped around a doubleness she calls a mestiza consciousness. In an interview with Andrea Lunsford, Anzaldúa describes how her flamboyant, self-styled, bilingual, code-switching mix of English, Spanglish, Tex-Mex narrative, fantasy, and critique actually creates identity: "Identity is very much a fictive construction: you compose it of what's out there, what the culture gives you, and what you resist in the culture. . . . So you keep creating your identity this way" (qtd. in Lunsford, 1998, p. 4). This special voice, she argues, is the grounding for individual liberation: "I am my language. Until I can take pride in my language I can not take pride in myself. . . . Until I am free to write bilingually and to switch codes without having to translate, . . . my tongue will be illegitimate" (p. 2). "Unearthing and nurturing that voice is part of the activism work" as well, Anzaldúa says. That voice must be spoken for others like the children who never see themselves represented in mainstream textbooks. "You're rewriting the culture," bring-ing something ignored into "the consensual reality" (p. 25). Writing like this is often fostered in what Canagarajah (1997, p. 173) calls "safe houses in the contact zone"—social and intellectual places in which minority communities or groups within a school, for instance, can find personal space and critical distance before plunging back into the fray.

These broad personal and social goals of cross-cultural discourse must of course be embedded in literate practices. Expressivism empowers indi-vidual or collective identity by nurturing a distinctive written "voice," but as it moves into the charged atmosphere of race talk, that expressive "voice" is often transformed into a lightning bolt of critique. "I think disruption is a primary prerogative of those of us who are paid pests," says self-styled, "hip-hop intellectual" Eric Dyson in a *JAC* special issue on "Race, Class, and Writing." "Our function is to disrupt and intervene upon conversations in ways that are disturbing, that in their very disturbance force people to ask why they frame the questions in the way that they did or make the analysis they do" (qtd. in Dobrin, 1997, p. 166).

This vision of a sharp-edged "special voice" (drawing on the accents of street talk, new music, radio shows, and church voices) is at the heart of the Black Public Sphere, writes Gwendolyn Pough, who brings the Dyson agenda to the classroom (and the campus). Using Black Panther Party documents helps her "not only to spark social change and empower students but also to cause disruptions in the academy through public debate and protest" (2002, p. 468). The discourse of disruption is both literal, such as students blocking traffic in Miami, Ohio, over unmet demands for a more diverse campus, and intellectual, "forc[ing] academics to reflect on their actions" (p. 468).

Some Problems in the Paradigms of Expression and Resistance

The empowerment scripts within expressivist and cultural-theory paradigms have taken writers well beyond the plan we saw in communication studies that would enable strangers to anticipate very broad cultural differences and communicate more appropriately adapted messages. The scripts in composition studies have created intense personal and political agendas and supported them with a set of powerful literate practices that include self-reflection, inventive literate performance, theory-based literary analysis of texts, media, and social events wedded to critical analysis of patterns of domination. They have taught writers to speak up in spite of difference and to speak out against oppression in its many guises.

One limitation they also have in common (often seen as an academic virtue) is the tendency to maintain a critical distance from a genuine problem: students come home from a service-learning experience to reflect in tranquility; self-expression allows writers to resist or escape the discourse of dominating others; vigorous critique is done from the safe house of theory, which can create not only a physical and institutional distance from the marginalized folks it speaks for but also, at times, an unchecked tendency to moral certainty. In both these paradigms, the cultural Other that inspires reflection or critique rarely speaks back. In "speaking up," we are often in a dialogue with ourselves, our past, our assumptions—we are not obliged to deal with the response of the Others to our words. And in "speaking against," we are typically in a dialogue with the theory, speculations, and injunctions of other academic writers. We are not obligated to be in dialogue with the Others for whom we speak. We are not accountable to them for our interpretations of *their* situation or our claims for what *should* be done.

What is missing in these scripts is a more fully articulated rhetorical agenda for *inquiry* and *argument* across cultural differences. This more fully rhetorical image would need to offer us:

- an explanatory theory of what is being empowered
- a literate practice—that is, an art (or techne) grounded in social contexts, textual models, and workable rhetorical strategies
- a way to scaffold the process in different settings, from a classroom to a community center or policy forum

A second thing missing in this script is a sense of alternatives worth working for. The debate over cultural literacy is a good example of how resistance without such alternatives can lead to an academic dead end. Critic Patricia Bizzell says that, on the one hand, we need to see beyond the Anglo, male, middle-class notions of cultural literacy promoted by conservatives. On the other, we need to go "beyond the simple anti-foundationalism" of the critics of cultural literacy. Confronting this Scylla and Charybdis then, classroom teachers, curriculum developers, program directors, researchers, and policy makers have to decide: what kind of scaffold should we build for learning, toward what end? If being "culturally literate" in a certain mainstream tradition won't empower all students, how do we decide what will?

Bizzell's critique concludes that we need to "articulate a positive program legitimated by an authority that is nevertheless nonfoundational" generated through a rhetorical process that is pluralistic, willing to speak of civic virtue, and to take the risk needed "to create and share utopian rhetoric" (1992, pp. 271, 275). The current dead end as she sees it is the familiar problem of resistance. We are caught up in

> the project of sniffing out foundationalism assumptions in every area of academic life. . . . We spend our time exposing truth claims as historically, ideologically, rhetorically constructed; in other words we spend our time in the activity called deconstruction. (pp. 218, 261)

And then, when we don't have a positive alternative, "once the ideological interest has been pointed out, the anti-foundationalists throw up their hands . . . [and] end up tacitly supporting the political and cultural status quo" (p. 265).

Bizzell's portrait shows how resistance without real alternatives can end up supporting the status quo. The educational scaffold Bizzell proposes is not unlike Jarratt's. It leads students to explore the historical rootedness of their own positions and then seek points of contact with other positions and interest groups (1992, p. 292). But in place of the rhetorical action Jarratt envisions (drawing her students into public speech), Bizzell would have us focus on how the liberal teacher creates her rhetorical authority and uses the tools of persuasion to convince students of her own egalitarian views. As useful as such critique may be, it won't produce the kind of intercultural empowerment the next group of writers (many writing out of their minority experience) is asking for.

Speaking With—Empowerment through Dialogue across Difference

Although Paulo Freire is rightly identified with a pedagogy for critical consciousness based on historical and structural analysis, his larger vision is inseparable from dialogue and transformative rhetorical action. Ira Shor's astute synopsis captures how a complex agenda for the empowerment of both students and teachers, oppressed and privileged works on many fronts:

> When pedagogy and curricular policy reflect egalitarian goals, they do what education can do: *oppose socialization with desocialization;* choose critical consciousness over commercial consciousness, transformation of society over reproduction of inequity; promote democracy by practicing it and by studying authoritarianism; challenge student withdrawal through participatory courses; illuminate the myths supporting the elite hierarchy of society; interfere with the scholastic disabling of students through a critical literacy program; distribute research skills and censored information useful for investigating power and policy in society; and invite students to reflect socially on their conditions, to consider overcoming the limits. (Shor, 1987, pp. 14–15; italics in original)

A Freirean democratic dialogue happens first with other learners, achieving critical insight by reflecting on shared situated themes (ranging in Shor's collection of essays from mathematics and statistics teaching, to work, to wife-beating). Consciousness-raising then goes public, in transformative action that draws others into a dialogue of possibility.[6] The legacy of Freire's work as Shor continues to extend it is an intellectually generous inspiration that invites many efforts at dialogue (Shor & Pari, 1999). Yet, as prophetic pragmatism reminds us, transformation is not the inevitable outcome of an exchange—of "you talk, I talk," as Royster calls it (1996). In classrooms and communities, the meaning of dialogue (like that warm abstraction *empowerment*) emerges in actions and outcomes, which will in turn be shaped by the activity we choose to scaffold. Consider some options.

Creating a Community of Knowers

In *Latino/a Discourses: On Language, Identity, and Literacy Education*, many of the academic essays by Latino/a writers (survivors of the monolingual, monoliterate English classrooms of the 1960s and 1970s) are themselves stories of empowerment (Kells, Balester, & Villanueva, 2004).[7] And one wonders, how did they do it? The path Juan Guerra describes and Michelle Hall Kells documents seems to depend on a sophisticated literate practice of code-switching and transcultural positioning—on an astute and agile reading of social and rhetorical scenes and a flexible choice among competing discourses. Although discourse miscalculations can be dangerous, this ability allows these speakers to move among cultures on their own terms. So many educators try to scaffold a version of this cultural mobility.

For example, Joseph Harris's classroom would not be a safe house insulated from conflict. The demanding literate practice of critical consciousness is not achieved by reading about difference. It requires a scaffold more dangerous than the benign world of Louise Pratt's contact zone (1991) yet short of a combat zone. It requires

> a sense of how to make such a meeting of differences less like a battle and more like a negotiation. We need, that is, to learn not only how to articulate our differences but how to bring them into useful relation with each other. (Harris, 1997, p. 120)

Kurt Spellmeyer makes a provocative argument about how this could happen in composition classes, where instead of a focus on the establishment rules of discourse, students are first recognized as meaning makers in their own right, *involved* in the work of reading and writing because it addresses questions that matter to them. Their class is a site of competing truths and real differences, where the goal is not to preserve or transmit knowledge but to appropriate it—to use writing to discover what these differences mean for each individual.

It is Spellmeyer's hypothesis of what happens next that speaks to empowerment. In this *involvement* with ideas and experience, writers enter a "community of knowers," acknowledged as meaning makers, not just acolytes (Spellmeyer, 1993, p. 118). They retain their own voices and work on their own questions but do so within an enlarged world, achieving what Spellmeyer's book title calls *Common Ground.* But how does one make the leap from personal involvement and appropriation to a common understanding? The answer for Spellmeyer is in the active pursuit of difference, because it is difference that produces an expanding horizon and involvement with a greater and more intersubjective life world (p. 98). In his dialogic pedagogy, difference emerges because students are enfranchised as knowledge makers.[8]

> I will argue for a dialogical pedagogy that recognizes individuals as real players in the social game, conscious agents who are never altogether powerless, unaware, or passive in their relations with others; never just creations, always reflective creators of both their own identities and the social worlds they inhabit. (1993, p. 32)

In contact with different ways of knowing, silent assumptions get confronted and "reified 'knowledge' becomes conscious knowledge" (p. 53). The play of difference yields a "productive restructuring of knowledge" (p. 58), unlike the transmission of abstract truth, convention, or institutional wisdom. (p. 97). This "community of questioners" is marked by an openness that instead of suppressing difference searches for the sources of dissimilar motives and a new conceptual horizon beneath which we all stand (p. 127). Finally, in perhaps his most optimistic statement, within this "achievement of understanding," we will be able to "jointly reconceive the idea of 'life' to make room for the lives we each wish to lead" (p. 271).

There are some obvious parallels in this script to community literacy. The rival hypothesis stance is one way to unpack the cognition of what Spellmeyer calls *involvement* and scaffold the strategic thinking that helps writers actually embrace difference and seek out a common ground. The negotiated meaning emerging from dialogue is not a body of preexisting knowledge (a canon, a cultural literacy, a tradition) to which we gain access. It is an understanding we achieve. And the community of inquiry created in both experiences is not the sort of place (such as academic discourse) that one gains entry into but is a place (and a body of knowledge) that we construct at the intersection of differences. It is at this point that community literacy takes a different path, moving beyond the classroom to acts of public dialogue, developing an image of empowerment based on rhetorical action.

Taking Rhetorical Action

Recall Gloria Anzaldúa's vivid image of composing her own identity with the "special voice" of expressivism and critique. However, she makes this script and its educational scaffold considerably more complicated when she goes on to write:

> But it is not enough to stand on the opposite river bank, shouting questions, challenging patriarchal, white conventions. . . . At some point on our way to a new consciousness, we'll have to leave the opposite bank, the split between the two mortal combatants somehow healed so that

we are on both shores at once and, at once, see through serpent and eagle eyes. (1987, p. 78)

Anzaldúa describes her cultural cross talk as a deliberate, crafted rhetorical act: "I wanted a book which would teach ourselves and whites to read in nonwhite narrative traditions" (qtd. in Lunsford, 1998, p. 4). As a result, Anzaldúa is herself negotiating some of the contradictory goals of empowerment identified with intercultural dialogue and the consequences of a "special voice."

> Say my goal is a liberatory goal. . . . It's a feminist goal. But then I have to weigh things: OK, if I write in this style and I code-switch too much and I go into Spanglish too much and I do an associative kind of logical progressing in a composition, am I going to lose those people that I want to affect, to change? Am I going to lose the respect of my peers? (pp. 6–7)

Anzaldúa's attempt to negotiate these goals asks us to question the assumption expressed in the phrase, "the subaltern can not speak"—that is, a person who is subject to a dominant culture is also subjugated by its discourse and therefore cannot speak with personal agency, in her own voice, *unless* she also rejects the language of that dominant discourse (Spivak, 1988). This subaltern speaker, it is assumed, is immediately co-opted if she uses the language of power.

Ellen Cushman poses a direct counterclaim to the assumption that empowerment requires an expressive/resistant "special voice." Working with low-income women applying for jobs and housing, Cushman scaffolds a discourse of empowerment that operates *within* a hierarchical mainstream, by helping women strategically craft their talk and writing to negotiate the webs of a welfare bureaucracy (Cushman, 1999, p. 13).

For Richard Scott Lyons, the target of empowerment is an even more explicit act of negotiation within a public forum: "What American Indians want from writing," he says, is *rhetorical sovereignty*" (2000, February). His definition imagines a special voice that is, however, no longer the disrupter but the codeveloper of a rhetorical process.

> [R]hetorical sovereignty requires above all the presence of an Indian voice, speaking or writing in an ongoing context of colonization and setting at least some of the terms of the debate. Ideally, that voice would often employ a Native Language. (p. 462)

There is a necessary tension in this agenda. Thinking with one's own language and cultural referents, he argues, "helps decolonize the mind," and yet the forums in which this discourse must succeed include legal courts and government reports. Success comes from "Native people who learned how to fight battles in both court and the culture-at-large, . . . generate public opinion, form publics, and create solidarity with others" (p. 466). Susan Wells's discussion of public writing frames the problem as a necessary difficulty.

> Rhetorics associated with identity politics would prescribe that we resolve that difficulty [which marginalized speakers feel] by searching long and hard for ways of talking that would make things less difficult. Such a reconfiguration of ways of speaking is certainly humane and necessary. But a rhetoric oriented to public discourse might begin by valuing what is difficult, and direct itself to the connection between discourse and action, rather than to the connections among speakers. (Wells, 1996, p. 337)

If Wells's image of an intercultural rhetoric values "what is difficult" over the expression of a special voice, Jacqueline Jones Royster, delivering the 1995 Chair's Address to the CCCC, raises the ante even higher. To begin, she is critical of (actually incensed at) assumptions that relegate her to any one "authentic voice" (1996, p. 37). She echoes the problem bell hooks defined so succinctly—"Certainly for black women, our struggle has not been to emerge from silence into speech but . . . to make a speech that compels listeners, one that is heard" (1989, p. 6). The problem of cross-boundary discourse, Royster says, is how to "negotiate the privilege of interpretation" (1996, p. 36). Like Lyons, Royster seems more interested in empowering action than voice, more interested in issues than language. Without losing the edge of critique, her sense of "negotiate" does not seem to depend on the adversarial power moves associated with the discourse of advocacy.

> How can we teach, engage in research, write about, and talk across boundaries *with* others, instead of for, about, and around them? . . . The goal is not, "You talk, I talk." The goal is better practices so that we can exchange perspectives, negotiate meaning, and create understanding with the intent of being in a good position to cooperate, when, like now, cooperation is absolutely necessary. (1996, p. 38)

Like Lyons, Royster's rhetorical stance puts her voice within a circle of collaborative meaning makers, as a co-constructor of the scaffold. This stance would empower a teenage speaker like Andre (chapter 7) to say, "I have been studying the curfew policy" and to be heard with the same serious, skeptical attention afforded to everyone else in the circle of problem solvers.

A Working Theory of Empowerment

So where do these competing images of empowerment leave the teacher, activist, mentor, or community partner hoping to empower themselves and others? One can hardly afford to ignore *any* of these voices or their underlying goals, yet each asserts its own priorities and distinctive literate practices.

The contradictions confronted CLC mentor Robert Dixon in a public way.[9] As Dixon reflects, his premise was that literate action is a playing field for the exercise of power. And like other college mentors Long (2000) described, Dixon locates power in academic literacy—in his ability to create crafted, autonomous, mainstream texts and impart that skill to his mentee. But another voice in his inner dialogue echoes from his reading in cultural theory and its critique of colonizing practices that impose one culture's language on another. Yet another voice argues the collaborative philosophy of the CLC with its vision of hybrid texts and intercultural conversations in which all parties are learners.

These alternative images of power and empowerment came head-to-head on his first day at the CLC. On the one hand he was a card-carrying scion of textual literacy—a mentor and professional writing major and an experienced editor from Carnegie Mellon who had "power over language and the institutional credentials, the authority to exercise that power." On the other hand, he also wanted to assume the role of collaborative-planning partner and supporter. How would he "construct" himself as a writer? As he puts it, "afraid that I would slip into the things I said I would not do, I was afraid of pandering or patronizing out of getting stuck or being unsure about what to do."

From the very first session, Dixon began to notice how the literate acts of writers had a way of shifting power relations in unexpected ways. In these sites of negotiation, literacy created a subtle but intriguing friction between the different communities at the table, a surprising spark that often realigned the power relations. For instance, we were all sitting at our large oval table discussing a recent interview the writers had with the superintendent of schools, asking how they could have made him listen *to* them instead of talk *at* them. Dixon passed a note to Ebony, his mentee: "If they do not take you seriously, who do they take seriously?" His note was intended to help her bring an issue into the discussion—an issue he wanted to come from her. But this literate move backfired.

> After doing this I noticed that I got looks from some of the Mentors and Literacy Leaders. I suddenly felt like I had been caught in grade school

passing cartoons of the teacher to my neighbor, only worse, because I was a senior in college, responsible, a good student, supposedly a Mentor-type role model. In the drive back to Carnegie Mellon, I spoke with the Mentors in the car pool. They said that they noticed what I had done and were wondering what I had been doing "passing notes." My reason for passing notes to Ebony was to get her to ask the questions to the round table rather than me. I was hoping to shift the power of asking a question I thought important from myself to Ebony.

But when Ebony did not respond, Robert tried to raise this question about power himself, which did indeed lead to a power shift but in an unexpected direction because the worst of all possible things happened—nobody responded. "As a Mentor, having a question which I formulated left hanging in silence shifted my own position of power in the round table. Mentors are constructed as authorities on writing and planning, a lack of response from the writers devalues that authority, at least to the Mentor," rearranging authority relations of mentor and mentee. The normally outspoken Ebony, it appears, simply did not see the problem this way.

As Dixon discovered, empowering someone else takes more than creating a place at the table and "passing notes to Ebony" to prompt rhetorical action—especially if you are expecting them to speak from *your* script. In this final reflection, Dixon is choosing to embrace rather then ignore such conflict—building a working theory that responds to his own competing theories of empowerment while remaining grounded in the experience of mentoring. He is trying to construct a *negotiated* meaning.[10]

To Empower Rhetorical Agency

In the decade of community-literacy projects I am describing, a working theory of empowerment emerged at the CLC that has much in common with Royster's (1996) and Lyons's (2000) vision of publicly negotiated meanings. With this priority, the CLC adopted but adapted the literate moves valued in other stances. For instance, CLC writers worked at achieving membership in a discourse, but in this case, it was one of increasingly public deliberation. They were encouraged to speak with a "special voice" (of urban, teenage expertise) that allowed them to name the attitudes, assumptions, and actions by which people in authority marginalize them. But unlike scripts that aim to disrupt or dismantle the discourse of authorities—and stop dialogue—community literacy attempted to scaffold a joint, action-oriented inquiry into options for individual growth and social change. And unlike a public rhetoric built on the force of unassailable arguments, it built an inquiry on a vivid understanding of the values, experiences, and understandings of culturally different Others. This is not to say that this script necessarily achieved all its goals, much less the personal and social transformation it sought. It is simply to say this is how community literacy defines its particular ends-in-view.

In response to the question of who is being empowered, to what end, by what means, community literacy made some significant choices. Its end-in-view was neither acculturation, self-expression, resistance, nor critique. Rather, the central thing one is empowered *to do* in community literacy is to take *rhetorical agency*. As we will see in chapter 8, this came to mean two things at the CLC: one was taking initiative as a writer to create a negotiated, dialogic understanding of a shared problem (as both Shirley and Robert do); the second was to go public with that understanding in live dialogue with an expanding set of communities.

Working theories attempt to negotiate competing voices. They try to acknowledge, articulate, honor, and respond to competing images of the good as well as constraints and conflicts. They also guide, even call for, action. At the CLC, empowerment was grounded in a complex set of visions, values, and practices from the beginning. These included Joyce Baskins's deeply African American perspective on the struggle urban teens would face, Wayne Peck's prophetically motivated, deeply compassionate value for individuality, my faith in personal strategic awareness and public rhetorical power, as well as the resistant, cautious stances of teenagers like Ebony and Shirley from chapter 2 ("Just talk to yourself").

But such negotiation is not just a theoretical exercise, for the voices and conflicting demands of big institutions were also key players in this story. In particular, the institutional voices of foundations and research funders entered this negotiation through the very material, annual rites of proposal writing and progress reports. By demanding accountability in terms of their notions of "results" and "impact," they added some highly conventionalized images of what empowerment looked like. On the surface, this might seem compatible with John Dewey and pragmatism's investment in outcomes. But in practice, this conflict within our working theory pushed us to ask: how could one nudge such institutional scripts not only to include the voices and values of teenagers but also to value evidence of their personal and public sense of agency? As seen in the case study below, it drew the CLC into a public effort to rewrite these institutional scripts for impact and empowerment.

Rewriting Public Scripts for Empowerment

An impact report entitled "Where Have We Come? What Have We Learned?" and written for the Howard Heinz Endowment in October 1995 reviewed what the CLC had proposed to accomplish. The proposal had promised to show that innovative urban education could (1) support learning and problem solving, (2) motivate teenagers (in comparison to the structure of school), and (3) model change for other educators. The report begins by responding to the large categories by which institutions measure change: the school performance and social behavior of youth and the visibility and impact of the project on other service providers. One can see this in its effort to document:

- unexpected levels of engagement with learning, with 88% attendance across projects from students who are consistently labeled as "uninterested" and "unengaged" by their schools
- value for learning in a follow-up assessment in which students from the past five years of INFORM rated what they valued on a 1-to-5 scale, with 5 being the best value. In it, 70% of these "at-risk" teens gave a rating of 5 to the CLC educational activities (e.g., learning to rival, publishing a document, and planning and setting goals).
- evidence of capacities for success in school and workplaces—from building working intercultural relationships, to meeting real deadlines, and completing public products
- evidence of wider impact and visibility: thirty-five writing projects in the first four years; four thousand Pittsburghers from government, schools, community-based organizations (CBOs), and neighborhoods involved in community conversations on youth issues; evening news segments reaching an estimated three million television viewers; a PBS teleconference reaching twenty-five thousand viewers, and newspaper and professional journal coverage

However, this apparently conventional section of the report was titled "Actual Results—And Some Things We Didn't Anticipate," opening the door to *alternative* ways of articulating impact that would identify empowerment with rhetorical agency.

For social-service institutions, the beloved major indicator of impact is mainstream social behavior. If the resistance script wants to see a monkey wrench deftly inserted in the machinery of the system, the funder's ideal sees urban youth socialized into middle-class values or at least domesticated into its code of behavior. Empowerment is equated with buying into the system (ironically, into a system that oppresses you even as it offers a promised "way out"). We were always a little taken aback when asked whether the CLC had produced a change in students' grade-point averages, pregnancy, or incarceration rates—as if a direct causal relation was either likely or traceable. Such indicators are not only difficult for small community organizations to come by (without access to large numbers of clients tracked over a period of years), they are crude measures of a much more complex experience. The CLC's Five-Year Follow-Up study had combined ratings with open-ended questions about impact, asking students what they remembered and took from the experience. The report used these to make a necessary nod in the direction social behavior but did so by transferring the agency from the program to children dealing with what our society had dealt them, as the following excerpt shows.

What Happens to CLC Teenagers?

For most of its teenagers the CLC is an education in community building. But for many it has a much stronger, personal impact. For teenagers on the edge, the CLC offers support in making critical life choices in periods of crisis and decision.

- Martin had a history of school suspension, had dropped out of high school, and was battling gang and neighborhood pressures. He found a new role for himself as a rap artist and spokesman for teens in a series of CLC projects, and has now re-enrolled in high school while holding down a job.
- J.R.'s old friends are now in prison for murder. The CLC weathered him through his period of decision and his separation from street culture, offering him an alternative image of his role in the community.
- At 15, Olivia is struggling to stay in school, to care for two younger siblings at a time when her mother is hospitalized for substance abuse, and to stay safe in the volatile housing project where she lives. She takes three busses across town to attend CLC projects—in her words, one of the few positive experiences she can look forward to.

Although the second major goal of institutions was school success, defined as grades and graduation, success was also identified with one indicator on which everyone—mentors, leaders, funders—could agree: the evidence of engagement. Engagement was the prerequisite to all of the scripts of empowerment we have reviewed. In addition to offering strong attendance and survey data, the CLC report tried to shift the focus from its efficacy as a program to the writers' perceptions of themselves and to what educational researchers see as the enormous power of *self-efficacy*—that sense that the motive force in one's life can come from *one's own* actions. Although such comments are subject to an "experimenter effect" (subjects tell the questioner what they think she wants to hear), the Follow-Up study had tried to mitigate this with an open-ended question: "What do you remember most?" For many teens, it was gaining self-esteem and the discovery that writing can change things, which the report documented as a category of evaluation and in the teens' own words:

SELF-PERCEPTION: Public success—as published writers—changes teenagers' perceptions of themselves, of the potential for change, and of the power of literate action.

When the assessment team asked, "What do you remember most?" for many CLC teens, it was gaining self-esteem and the discovery that writing can change things:

- "When we had the presentation with the Mayor, I felt a lot of pride in my work. I never got recognition like that before, and it was good to see that even important people were interested in what we did."—Rochelle Holloway
- "I learned that it's important to voice my own opinions. I shouldn't always just back what other people say, because if I have an idea, it might not be perfect, but it's important, and it's not wrong. Someone might even be able to learn something from what I say."—Leanna Lyle
- "I gained confidence. Overall confidence, and also confidence in my writing."—Tomika Benning
- "I have learned that through writing and talking about things you can bring about changes."—Steve Hale

---

This foundation report is an exercise in acknowledging but redefining some standard institutional images of empowerment. It challenges the limited script of school performance (with its expectations for correct, insignificant text) by evaluating the teenagers' work in terms of critical thinking and public rhetorical action. It rewrites desirable social behavior not as conformity to social norms but as assertive, public problem solving and a confident contribution of expertise to social decision making. It sees engagement reflected not in attendance but in the child's own sense of engaged self-efficacy.

Empowerment in Personal and Public Action

Reshaping the discourse of a progress report probably had more impact on our thinking than on the foundation's, but it suggested ways a more institutionally visible "formal" study could rewrite empowerment as personal and rhetorical agency. The project, dubbed the Transfer Study, followed the lives of fourteen teenagers from an INFORM project. One year after their participation, we invited the writers back for a sustained interview conducted by Joyce Baskins. To mitigate the experimenter bias with an adult they trusted and admired, we avoided requests for evaluative statements or opinions.

Using a technique called "critical incident" interviews (Flanagan, 1954), Mrs. Baskins asked teens to probe their memories for "specific instances or actual events" in which they saw themselves using what they learned at the CLC. From these transcripts, the only comments coded as evidence of transfer were ones that could locate such choices in a specific incident. The results for the first year of this study follow in "Community Literacy Transfers: A Tracking Study of CLC Teenagers," which is included in full because I believe the incidents teens describe speak even more clearly to the realities of agency in their lives than do the more generalized comments which follow.

Community Literacy Transfers
A Tracking Study of CLC Teenagers

This is the first phase of a five-year study to follow the lives of fourteen teenagers from Pittsburgh's inner city. To observe a naturally occurring sample, we focused on an intact group from a single recent project. And we began with what is perhaps the hardest question to really answer—but one of the most significant: How does the CLC experience affect the attitudes they take and the strategic choices they make after they leave the CLC?

PROFILE OF THE CLC FOURTEEN

The teenagers in the project come from Pittsburgh's poverty neighborhoods. They are predominantly African American, and their self-reports provide a window on the struggle of urban teenagers to come to maturity within some of Pittsburgh's most troubled neighborhoods. Two of the young women in this project were emancipated minors—the courts determined they were better off living on their own than remaining in a current home situation. Although both were in the 12th grade, one was 17 and the other—whose life circumstances were bleak at best—was 19. Their determination to graduate demonstrates a high degree of personal responsibility. At the time they joined CLC projects, two of the young men had been recently living in a shelter. As their mother signed herself in and out of a Mental Health Center, they had experienced various temporary "homes" with relatives and friends. (A CLC staff member in fact ended up taking them in for four months to offer them some stability till the end of the school year. For Daryl, the effect on school performance was striking.) Five young people in the group live with both parents. The remaining five live with single mothers, some of whom are highly motivated and have strong extended family support.

Many of the parents we talked to were attempting to instill a sense of motivation and pride in their children in the face of realities that breed cynicism. Two of the young men living in single-parent homes with their mothers spent time daily figuring out how to avoid the gang violence and police intimidation that has become part of the fabric of their lives. One of these teenagers had lost two friends within five months to drive-by shootings. All of the families live in mid- to high-crime areas, and the teens speak clearly about the dangers of navigating through dangerous areas in order to find safe places to be with friends. Unprompted, they talk and write of the "stress" of avoiding danger and persisting in the face of racism. Roughly half of the teenagers are not comfortable in school. For them this institution is failing to foster images of achievement or future.

These are Pittsburgh's everyday teenagers whose life stories and self-reports shed light on the accelerating social fragmentation in our city. Their choice to seek a safe place at the CLC and to respond to its offer to learn (perhaps in a different way than school) demonstrates a high degree of individual responsibility and provides grounds for hope in the face of urban devastation.

THE QUESTION

In structured, taped interviews teenagers were asked the question most educational institutions never ask: Does this educational experience transfer?

We encouraged them to think about their experience at the CLC in at least three ways:

- **Strategies**. Skills learned, including planning, writing, and speaking in groups, analyzing problems, rivaling, and considering options and outcomes
- **Collaboration**. Entering into a intercultural relationship with a mentor and a productive, working relationship with adults and teens
- **Community.** Finding your place and seeing a responsibility to deal with problems and recognize multiple points of view

Remember your experience at the CLC—what you learned there about problem-solving strategies, about collaboration, or about community issues? Now think about what is going on in your life—at school, at home, on the streets, or at work? Problems, struggles, accomplishments. Or think about goals and life plans for where you want be going? Can you describe any specific instances—actual events—in which you used what you learned at the CLC?

EVIDENCE

Although students were often quick to say, "Yes" or even offer heartfelt testimonials about the value of their experience on tape, the only comments we counted as evidence were specific instances and examples in which they used this experience. Responses that met this criterion were tabulated for each teenager on the matrix shown below.

Of course, we weren't there to see what really happened. What these examples reveal is this: a combination of changed behavior and changed perception about their behavior, which says that these teenagers see themselves transferring learning from the CLC to their lives.

HOW MANY TEENS CAN SEE AN IMPACT ON THEIR LIVES?

How many teenagers cited at least one instance of transfer in a given area? (Some offered multiple examples in each area.)

IN SCHOOL	AT HOME	IN SOCIETY	ON LIFE PLANS	CLC's TRANSFER INDEX
13 = 93%	12 = 86%	11 = 79%	9 = 64%	80%

HOW DOES TRANSFER CHANGE BEHAVIOR AND TRANSFORM ATTITUDES?

We quote some of these comments to point up a critical finding: CLC teenagers internalize the problem-solving strategies they have learned.

Note: Many of these comments are a direct response to questions about using one of the CLC's three hallmark strategies: (1) seeing the story behind the story (SBS), (2) using rival hypothesis thinking to generate alternatives (rivaling), and (3) examining options and outcomes in decision making (O&O). The strategy to which they were referring is indicated in parentheses.

1. CLC problem-solving strategies transfer to school; they support achievement and change attitudes.

- I'm getting good grades now because of my writing and decisions about what I do. . . . (pause) Probably why I'm getting good grades now. I get along with teachers; before I'd go to class to cut up; not let teacher do her job. Now I get more out of it & grades coming up. [Tony]
- (On using SBS) Yes, in math & science. You need to see the story behind the story in an experiment. [Cara]
- Used to breeze past; I know now you got to put in 110%. [Leon]
- (On O&O) You come in late and teacher says "you're disrupting my classroom" & that's a strike against you. But if you just

sit down and start doing your work, they have no reason to try to mess with you even more. So before I walk in, I think, as I'm walking down the hall. I think, well, if she tries to say something, then I won't say nothing, then I won't be in trouble even more. That's like a different option for me. I also stopped saying smart things to football coach. It's a whole different outcome. [Leon]
• Didn't used to care about grades, but now I've got a lot to look forward to and grades up to 3.8. [Shari]

2. CLC teenagers describe a new sense of responsibility—and others are seeing it, too.

• Coming in on time. CLC helped—you have to be here on time or kicked out. My family sees me as more responsible. I showed I could do all the work and get grades. More trust. [Roland]
• Getting to school for that first class at 7:00 am, clothes ready, hair done. Used to be "when I get there, I get there; when I go, I go." At CLC you had to be on time, ready. Late, you in trouble. [Kristin]
• She [my mentor] showed me what responsibility is. I think I knew, but she showed me what responsibility to something is. . . . I learned to show respect; would have been hollering when we differed. [Arlena]
• Me and my dad just put a kennel up for our dog. And he was hollering about [how to level it]. And the way we collaborated—I sort of figured out [how to do it] the way he wanted it and the way I had thought. We put our ideas together . . . I told him, "we're collaborating, Dad." [Roland]

3. Teenagers see the option to resist social pressures.

• (On rivaling) At the community picnic, they tried to get me to drink, but I looked at it from all sides. [Tiffany]
• Was asked to be in gang, could have dropped out of school. But had a lot of people helping me. [Daryl]
• (On rivaling) When my friends invited me to do something [involving a fight], I didn't. [Roland]

4. CLC teenagers are developing a strong sense of community—people help you and you help others. Moreover, problem-solving strategies help you deal differently with the pressures of urban life.

• Used to be by myself. Don't want nobody to help me, I know everything. Now working with mentors & groups, I see they can help & I'm not afraid to ask questions. . . . I have made some wrong decisions, so now I ask advice—from a *couple* of people. [Tracy]

• (On rivaling) My girlfriend's boyfriend was beatin' her up and she was trying to stay, but I was tryin' to help her see it in a different way. She's saying if they stay together long enough, things will get better But I was tellin' her, I mean, if it's already happenin' now, then most likely things aren't gonna change—it's gonna get worse, and I was just tryin' to help her see that. [Tiffany]

• Before, when I had nowhere to go [for help], I couldn't say nothin' because nobody would listen. (On rivaling) Before I wouldn't rival nobody; I thought it in my head, but couldn't talk. (On SBS) When my brother & I didn't have a place to live and nobody would take us, I tried to understand their side—my aunt didn't have money; my dad had no room. [Daryl]

• (On rivaling) One of my friends got shot and died. And people were saying how this happened and how that happened, and I stated my point of view . . . They was sayin' all kind of goofy stuff, and I had to go to one of my serious thoughts. . . . Everything I'm thinkin',' I let them know. I don't know why. I do. Cause sometimes I used to just keep stuff to myself—cause I might think whatever I got to say might sound goofy or dumb. [Roland]

• (On rivaling) When you're having a conversation with your kids, it always sticks in the back of your mind. Downtown two weeks ago, Mike owes me some money. First he said he was gonna give me the money the next day. But then the day after that went past. Then 3 or 4 days went past. So, I told Mike, "We are friends, but if it was somebody else, they might get violent or something." I tried to tell him how people feel about their money, and then he told me—well, he had all these excuses and I tried to understand his excuses before I did anything else. [Leon]

• (On O&O, after moving to a new neighborhood where white guys at school were "overheard" saying, "Niggers gonna come up here and take over") I could fight and get suspended, but I stop & think, if I don't they might get caught and I go on. My friend always be fighting white kids. I tell him just chill, be cool. (On using SBS) And I try to see why he act like he do. Some say not enough attention from his mother. Maybe he think he bad; not want to be thought a punk; low self esteem. . . . When I'm about to fight, I would now say, he just wants to fight because he's jealous. I look for reasons; before I wouldn't even think about that. [Jason]

• (O&O) My roommate wasn't sure that she wanted to go to college. She was tryin' to put it off, you know, like . . . "Well, after I do this—after I finish here I'm gonna go to college."

And I told her, "I understand you workin,' but you can work and go to school. But if you just sit on your butt and just keep puttin' college off, you're not really gonna go, you know. Cause you gonna get lazy, and then you gonna get pregnant and this and that." And I was tellin' her, go to college, do whatever you're gonna do, and own your own hair salon. I was really helpin' her out, because she wasn't sure she really wanted to go to college or not. [Tracy]

5. CLC teenagers are setting new expectations and life plans.

• (On O&O) I didn't want to go straight to work out of school; wanted to chill a little. But I knew there were things I wanted & needed and the only way to get them was to work. So I sat down and made a list, of "if I don't work (can't get this); if I do work (can get this)." [Arlena]
• (On grading self at CLC): Before I thought it was *possible*, but didn't think it *important*. I use it at night before bed. [Leon]
• I'm gonna make straight A's. [Daryl]
• I changed my major to communication. [Shari]
• The questions you ask me, I've asked myself ever since I left here. [Kristen]
• A whole bunch of things my mind had got opened up to. I can do this; I can do that. I can be what I want to be. [Tony]
• (On O&O and her decision to go to school) I tell myself, "if I go something good can happen." CLC's the only reason why I think that. [Tracy]

WHAT DOES THE TRAJECTORY LOOK LIKE?

1. Stayed in school   14 (100%)
2. No suspensions   14 (100%)
3. No incidents involving the police   14 (100%)
4. Waited to start your family. Female/Male   7 F (100%)   6 M (93%)
5. Applied for a job   12 (86%)
6. Got a job   6 (43%)
7. Did community service   4 (29%)
8. Chose not to use drugs or alcohol when your friends were using or abusing them   14 (100%)
9. Took steps toward further education (apply, get info)   13 (93%)
10. Got further education (workshops, training, college)   9 (64%)

In institutional terms, this study carried some good news: teens saw a robust transfer of their CLC experience to everyday life. Even more interesting are the distinctive images of empowerment the transfer creates—the ways writing, collaboration problem solving, and a public voice appear to support agency across the contexts of students' lives.

The report's simple statistical index shows that on average 80% of the teens are able to cite a specific, codable instance of literate strategies transferring to school, home, social experience, and life planning. Moreover, the teens are often quite self-conscious about their strategic action. (School evaluation, by contrast, is normally a closed circuit that only asks if students can repeat back what was presented to them. Schools rarely ask whether their instruction transfers outside its walls, much less if students have developed a metacognitive awareness of their strategic choices.) Secondly, the report highlights four ways that transfer (what we might call empowerment in everyday action) seems to be working:

- CLC problem-solving strategies transfer to school; they support achievement and change attitude.
- CLC teenagers describe a new sense of responsibility—and others are seeing it, too.
- Teenagers see the option to resist social pressures.
- CLC teenagers are developing a strong sense of community—people help you and you help others. Moreover, problem-solving strategies help you deal differently with the pressures of urban life.

In concert with academic and institutional images of empowerment, the teens cite achievement in school. However, their comments suggest that this difference is not linked to learning a given academic discourse but to changes in self-perception and attitude, often expressed as a new sense of responsibility and connectedness. There are, of course, many social skills one could highlight in these comments, but what stood out to us was how teenagers saw community-literacy skills helping them to *respond differently* to the world around them—from parents, teachers, and friends to the pressures of urban stress and even violence. This report shifts the locus of agency from the program to the young people. It translates the conventional indicators of success (in which empowerment is equated with meeting behavioral norms) into acts of personal decision making, reflective understanding, and rhetorical action.

The chapters that follow ask how such agency-under-constraint might work. In chapter 8, we will reframe the question to ask: How can community partners learn to recognize and affirm the sometimes indirect indications of rhetorical agency already present in others?

Part 3

Rhetorical Tools in the Rhetoric of Making a Difference

Rhetoric places its bets on the power of transformative knowledge, on knowing that how we represent and re-represent our shared reality can change that reality. Community literacy goes about the rhetoric of engagement in a distinctive grass-roots fashion in which transformative knowledge is constructed one person at a time in a set of negotiated and transformed understandings.

In shorthand, the community literacy script—its ideal, its end-in-view—goes something like this: Intercultural inquiry (supported by the rhetorical strategies and literate practices of community literacy) takes us into contradictions and generative conflicts, calling its partners to interpretation and a meaning making that embraces difference. Such inquiry can uncover the hidden interpretive logics and situated knowledges of others. Going public in community literacy is not limited to finding a voice. It is more akin to creating a public—to constructing a discursive process and a space of dialogue and deliberation in which everyone who engages in this process is recognized as a legitimate partner in discovery and change.

The new cultural politics of difference, Cornel West argues, is an affirmation of the agency, capacity, and ability of people who have been degraded, oppressed, and exploited by our status quo. I will argue that the rhetorical agency of everyday-people-acting-within-constraints is manifested here in two ways: in the capacity both to construct an engaged, negotiated understanding and to go public in dialogue and deliberation. The problem is often our inability to recognize such agency and our failure to affirm it in others. One of the critical roles for partners from places of privilege, I argue, is to become rhetorical agents who do not speak *for* others but affirm and nurture and document the rhetorical agency of marginalized people. And who support the counterpublic work of drawing us all into a transformed—and transforming—understanding.

All of these ideals are best understood as actions. The following chapters explore some rhetorical tools that let us engage in this rhetoric of making a difference.

6 *Intercultural Inquiry and the Transformation of Service*

The revival of community service on college campuses appears to offer an alternative to the hubris of university expertise and the ineffectuality of academic critique.[1] Community outreach brings idealism and social consciousness into the academy. It brings a human face and complex lives into the discussion of issues and ideas. But it can also plunge teachers and students into its own set of contradictory and sometimes profoundly conflicted social and literate practices.

> Scott's freshman writing course taught argument by immersing students in the academic debate on literacy. But, according to Scott, it was tutoring at an urban school unconnected with the course that revealed "where certain things fit and others didn't. . . . What a beautiful opportunity it is to be able to understand a class through real world experience."

> In her first semester at college, Lisa signed up to do volunteer work for an afternoon. "They didn't tell us where we were going; we just got on the van. And it turned out we went to my own neighborhood—which we were supposed to clean up. I could hear the other students talking about 'them' and . . . I never had anything to do with service after that."

Guerrilla service, those short forays into soup kitchens, nursing homes, and Lisa's neighborhood, reinforces the distance between the giver and receiver, especially if the contact is superficial and the junket uncomplicated by preparation or reflection.[2] Many current approaches to service-learning avoid this dilemma by embedding personal and social consciousness in academic work—in "professional" performance for a nonprofit client and/or broad critical analysis (Adler-Kassner, Crooks, & Watters, 1997; Waterman,

1997). But a fundamental conflict remains unresolved when students (fired up with certainty for social change) confront the suddenly realized limitations of their own understanding. They find their academic agendas for service and action failing to connect to the alternative expertise of the community and to its own resilient cultural agendas. They came prepared to act; they really needed to inquire.

At the Community Literacy Center, inquiry—in particular, intercultural inquiry—offered a way to be in relationship across the community/university divide and a role for mentors that was philosophically rooted in the practice of prophetic pragmatism. Such pragmatism, of course, raises the question of outcomes: to what end does such inquiry lead? When the mentors in this chapter, Scott, Anne, and Nichole, write about their efforts to understand, inquiry appears to be supporting two significant possibilities. First, it provides a space for students and teachers to face and negotiate some of the conflicts community service itself poses. Secondly, I suggest, inquiry leads to a transforming and possibly transformative knowledge.

Facing Some Contradictions in Community Outreach

The practice of inquiry must start, as we will here, by confronting the conflicts within the everyday practice of outreach. These become clear when we look at service-learning as not simply a set of programs or theories but as what activity theorists call a *sociocultural activity*—a whole system of actions, thoughts, feelings, and values that take shape not in theory but in a socially, historically, and culturally located meaningful activity.[3] Activity researcher Yrjö Engeström shows that social-cultural activities (such as a doctor's visit at an HMO or sentencing in traffic court) are rife with internal contradictions. To understand what is really going on in an activity, he argues, we need to recognize the "multitude of disparate elements, voices, and viewpoints" that emerge as contradictory voices, ideologies, and practices within events and the activity systems that shape them. We have already seen some of these in the decidedly mixed blessings of social-service institutions and the checkered history of community/university relations.

Our first response to the inevitable mixed motives and problematic assumptions within community outreach might well be a theory-based cultural critique. Indeed, an activity that proposes to enter the lion's den of social difference armed with idealism is an easy target. Yet simply unveiling suspect ideologies and assumptions can become an academic exercise that takes the place of the more vulnerable stance of engagement with these conflicts. Entering the crosscurrents of a turbulent social, cognitive, and cultural activity, such as, community outreach poses hard questions, such as, why are we here? And who am I in this relationship? These will be answered in practice in one way or another—even though the answers will pose new problems. It is significant that some of the most probing accounts of these contradictions come from teachers and students most committed to negotiating these tensions in practice.

Take for instance the question, why are we engaged in community outreach? And why do we disagree about the answer? Sustained engagement, like Scott's semester of tutoring, can lead to self-discovery and caring relationships. However, Bruce Herzberg (1994) and Aaron Schutz and Anne Ruggles Gere (1998) argue that these private experiences often build merely personal stories: they fail to challenge the public representations of the Others a student serves; they define social problems as personal ones, and they place agency (knowledge, power, and self-determination) with the tutor. These educators hold a different vision of public service that goes beyond private caring, in which the personal growth of the tutor does not take precedence over public, collaborative, or social action. They privilege "practices that might both foreground inequality and take advantage of 'difference'" (Schutz & Gere, 1998, p. 144).

College students also arrive with competing images for how literacy should support social justice—images all the more powerful for being largely unarticulated. In Elenore Long's (2000) in-depth study of college mentors, these assumptions and dilemmas emerge in students' electronic bulletin-board posts and papers. We see them wrestling with conflicting priorities that range from teaching grammatical correctness to supporting emancipation to inviting free expression to encouraging action-oriented problem solving. Long's study then takes a revealing turn when she shows how the conflicts emerging in students' personal experiences parallel (and extend) the scholarly debates within rhetoric and composition.

Differences like these translate into programmatic choices. Thomas Deans's insightful analysis documents how outreach programs are organized around the philosophical fault lines in service-learning, dividing programs into those committed to writing *about* versus writing *for* versus writing *with* the community. The stance Deans (2000) and others take to these alternative relationships can be generous and open—but in the practice of outreach, it will always be necessary to set priorities even among competing goods.

The social history of community outreach also shapes our position and options in the community. With its roots in both the conservative soil of charity and the rocky ground of activism, outreach is itself a story of contradictions, good intentions, and unintended outcomes. It was the settlement-house movement—the committed people of Jane Addams's Hull House living *in* neighborhoods of need—that gave rise to the bureaucratic machinery of social services (McKnight, 1995; Peck, Flower, & Higgins, 1995). Later, the rise of community/university collaborations translated the ancient tensions of town and gown into the progressive agenda of the 1940s in which academic "experts" brought their expert knowledge to redesigning the neighborhoods—and the lives of others (Harkavy and Puckett, 1991). In the 1960s, we began building walls around our urban ivory towers to protect them from the decay our flawed expertise hadn't averted. The renewed social responsibility of the 1990s brought with it the impulse to critique patterns of domination and/or to engage in a new dialogic relationship. But this impulse is now trying to operate within social histories and institutional practices that are strangers to collaborative relationships and ill equipped to recognize community expertise. And academics, Ellen Cushman argues, are part of this divide: in our own drive to specialization (and status), we have replaced the role of engaged public intellectual with the more distanced practice and pedagogy of critique (2003).

Just as activity theory predicts, outreach exists amid a chorus of diverse voices arising out of its historically shaped and socially embedded assumptions, practices, and values. The dilemma this creates is also a personal and cognitive one for many students asking, who am I in this role, in this intercultural relationship, in this society? Schutz and Gere see this posing a choice between the competing calls of service and activism—between a "caring" and a "critical" stance. However, I suggest, neither of these postures is well designed to catch another central voice within this activity—the voice of the community partner, who is asking, why are *you* here? And who are *we all* in this relationship? Neither care nor criticism recognizes the option of inquiry with others. The research on service-learning is indeed preoccupied with *our* expertise: with developing pedagogical agendas, with interrogating our middle-class ideologies, with producing satisfying academic dichotomies and incisive critiques (Waterman, 1997). In the twenty-nine studies reviewed in an annotated bibliography of *Community Service and Composition*, the option of seeking out the agendas, the assumptions, and the interpretations of community partners is rarely recognized as a goal; service is never addressed as a critical inquiry process (Bacon and Deans, 1997).

Hearing the voices from the community could pose some new contradictions that are at the heart of understanding our role and identity. Consider the "call of service." Robert Coles describes it as a deeply motivated desire to connect—a commitment to seeing the humanity in others and engaging in what Paulo Freire would call a dialogue of love and respect. But organized service activities often erect a protective glass wall of charity between "us" and "them." Survey studies suggest that freshmen may be primarily attracted by the opportunity to socialize with peers—the van ride to Lisa's neighborhood (Chai, et al., 1999). Others seek personal empowerment (Serow, 1997). Dialogue is not the mere outcome of contact; it is an achievement (Flower, 1997a).

For other students, the impulse to outreach bursts from an emerging critical consciousness—an awareness of the social and ideological forces that oppress some and shape us all. Yet, the political certainty of critique or of feet-first activism can be an elephant in the teashop of complex urban or cultural realities. "We" may find that "they" fail to fit our schemes for them. For instance, as Ellen Cushman (1998) argues and her research so dramatically shows, our certainties can be challenged when we recognize community partners as agents in their own right, rather than as the recipients of our service and empowerment. We may discover that their expression of critical consciousness operates on its own oblique, adaptive terms, not our academic ones. What's worse, their strategies for resistance and action, for getting over and for keeping on keeping on are not those we felt called to impart. Clyde Moneyhun documents a similar contretemps in which a community organization took a cautiously conservative stance to our more radical, liberatory, or simply middle-class notions of education, service, or social action coming (1996). Intent on maintaining their support with conservative donors, the community resisted agendas that could rock the vulnerable boats they had to use to navigate unreliable funding streams.

If theory-based social-action agendas find themselves in tension with community practices, even the identity many mainstream students claim (as tutors and mentors who at least know the *educational* system) faces challenge. Service in urban settings, Novella Zett Keith argues, should attend to an alternative community-sensitive model of education emerging from successful urban sites (1997). This model takes a page from the identity-building success of street gangs and the sustained relationships of urban sanctuaries (Virgil, 1992; McLaughlan, Irby, and Langman, 1994). It thrives on an authentic pedagogy that enables "knowers to recognize themselves, name their experiences, and learn how to change existing conditions for themselves as well as others in the community" (Keith, p. 137). But who then is the college student in this model of learning that dramatically diminishes the significance of mainstream institutional practices (and their representatives, such as, college tutors)? And just where do they fit in Keith's vision of service-learning as "'service with' rather than 'service to'" or her claim that "service must be based on reciprocity" (p. 131)?

From Contact and Contradiction to Transformed Understanding

The field of contradictions just described is not unique to community out-reach. Like any vigorous activity system, it is a site of diverse voices and agendas. But advocates and critics of service-learning often fail to recognize the full range of contradictory voices that students and teachers alike *need* to encounter within this space. Booster projects (like Kendall's 1990 two-volume resource book) generally avoid conflict by combining philosophical asser-tions and encomiums with programmatic advice. The practice of critique takes another kind of evasive action, probing for problematic assumptions but holding itself above the (inevitably problematic) decisions and (critiquable) actions social actors must take. These diverse voices and contradictions are a necessary part of the territory in intercultural engagement. They are a point of departure for inquiry—not into "teaching the conflicts" for their own sake—but as a basis for personal and collective action built on negotiated meanings. And they could be an entry into the difficult transformation of service into a reciprocal activity.

Louise Pratt called this territory a "contact zone" when she described a Stanford course in which college students felt the friction of difference through their exposure to competing readings of history (1991). In the analy-sis of texts and cultural issues in Phyllis van Slyck's basic writing class, it is "a space in which complex feelings and attitudes on different sides of a question are dramatized" and students recognize that "neutrality is an illu-sion" (1997, pp. 167–68).

Such awareness is the necessary place to begin, but are we stopping short? My concern here is with students and teachers prepared to go beyond the uncertainty, disequilibrium *and safety* of the contact zone and who are ready to move from the observation of difference into the interaction Victor Vil-lanueva calls the "struggle to understand" (1993). Working with an urban writing project, he writes:

> I also discovered how much the teachers could not understand about being of color and of poverty, but how much they would change if they could make real changes. I discovered teachers' desperate struggles to understand. (p. xvi)

He argues, in the language of Freire, "Just giving voice to the consciousness is struggle, is action, is praxis. . . . The power of the conscious intellectual (a rhetor) is in discourse: talking, writing, listening" (pp. 58–59).

But why is such understanding such a struggle? It is not merely a lack of knowledge: it is because understanding means somehow *dealing with the contradictions.* It means fashioning a tentative and probably problematic negotiated response to the social and cognitive, historical and material conflicts within this human activity. Engeström sees contradiction as not only the defining feature of an activity system but also as its source of transformation (1993). In my own research with writers, the attempt to construct a *negotiated meaning* is not only one of the great challenges of this social and cognitive process, it is its most creative act (Flower, 1994, pp. 36–84). So if teachers are frustrated when their course doesn't produce the informed and activated social imagination they envisioned, students may be struggling to accommodate other contradictions. In my own class, mentors enter an urban community house anticipating an experience of transformative understanding. They are unprepared for ways the veil of cultural difference can quietly resist their appeals to common humanity and the sheer force of caring. I face my own dilemmas. As I moderate a session of the Carnegie Mellon Community Think Tank on welfare-to-work, I hear women in that transition tell the story-behind-the-story of their work life—of feeling unprepared, insecure, unconnected. And I see my own "understanding"—my unquestioned sense of the supporting, intimate, inevitable connection between work and identity—begin to unravel in the light of their experience. I, like my students, stand in the need of negotiated, transformed understanding that in some way embraces these differences.

Transformative understanding is an activity, not a statement. It is a form of praxis—a kind of knowledge-making that names problems in the world and transforms both our representations of them and of ourselves, opening the door to informed action. But in a multicultural context, the stakes are raised, for here, I wish to argue, the challenge is to build a new and mutual, *intercultural* representation of that problem, its meanings, and consequences. The community literacy practice that we called *intercultural inquiry* is a literate action defined by its open-eyed, against-the-odds, self-conscious attempt to engage in collaborative acts of meaning making that are mutually transformative. Intercultural inquiry is unlike an act of self-discovery or service, of cultural critique or social action alone, as critically necessary as these are. Nor is it the attempt to understand the nature of difference for its own sake. Rather the partners in an intercultural inquiry attempt to *use* the differences of race, class, culture, or discourse that are available to them to understand shared questions.[4] Whether the issue at stake is education, work, social identity, racism, risk, or respect, an intercultural inquiry seeks rival readings of that issue that have the potential to transform both the inquirers and their interpretations of how it works in the world.

Such an inquiry can also put some of the contradictions inherent in outreach and service-learning on the table, inviting students into a space for negotiating them. For example, many students are quite comfortable with integrating their sense of social action and personal service. Yet they draw a line that firmly separates these two from academic endeavor—from reading, research, theory, or from an intellectual commitment that not only seeks out rival interpretations, but embraces contradiction. Service is conveniently separated from these students' professional and educational lives. In the case studies below, students use the practice of intercultural inquiry to go beyond a contact zone into confronting contradictions, inviting rivals, and constructing and negotiating meaning through the eyes of difference.

When Scott, Anne, and Nicole tell the stories of their own struggles to understand, we hear some of the multiple motivations that led them to Pittsburgh's urban community and the conflicting voices that shaped their attempt at an intercultural inquiry. More importantly, these stories offer a ground for inquiry into the negotiated, situated meanings these students construct—*out of* racial and culture differences *with* urban teenagers. They show students reaching for a kind of understanding that could support literate and social action.[5]

Starting Points for Inquiry

Anne was a first-time mentor highly aware of the limited grounding her own assumptions offered her. Her inquiry replaced those assumptions, not with new certainties but with a growing need to know.

> I was brought up with a very traditional view of what a family is and does. In my small rural hometown, a "family" consists of a mother, a father, and several children. When one parent is absent, it's usually for either a sad or socially unacceptable reason, neither of which is discussed freely. . . . My family eats dinner together every night. . . . Erica and Shawana's family is comprised of four children, each with a different father. . . . When I brought up the girls and their family, my mother said, "Oh isn't that too bad, those poor kids have probably been through so much. . . ." I tried to go into this inquiry with an open mind. However, I definitely had assumptions as to what I thought I would find out about family structure as a measure of support. As the inquiry progressed, and I found that the vast majority of those assumptions were incorrect, I began to wonder why I had thought such things.

Scott, by contrast, entered the course with a history of mentoring that echoes with the multiple voices of outreach. He began tutoring as a personal escape from the stress of a freshman year, little expecting he might end up finding a new sense of himself in the call of service. Scott certainly had no illusions about his knowledge base: "Being from rural Vermont, these problems [of growing up in the inner city] only exist on the television news."

In a reflection written at the end of his sophomore year, Scott was still tutoring in an urban elementary school, but his motivation now came from seeing what he could contribute. Drawn by the "great need for positive role models and mentors," he saw "how big a difference just a little bit of time and effort can accomplish." Despite an after-school science club in which "Todd wouldn't glue and Peter wouldn't cut," and the boys' only stated preferences were "to 'blow things up,'" Scott says, "I approached the program with the belief that if I could make a difference in the life of just one of my tutees, then that would be enough."

By the time Scott joined the Community Literacy class as a junior, he had tutored every semester, taken a summer job at an urban YMCA, and was helping set up the university tutoring program as a student-run organization. He now knew much more about those "problems" of growing up in the inner city than most students—enough, in fact, to realize some of the contradictions within his own understanding:

> It seems a truism that is growing more true each day. Black male urban youth are growing up in an environment depleted of positive male role models. The U.S. Bureau of the Census states that only 28 per cent of Black children today are living in a two-parent household. [And yet,] there are many cases of Black male teens accomplishing great success in the classroom and the workplace. . . . What, then, has helped these individuals to form their own notion of work ethic?

The starting point for Scott was a troubling sense of contradiction telling him there was a more complex reality to grasp.

Like many students who enter community-outreach projects, Scott and Anne are walking into Pratt's contact zone of cultural difference hungry to learn but already well provisioned with media images, faceless statistics, personal histories, and underqualified generalizations naturalized to truisms. As an industrial-management major, Scott is also headed toward a professional life in which these standard representations of the urban workforce (with its underprepared youth and unsupportive families who are not "work-ready") will also shape decisions and policies about hiring, training, and management. Nevertheless, as these students became critical of the conventional wisdom (and brave enough to venture beyond critique to praxis), they became increasingly aware that good intentions toward others do not give one easy access to accurate representations of those others. And when talk turns to work, family, or identity, we are even less likely to accurately infer the *representations of these issues that those others hold.*

Seeking Voices and Rival Representations

At the Community Literacy Center, students reach for what Schutz and Gere describe as "public practices" in "public spaces" where people join a common effort around a common project (1998, p. 141).[6] For seven weeks, mentors (like Scott and Anne) and teenage writers work to tell the story-behind-the-story of an urban issue. The project then moves from inquiry to action, culminating in a ten-to-fifteen-page published document and a public Community Conversation led by the teens. The college course culminates for mentors in an in-depth inquiry of their own.

The model for the mentors' written intercultural inquiry is the table in figure 6.1, which brings the insights, expertise, and the rival hypotheses of multiple "voices" into meaning making. As a metaphor for the dynamics of such listening, this model requires a deliberate search for voices that are typically not at the table or that because they fail to speak the dominant discourse are not heard. Unlike personal reflection, it must seek these voices artfully in text, talk, and observation.[7] As the table also suggests, intercultural inquiry is not a study *of* others but a collaborative inquiry *with* others into shared, mutually significant questions. It seeks the grounds for understanding and action in alternative readings of the world that are based on diverse racial, social, cultural, class, and gendered experiences.

One foundation for this model was our five-year study of how the rival hypothesis stance was used by minority students in college classes across the curriculum and by urban teenagers in a community literacy project. In *Learning to Rival: A Literate Practice for Intercultural Inquiry* (2000), Elenore Long, Lorraine Higgins, and I had traced how students transformed this mode of academic inquiry into a strategy the teens dubbed *rivaling*. Grounded in John Dewey's vision of provisional, experimental ways of knowing, *Learning to Rival* went on to argue that intercultural inquiry demands what we called a *strong* version of the rival hypothesis stance "in which *an active search for diverse rivals is essential to understanding*" (p. 50; italics in original). In the spirit of Cornel West's prophetic pragmatism, this strong stance "exists 'in order to disclose options and alternatives for transformational praxis'" by strategically "embracing plurality, invoking agency and action, and constructing meaning in contested contexts" (West qtd. in Flower, p. 77).

> A strong [rival hypothesis] stance, then, is not just a theory of knowing that privileges uncertainty and rival views; it is an educational, literate practice that calls for the construction of supported meanings in the midst of uncertainty. (Flower, Long, & Higgins, p. 79)

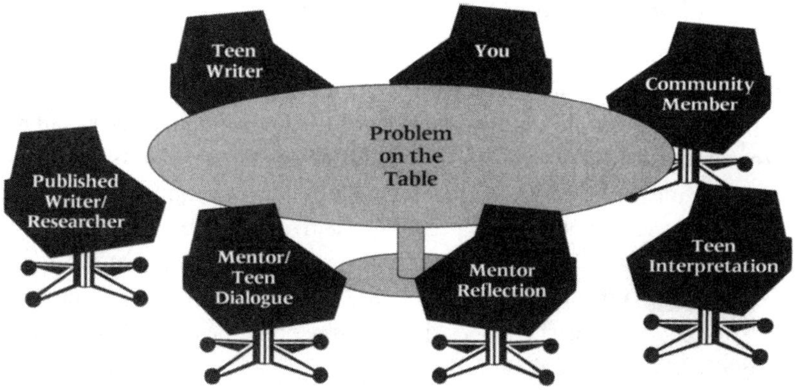

Fig. 6.1 Multiple voices at the table. From Linda Flower, *Problem-Solving Strategies for Writing in College and Community*, Harcourt Brace College Publishers, 1998

Scott's inquiry into role models invited some diverse voices to his table, including the published voices of Shirley Brice Heath and Milbrey W. McLaughlin (*Identity and Inner-City Youth*, 1992), Alex Kotlowitz (*There Are No Children Here*, 1991), Keith Gilyard (*Voices of the Self*, 1991), and others who share the floor with Scott's own growing network of urban teens—working Javon, drifting Bobby, the resistant Sharod, the realistic Charise and others. They bring their claims, reasons, stories, and motives for telling them to Scott's inquiry, offering diversely situated answers to Scott's questions, complementing, contradicting, and conditionalizing one another.

In a multivoiced inquiry like this, published writers step down from their status as authorities, arbiters of truth, or controllers of legitimate facts. This is not to say that the teens speak from a privileged standpoint on the truth. Rather, both groups become significant voices in dialogue and the source of rival hypotheses (well or weakly supported) about complex open questions. What matters is that marginalized participants are not merely objects of study but self-conscious partners in an inquiry, with inside knowledge about issues that concern them. Scott did not "interview" his teen and mentors but asked them to deliberate a question with him. He sought their rivals in order to situate his emerging image of role models and work ethics in multiple contexts *and* in the meanings those ideas held for young men in their lives and world. As a result, this story does not necessarily "add up," letting Scott reduce his inquiry to a tidy thesis supported by authoritative quotations. Rather, these voices drew Scott to construct a more complex and diversely situated, if always tentative, negotiated meaning around the topics of his inquiry—and a newly negotiated understanding of his own place in the story of mentoring and modeling.

An Intercultural Reading of "Networks of Support"

At this point in my account, Scott is now a college junior and mentor in the community-literacy course, focusing this term on the networks supporting youth. He is still thinking about the power of role models and mentors, but his representation of the problem has changed. He has reframed his sophomore preoccupation with *being* a role model into an open question about the role African American men already played in the lives of the black teenagers he now knows. In addition, he has begun to shape an on-going question about his own place in this story as a white middle-class college boy from rural Vermont. At the same time, Scott is also developing new tools for inquiry, learning strategies for collaborative planning, research methods for collecting rival readings, and a set of broader literate practices that support rivaling and intercultural interpretation (Flach, 1999; Flower, 1998; Flower, Long, & Higgins, 2000).

In what follows, I quote from "5 O'clock World," Scott's inquiry project, which he describes as an "examination of role models and work ethic in five urban communities." The voices at his table bring rivals from his freshman year of tutoring, the summer job at an urban YMCA, and the current Community Literacy Center project.[8] In a first step toward intercultural meaning, Scott begins the paper by grounding this "mutual inquiry in my own personal history with the culture of work."

> As a student at Carnegie Mellon, I typically work 16 hours a day. Classes begin for me each day at 9 A.M., and before I crawl into bed at night the clock usually reads 2 A.M. the following morning. . . .
>
> Back in Vermont, it will be well below freezing tomorrow morning at 5 A.M. when the alarm goes off in my parents' bedroom. My father, at age 47, who has worked since he was 14, will crawl from bed and start his day. He owns two companies, one of which is a home heating fuel dealer, and wintertime in Vermont is prime time for him. . . . By the time he gets home from work it will no doubt be the better part of 7 o'clock . . . I can remember only one day that my father missed work, so sick that he could not move himself from our couch. Much to the chagrin of the ten year old in me, I am slowly becoming my father. To the credit of the 20-year old me, I don't really mind.

From the beginning, it is clear that few of the urban teenagers at the Community Literacy Center have come with twenty-year-old Scott's experiences, assumptions, and attitudes about work. Some had joined the project (called Roads to Learning/Roads to Work) because their friends did, because they wanted get at the computers and the Web, or because "work" meant a little money in the pocket. So what shape does "support" take? What is the mentor's job? Is it to be a role model who could impart his own Yankee work ethic? Is it to teach what the service agencies call work-readiness skills? Or is it something yet to be discovered? For example, Keith Gilyard, one of the powerful voices at Scott's table, urges him to recognize the agency in others before attempting to reorganize their lives. Scott quotes Gilyard.

> School records indicate that my outstanding disability was "father not living with family." . . . Sure there were family difficulties, but the contention that they were directly translated into school problems is ludicrous. To label my "broken home" a learning disability represents, among other things, a failure to view me as an active participant in my own reality. . . . I will state unequivocally that the consistent belief in my ability shown by both of my parents was a major reason I was always, for one thing, in better shape than the school system itself. (1991, pp. 109–10)

Scott's paper is an attempt to transform service into inquiry—to create a collaborative intercultural representation of what work, success, and role models mean in the context of adolescent lives. As the narrative of Scott's inquiry unfolds, we see him hearing—and testing—some voices of conventional wisdom from his background that assumed families without men were necessarily "broken" and that influence depended on proximity—the man in the house. Then, as Scott puts it:

> Enter Javon. Sixteen years old, honor student, and employee at Foot Locker in a suburban mall. Not just an employee, moreover, but both the youngest employee and the employee with the greatest number of sales, to be exact. . . . Javon seemed to be the diametric antithesis to the stereotypical image of the Black urban male teen that led me to my inquiry, therefore making him the perfect place to begin. What's more, Javon lives in a single parent household headed by his hard-working mother. . . . Javon felt that a great deal of his work ethic, which he felt to be strong, came from the example that had been set by his dad [now living in another city].

According to Javon, the out-migration of black professional males was indeed bad luck for teens like himself—"white suburban males had a much larger pool of role models to draw from." In *Urban Sanctuaries*, Milbrey McLaughlin, Merita Irby, and Juliet Langman elaborate the same observation, describing how effective youth leaders make a strategic choice *not* to live in the projects: "Any credible role model embodying an appealing future would live elsewhere" (1994, p. 41).

Scott's interviews with teens turned up story after story of fathers, jazz-playing grandfathers, brothers (one of whom was "one hell of a 'baller'" with a college scholarship and job), and volunteers who mattered. However, these pictures of working (if nontraditional) support were rivaled by other voices.

The strongest was thirteen-year-old Bobby. Scott had been working with Bobby for three years since his freshman tutoring days and invited his young friend into this inquiry.

> Bobby is a better-than-average student [in middle school], all things considered, however he usually finds himself in some sort of trouble with the administration due to insubordination or insolence of varying degrees. Bobby talks incessantly about his father, however the incongruity in his stories leads to the impression that it has been a very long time since he last saw the man. . . . Although no one in the household held gainful employment, . . . the living room was furnished with black leather sofas and chairs and the dining room contained an immaculate glass dining table with matching chairs trimmed in brass. The tags from Rent Way were still attached and in plain view, revealing the temporal existence of this furniture in the apartment.

The economist in Scott questioned whether Bobby saw "a direct link between the notion of labor and that of material possession." "I asked Bobby who the role models in his life were, and unfortunately he did not seem to feel he had any."

In the next breath, it is clear that the story of men in his life was more complex that that. Scott asked him about being in school: "Even I was surprised when he said . . . he did not see a real advantage to staying in school because most of the men in his neighborhood, regardless of whether or not they had completed high school, could not find employment at places other than fast food restaurants or gas stations"—an argument Scott had also heard in John Ogbu's research on the "employment ceiling" (1992).

This growing body of rival interpretations at Scott's table was challenging his image of support networks and qualifying his hypotheses about the ways role models created images of work and success. So he took his inquiry a step further, into the influence of more distant role models, asking four teenagers to do a "rival reading" with him, interpreting a *Fortune* article on the New Black Power and its profile of Buppies.[9] Were these available images of success moving up or selling out? Would they be dismissed as "acting white"? "In contrast to my initial belief in the importance of readily accessible and visual success stories in these communities, Javon echoed the sentiment [found in McLaughlin's interviews and the *Fortune* article] that the move was necessary to fulfill the image of 'success.' . . . Charise, Javon, and Nahmel . . . felt that these people offered hope to youth that they could succeed in a world of adversity." When asked flat-out, Javon argued against a double standard—the expectation to remain in "urban confines" should not be greater on successful blacks than whites.

But when Bobby looked at the pictures in the *Fortune* article, to Scott's surprise, he didn't seem to see success or even material wealth. He felt that the suits that the people in the article were wearing made them look "'White' . . . they dressed 'a lot like you do,' referring to me."

Bobby: [The people in the article] live in the suburbs, I know that much.
Me: Why do you say that?
Bobby: 'Cause don't nobody dress like that in tha ghetto.

Underneath this inquiry with teens about their role models and images of work was, of course, the inevitable question mentors ask themselves—what is my role, if any, in this process of developing images of identity? Javon was, as always, diplomatic.

Javon: Like that tutoring work you do, that's really cool and all, and you're probably really making a difference, but . . . (*hesitates*)
Me: But I would be making more of a difference if I were a Black Man going to Carnegie Mellon University and going out into the inner-city schools to work with these kids.
Javon: Yeah, definitely.

And yet, for Bobby, Scott had actually been a reliable supportive presence for three years. Scott's paper goes on, "Then I asked him matter-of-factly if he felt that I could be a possible model for him. He was quick with his negative response, and when pressed for a reason, he paused, shrugged, and said that although he liked me, 'I ain't white and I don't wanna be white.'"

Scott's paper closes with the heading, "Observations, Not Answers." Like Anne, he has had to revise his assumptions about family structure and the role of men who are not "in the actual home." And he has shaped a more complex understanding of how he is read by the teenagers he mentors from their positions shaped by race and class. He had maintained his sense of commitment and faith in connecting but reinterpreted his place in these layered relationships.

Scott has arrived at a "negotiated understanding" that situates public is-sues attached to youth (support, work ethic, identity) not only in his cultural context but also in glimpses of theirs. His inquiry let him begin to see ideas as actions shaped by the conditions of the teens' lives and leading to consequences in their attitudes and choices. He has begun to construct the situated meaning of support. And he has gone public, entering a dialogue with the class, with future mentors, and with other contributors on the Web site.

Inquiry and Transformation

The transformation of service into praxis starts with changing the expectations we set for service-learning courses and community outreach projects. Having entered the contact zone of cultural difference, we must be prepared to go beyond contact into the struggle to understand with others in a collaborative intercultural inquiry. We must be ready, as Scott and Lisa were, to step beyond the safe distance of critique to the active negotiation of the inevitable contradictions within service and the conflicts within our own thinking and understanding. Secondly, we must set for ourselves and our students the explicit goal of creating a *transformed* and *transformative* understanding, not as a lofty ideal but as an operational, achievable, and profoundly significant expectation.

More specifically, one way to move out of the catbird's seat of expert and advisor is to take a critical look at the discourse strategies we use to learn from others. For Eugene, another CLC mentor working with urban teens, the problem was resisting the impulse to appear knowledgeable, to fake it, to fit in. He developed a discourse strategy he called the "clueless approach," which reordered the relationship of mentor and teen.

> I saw that I would not benefit from this experience by just "getting by." I realized how much there would be to learn if I asked more questions and accepted my position of no knowledge (instead of just trying to silently extricate myself from situations when I didn't "get it.") As a result, I adopted a "clueless" approach to learning and teaching. I questioned everything that I was uncertain about, and both I and my writer learned more about each other and the task at hand. (qtd. in Flower, 1998, p. 414)

Eugene was not only honoring the expertise of his teen; he was working through one of the demands of this discourse that student writers often struggle with. In asking them to pose and pursue a genuine, open question, inquiry asks them to violate the common sense of much academic discourse. Its reverses the golden rule that says, don't pose a problem you can't answer; propose a thesis you can defend. Assert what you already know or believe, then find the evidence (or authorities) to support it. Eugene, Scott, and Anne are success stories in large part because they choose the alternate stance of inquiry.

Perhaps it would be more accurate to say they persisted in inquiry. One of our revealing failures points to the considerable barriers discourse expectations can put in the path of good intentions. In Susan Swan's study of a graduate public-policy class, Sophie, a master's student, had announced her clear intention to "get involved instead of telling people what to do" (2002). But in the crunch of interviewing her community contacts, Sophie fell back on the familiar discourse of talking about *her* proposal for change, ignoring their very different sense of the problem. The next term, Swan expanded the instruction in inquiry methods, and an intriguing body of differently situated knowledge began to emerge from interviews that extended, challenged, disconfirmed, and/or qualified the findings from students' preliminary policy research. Their inquiry process was a great success—but the final reports told a different story. Writing for a professional panel in a genre that privileged large data sets and statistical analysis, students were unable to maintain the voice of this alternative expertise or integrate this new local knowledge into the discourse of their discipline. Knowing does not always lead to literate action.

Transforming Understanding

The goal of intercultural inquiry is a transformed understanding, that is, a collaboratively constructed meaning that does justice (as best it can) to the interpretive logics of all parties. Clifford Geertz argues that figuring out how to do this is the great challenge of contemporary anthropology. In *Local Knowledge*, he describes this challenge as turning away from "trying to explain social phenomena by weaving them into grand textures of cause and effect to trying to explain them by placing them in local frames of awareness" (1983, p. 6). The trick here is not empathy ("imagining myself someone else, a rice peasant or a tribal sheik, and then seeing what I thought")—"The trick is to figure out what the devil they think they are up to" (p. 58). It is "displaying the logic of their ways of putting [things] in the locutions of ours" (p. 10).

Paulo Freire's pedagogy of the oppressed also insists on drawing out this interpretive logic as a basis for critical consciousness in both speakers and hearers. Sitting in literacy circles, adult learners are asked to interpret key words and pictures as a way to "name" their own condition through stories and descriptions. "To exist, humanly," Freire argued, "is to *name* the world, to change it. Once named, the world in its turn reappears to the namers as a problem and requires of them a new naming" (1970/1985, p. 77). As these learners interpret a picture of a working-class man staggering from a street-corner bar, they express a richly situated knowledge that takes us beyond the familiar abstractions. They do not see a social issue, a moral decline, or the problem of alcoholism. Their sympathetic eyes see not only families without money for food but husbands who cannot support their families, who are drinking in despair and shame. The interpretations arising from this intercultural inquiry are attuned to contradiction and complex causality, weaving together the multiple threads of situated meanings.

On the other hand, when W. E. B. DuBois talks about double consciousness in *Souls of Black Folk*, this awareness of other people's interpretive logic as it is applied to *oneself* can become an oppressive, unavoidable awareness of racism (1903/1961). For African Americans, racism is not an abstraction or generalization but a situated understanding that produces an intense, abiding awareness of how you are seen by others. It is the constantly split consciousness of yourself—as the identity you feel within and as the diminished identity reflected in the eyes of the white world.

My point in this unlikely juxtaposition of Geertz, Freire, and DuBois is to suggest that grasping someone else's interpretive logic can be grasping a tiger by the tail. It has the potential not just to change our knowledge of the world but to challenge our image of ourselves in that world. As college mentor Nicole sketches it, her glimpse of someone else's situated of knowledge also created a heightened awareness of her own.

Her mentee, Elliot, was an urban teenager, labeled in school as learning disabled. He was tall, witty, and ironic, slow to trust, quick to defensive anger, no stranger to violence. For him, the daily trip to school through his neighborhood was hazardous. Going to school was a decision he had to make each day. As Nicole earned his trust, she began to focus her inquiry with Elliot on his situated knowledge of "responsibility"—in its telling juxtaposition with her own.

> In the past, I have always perceived responsibility on a superficial and individualized level: to clean a room or get up for school. I never viewed responsibility as a *choice*, but rather as something I had to do. Much to my surprise, however, the teens I interviewed at the CLC did not recognize responsibility as such a close ended, easily defined issue. . . . Elliot, for instance, responded, "School, well that is something you have to decide to do. . . . [And achievement makes] you feel more better, and that starts rubbing off on certain people." Elliot clearly identifies his responsibility to himself as a means of affecting society as a whole. Or, to paraphrase Elliot, to feel better about yourself and pass that on to other people. (qtd. in Flower, 1998, p. 337)

Nicole's encounter with Elliot's deeply and differently situated interpretation of responsibility was a critical step toward a transformed understanding. Motivated by this glimpse into someone else's interpretive logic, Nicole turns to look at her own with the words, "I now wonder . . ."

Of course, we may not be comfortable with the differences such inquiry can uncover. Dialogue can reveal that our progressive politics, our support of Black English, or our ideas of emancipatory education for others were not exactly what *they* had in mind.[10] We want to ask Javon if he is selling out for success in the system. We fear Bobby is failing to read its economics rightly. Intercultural inquiry is not focused on forging consensus, but it can let us put charged issues like these on the table as open questions, and doing so can rewrite the terms of difference. When we situate the meaning of a concept (such as justice, success, responsibility, emancipation, or role models) in culturally diverse readings, it becomes a qualified, conditionalized concept (for both the teen and the mentor). It becomes clear that our meanings are both partial and located in their circumstances and consequences. This does not mean they are necessarily isolated or solipsistic, if we accept a pragmatic vision of what it means to "understand." In Donna Haraway's apocalyptic language, understanding exists as "an earth-wide network of connections, including the ability partially to translate knowledges among very differ-ent—and power-differentiated—communities" (1991, p. 187).

When social issues are embedded in human actions, we are forced to reckon with—and are privileged to glimpse—the intentionality of others. Elliott's attendance at school is no longer a social statistic about an at-risk male; it is a self-conscious decision to cross gang territory, to save face but still work around his difficulty with reading, and to deal with his history of suddenly escalating conflicts with other young men. But transformed un-derstanding is not the result of service-learning courses, critical pedagogy, or any program. It is created when we *use* inquiry to seek out those rival readings of culturally charged issues and to challenge the attitudes we, like Anne's mother, mistakenly attribute to others. It becomes working knowledge when our representation of staying in school can accommodate the logic by which Bobby dismisses school, and Elliott chooses it. And most importantly, understanding means something when it leads to transformed relationships and actions, built on a grounded image of the agency and interpretive life of others.[11]

7 *The Search for Situated Knowledge*

Designing a community-outreach project around inquiry is a first step to the collaborative construction of transformed knowledge. However, the desire for dialogue is rarely enough without a dedicated search for difference.

When blacks and whites of goodwill in my city gather to talk about significant issues, they face hard questions, such as, why don't black youth find meaningful work? What would it mean to carry out a police-enforced youth curfew in the black community? And in these moments, the desire for intercultural dialogue is often matched by a sense of the distance between the ways we represent those issues. Hoping for a collaboratively constructed understanding, we encounter a chasm, for behind the words we use in common lie strikingly different life experiences that instantiate a concept (such as, police-enforced) with different flesh-and-blood realities. Such experiences may allow you, for instance, to make sense of that concept with an image of your own son, in his stocking cap and braids or whatever is the current urban fashion, who was recently harassed by police on his way to the corner store. As an inner-city resident, you may instantiate that concept of "police-enforced curfew" with the visceral feeling of what "no recourse" means in a confrontation with authority. Your mind automatically "enacts" that concept, drawing on neighborhood history and stories of demeaning encounters that are the grounding for presumptions you can hardly articulate—and I fail to imagine.

The question is, how do we talk about culturally significant issues across such differences? We stand within a history that has alternately marginalized and ignored the knowledge of the powerless and then (when we must listen) domesticated and assimilated that experience into mainstream and middle-class schemas. As academics, we stand in a profession more accustomed to speaking "for Others" than listening to their unanticipated, resistant meanings (Delpit, 1986; Cushman, 1998). When white, mainstream academics like myself begin to work with urban community organizations, the attempt to talk across differences must not merely acknowledge this history but must deal directly with the relationships of power and distrust it has left behind. We must also anticipate the barriers our dissimilar discourses can erect as they signal what is expected, invited, or allowed. We must recognize the way dialogue halts at the walls of the specialized discourses we bring (from policy, education, social services, critical theory) with their exclusionary concepts, categories, and styles of argument.

But beyond these things, there is often yet another more tacit barrier to collaborative understanding. It arises even in a climate of dialogue like the community conversation examined later, in which urban teenagers, their community supporters, and university partners have built relations of trust. It exists within the process of meaning making itself and in the body of powerful, unarticulated, experientially based interpretive resources both parties bring to what appears to be common, public topics of discussion. These are the resources I call "situated knowledge." Listening is a highly constructive, interpretive activity under the best of conditions, but in circumstances like this, are we likely to "hear" or infer the experientially shaped situated knowledge and the silent logic that Others are using to make meaning in the midst of our dialogue? And say I do begin to grasp something of your situated sense making, of the ways you are interpreting the meaning of a youth curfew (or interpreting me)—can a deliberate search for this difference make a difference?

This chapter takes us into a particular attempt to talk across difference and offers a preliminary theory, a hypothesis really, about what could happen were we to ground intercultural inquiry in a deliberate search for situated knowledge. I use *hypothesis* here in the sense of William James and John Dewey: as an explanatory account that functions as a guide to action, observation, and the revision of one's explanatory theory. *Intercultural inquiry* is both an attitude and a scaffold created by literate practices. We engage in such inquiry in order to go beyond those dialogues that merely swap stories, on the one hand, or rehearse familiar generalizations on the other. Partners in inquiry turn to literate strategies that help them to elicit something of the situated, affective, and embodied knowledge behind the speakers' words (where important differences may lie), to embrace these as rival interpretations, and to draw themselves into a joint, reconstructive negotiation with their own understandings. Such inquiry is, then, a deliberate meaning-making activity in which difference is not read as a problem but *sought out as a resource for constructing more grounded and actionable understandings.* In the spirit of Dewey's (1929/1988) "experimental way of knowing," I want to develop this theoretical account of inquiry pragmatically, that is, to explore its meaning as it *emerges* within a cultural/social/cognitive activity and as it is defined by its *consequences*. In this case, the activity is a Community Literacy Center Community Conversation, a public event designed with the explicit goal of embracing multiple voices, drawing out situated knowledge, and sparking a genuine intercultural dialogue.

The Dynamics of Public Inquiry

For many people in Pittsburgh's urban neighborhoods, the passage of a new curfew policy brought differences in culture and power to a flash point. Here is an excerpt from one urban analyst's attempt to get at the story-behind-the-story.

What Do I Mean by "Story Behind the Story"?

Sometimes adults (police) don't know what teenagers are really thinking, and they misunderstand teenagers actions and intentions. Since they haven't "been there," they can't see the hidden logic behind what teenagers do. This is what I mean when I say, "Story Behind the Story." . . .

How can adults (police) be helped to see the story behind the story? . . . I've been studying the curfew policy. If the curfew would begin right now, I think there would be a lot of conflict between teens and cops past curfew time. The curfew policy is not clear for everybody to understand, teens or adults. It only talks about the teens' conduct and attributes, but it doesn't talk about how cops should be. This is important because a cop can treat you any way because he is the police, and it won't be equal because teens will have to take it and show respect to someone that may not be showing respect to them. . . .

I don't understand the way cops feel, but I do understand the way teens feel because I've have had my own personal experiences. It seems like every time I see a cop car I feel angry, because they just want to harass me and pull me over for no reason. I've had this happen to me a couple of times. . . . [1]

Andre, the author, is an urban teenager trying to come to grips with being stopped and searched because (the police tell him) "his hair" (an ordinary short Afro) apparently makes him "look like someone in a picture." He stands in the midst of claims and contradictions that surround race and class, youth and adult relations in my city.

This young man, fourteen-year-old Andre Ashby, is also standing up quite literally in a public community conversation, reading this levelheaded analysis from a printed document called *Raising the Curtain on Curfew*. His text, developed in a seven week CLC project, moves from this essayistic analysis to a narrative that interprets the meaning this teen made of his own encounter, to a politic recommendation that the police academy teach its officers to seek the story-behind-the-story (a strategy he learned in the CLC project). It is timely advice because the audience who fills the small auditorium of the Community House includes the director of police training, a director of the curfew facility, other people from public service agencies, a city councilman, a state representative, the media, and family and friends from the neighborhood and university. They have come to a dialogue in which urban teens (supported by their college mentors) are holding the mike and dramatizing the issues.

From where Andre stands, directing this discussion, community literacy has taken the force of literate action. The teenagers have been using writing to initiate a community problem-solving dialogue—to raise and name a problem, to assert and demonstrate the expertise their marginalized perspectives can bring to the analysis of public policy, and to engage that public, as its best self, in a dialogue defined by inquiry.

Stepping back, looking at this event from where I stand, Andre, the other teen authors, and the people who came to their Community Conversation were also engaged in an unfolding experiment in intercultural rhetoric. This dialogue—in text and talk—was an attempt to construct knowledge at the intersection of cultural difference. It had set for itself the task of drawing out local expertise, using difference intentionally in order to build a more diversely informed, multivocal meaning. All of this was based on the premise that this room was, in fact, a vast archive of silent, culturally shaped, situated knowledge(s). However, this premise also identifies the problem, for the diversely situated local knowledges held by the mix of people in this room were just as likely to be submerged icebergs lurking in the route to cross-cultural understanding. Despite its potential, such knowledge operates with tacit uncertainties and a private process of meaning making. Typically, it is neither shared nor open to question.

Given the secretive habits of situated knowledge, the working hypothesis of intercultural rhetoric is that this silent knowledge *could* be transformed into a generous interpretative resource, *if* people could reveal more of the richly contextualized stories-behind-the-story at work in their own meaning making. The community conversation examined here is a practical experiment in knowledge building across difference—an attempt to embrace difference, conflict, and contradiction and in doing so transform understanding. To sharpen what we might learn from this experiment, it will help to recognize first some of the tensions that an intercultural rhetoric must negotiate, which include conflicting notions of the public sphere, empowerment, and community service. Then we look at how intercultural inquiry played itself out in a community conversation before we turn in the final section to thoughts about how embracing conflict can lead to new understandings.

As community members, family, teachers, and university friends begin to fill the Community House's intimate, 105-seat auditorium (which becomes the Community House Church on Sundays), they receive a copy of the teens' sixteen-page document, *Raising the Curtain on Curfew*. To initiate the dialogue, teenager Frank Boyd and his group are performing the sketch he wrote called "Bad Experiences After Hours." This is not only a true story dramatized with strong feeling; it is also a strategic literate act.

The Rivaling Stance

"Bad Experiences" uses the rival hypothesis stance to explore the personal dynamics of a curfew encounter from different points of view. Frank and Andre are inventing ways to turn this thinking strategy into some sort of textual and dramatic practice. In his published text, Frank had hit on a technique for revealing rivals by turning them into inner thoughts, italicized and placed within brackets. On stage, the teens decided to have these interpretive interior monologues boom through the PA system from a prerecorded tape while they stay in character.

As the sketch begins, two sixteen-year-old, "black males with braids, wearing baggy clothes, Dickies, and t-shirts," have unwittingly violated the curfew policy as they walk home from a football game.

> As the cops approach Dennis and Shawn, they say, "What're ya doin' in dis alleyway at dis time of night. Don't ya know there's a curfew?" {*Thinking: I know these two teens are neighborhood drug dealers cuz they're dressed like most drug dealers I see all the time. And now with this curfew we can catch 'em in the act and put 'em behind bars.*}

Although the boys try to explain, the cop is thinking, "Gimme a break, I've already heard that story" and comes back with

> "Get your ass home. This is ya first warning. Don't let me catch ya out here again." {*Thinking: I told them I'm not buyin it. We'll just follow them and pick 'em up.*}

The boys take the alley, which they see as a short cut, but which the police read as trying to avoid the warning, and the second encounter occurs. In Frank's script, the police act on their hasty interpretation.

{*Thinking: we got ya now!*}

These officers put the teens on the wall and search them aggressively. They're pushing, mugging, hitting them. Dennis and Shawn try to plead their case, asking what's going on. The cops say, "Didn't we already stop ya in the alleyway? This is your second violation. Get in the car before we throw ya in."

The teens hesitate getting into the car because they don't understand what they did wrong. {*Dennis and Shawn thinking: We shouldn't have to get in the car. We did nothin' wrong.*} They tell the cops they're still on their way home. One of the officers grabs Dennis by the arm and Dennis, afraid of getting hurt, quickly reacts to the cop's hand, smacking it away. The officer, thinking he has to quickly regain control, hits Dennis in the leg with his billy-club knocking him to the ground. The officer places his knee on Dennis's back to hold him. Shawn looks on in fear before trying to run. The other officer grabs him, slamming him on the car to handcuff him.

The bracketed interior monologues by the boys and the police are a technique Frank designed to locate rival interpretation in real-time action. This use of the rival hypothesis stance speaks in the mixed accents of rhetorical theory, educational research, and neighborhood savvy. As a strategy for critical thinking and deliberative inquiry into open questions, the stance is claimed by multiple academic disciplines, from rhetoric and philosophy to social and physical sciences. It is seen as an important but difficult-to-teach aspect of university training. But, as my colleagues and I observed in the Learning to Rival project, it is fitting that the verb form, "rivaling," was coined by the Community Literacy Center writers, who quickly appropriated it as a new strategy for discussion.[2]

Urban teens saw rivaling as a way to give presence to their own, often-silenced readings of situations. Rivaling let them go beyond the familiar rhetoric of complaint and blame that accompanies teen powerlessness, by giving them not only a justification to speak but a way to enter adult forums with a new strategy for civil discourse and inquiry. In group discussions among themselves, the freedom to offer rivals as *possibilities* to be considered also operated as a desperately needed alternative to adversarial argument and the imperative of advocacy that often locked them in the closet of "my opinion." Rivaling allowed mentors to draw out the teens' expertise and also challenge or disagree without dominating.

In this public community conversation, urban teens used the strategy to tell the frequently silenced stories-behind-the-story of neighborhood experience. This mutable literate practice then was one of the powerful "voices" shaping this inquiry. But another equally potent force was the voice of neighborhood history, which revealed itself most clearly when flashes of situated knowledge burst into the dialogue.

The Play of Situated Knowledge

Inquiries are driven by questions, concerns, and desires. This one was initiated by a history of worry and anger over racially focused police action in this inner-city neighborhood. The curfew legislation raised this unstated policing policy to a new level of exigency for the members of this audience. Frank's desire to tell his story was motivated by the experience of this urban community—which would, in turn, shape the way his story was interpreted. Nearly every boy in the group had been arbitrarily stopped by police; every girl knew of friends or relatives subjected to this demeaning experience. The pregnant daughter of a literacy leader was at that time part of an American Civil Liberties Union (ACLU) harassment suit after she had been verbally abused, choked, and pushed to the ground in front of her five-year-old boy by a white officer. Her female companion driving the car had stopped at a traffic light and had not followed a contradictory police order to move. Proposals for a citizens review board of police action (later passed by referendum) were in the news. Feelings ran deep around this everyday threat each young black male walked under, and the white mentors struggled to understand. The community conversation, then, was not simply about a curfew but about a policy of harassment, under the name of getting tough on drugs, that targeted this black community. It raised a racialized issue, rooted in the history of Jim Crow policies of "legal" oppression, in civil rights anger, and in the current generation's intense preoccupation with respect and being "dissed." It was about rival conceptions with a human face.

Situated knowledge refers here to a particular way people can *represent* their knowledge and experience—a representation that can have significant consequences for sharing that knowledge with others.[3] To begin with, the diverse sources of the situated knowledge(s) we bring to an intercultural discussion like this often guide sense making by turning public words into private dramatizations. Drawing on our situated knowledge allows each of us to represent a topic of discussion (e.g., youth curfew) not only as an abstraction but also as an imagined activity—as a social or psychological event in context, peopled by actors with intentions. Unlike abstract ways of representing what we "know," evoking situated knowledge is like playing a brief home movie of the mind.[4] Like any good drama, it fuses ideas with emotions, it supplies unstated reasons and hidden motivations for actions, and it plays out the meaning of those actions as consequences. In short, it embeds meaning in a rich matrix of human activity.

The problem is not that this situated knowledge (rooted in each person's cultural, social, and material history) guides interpretation of a topic like curfew but that both this mode of knowing and the interpretation it constructs remain tacit, uncommunicated. Like silent movies giving sense to our words, these private showings play before the mind's eye as we speak but remain unarticulated to our interlocutor. Meanwhile, that hearer may be blithely embedding our words in her own (differently) situated construction of meaning.[5] As Frank's sketch shows, Dennis, Shawn, and the "cops" were screening different interpretive films as they talked.

We can also contrast this *situated* knowledge with the stripped down, *abstracted* representations of knowledge we often share with one another.[6] Prestige discourses (e.g., academic journals) tend to value abstract and symbolic representations. We delight in rising to talk of principles, generalizations, and theory. And within most intercultural dialogues, the representations people share around weighty issues, such as, policy, race, or education, tend to gravitate to the dignified use of abstractions. Content to exchange familiar signs—the propositions of policy, the generalizations of theory, the concepts and commonplaces of the day—we can enjoy the illusion of understanding but fail to catch more than a glimmer of the situated knowledge that lies beneath the terms we trade. The paradox of intercultural dialogues is that the things dividing us that are hardest to share—the deep roots of history, the racially shaped experience, and the repertoire of interpretive strategies we use to make sense of that experience—may also be the ones we most need to communicate.

For example, Dave Coogan's richly detailed case study in an inner-city Chicago neighborhood documents a failed attempt to increase parental involvement in underachieving local schools (2006b). The advocates (a community/university team) built their campaign around the apparently motivating concept of "local control"—but failed to inquire into what Coogan calls the "rhetorical history" of that concept, the local situated meaning it had already accrued for these residents. Had they known, he argues, the extent to which this particular notion (or ideograph) had already been discredited or undermined in public discourse (in a local debate ten years prior to this project!), they might have built a very different argument. And in fact, Coogan's rhetorical research led to a new argument framed as "local responsibility." Attuned to neighborhood knowledge, it led to a far more successful campaign.[7]

John Dewey (1929/1988) suggests another reason for seeking out these situated representations when he argues that the *meaning* of an idea, concept, or claim (like the value of a curfew) does not lie in the satisfyingly clean logical patterns we are often pleased to construct with our ideas. Its significance does not derive from its connection to (or validation by) another theory or generalization. Rather, its meaning lies in the pragmatic existence this idea leads in human experience—in the personal and public uses to which that idea is being put. A situated representation of a concept, shot through with the drama of human intentions, actions, and consequences, is one way to approximate this more complex notion of meaning. It stands before the mind's eye of the speaker—and potentially of the hearer—as a meaning playing itself out in the world. Of course, as activity theory is quick to remind us, insofar as a situated representation captures the dynamics of a social/cultural/cognitive activity, it is also likely to be shot through with contradiction.[8]

Cross-Talk

At the community house, where we left each listener trying to make sense of things, constructing the meaning of this "curfew policy" or Andre's reference to "respect," it was apparent that diversely situated knowledges were coming into play. As these representations rose to the level of articulation, interlocutors could begin to glimpse one another's divergent contexts for interpretation, alternative images of people's motives, and contradictory visions of outcomes.

The first person to stand up following the teens' problem-posing dramatizations was Sala Udin, a prominent African American city councilman who had opposed the curfew measure. Taking the microphone, he addressed himself directly to the teenagers, appearing to all but ignore the rest of the room, in words that echoed Martin Luther King Jr.: "This is an unjust law. You know it, I know it. We will continue to oppose it." In that room, his words evoked powerful images of lunch counter sit-ins, of resistant, nonviolent protest. They emerged from the discourse of law, politics, and social activism. For my generation, they evoked images of Birmingham and Selma, Alabama, while the young were more likely to envision the police they had encountered last week up on Federal Street. At that point, Udin suddenly moved into the 1990s and the sober discourse of urban wisdom and personal savvy—a man speaking to his community. His advice was intense and direct, "Stay as far away from the system as you can. Don't expect it to treat you fairly, and most of all don't even give it a chance to do what it will do." His meaning was all about action in context.

On this night, kairos called out yet another layer of situated knowledge. For the councilman and many in the audience, the meaning of a police-enforced ordinance evoked vivid images of the recent, nationally reported death of Jonny Gammage, a black motorist who was stopped in a nearby white neighborhood for no documented cause and died as result of police brutality.

Two hours before the community conversation, the news broke that the jury had just exonerated the police. People began gathering in protest on the steps of City Hall. With all the major-news cameras rolling downtown, no one expected Councilman Udin, a key spokesperson for the black community, to appear at a local community house. Like a dark cloud, the Gammage decision seemed to elicit a feeling of "nothing changes," angry despair in the middle-aged, and angry shock in the young. It was a surprise when Udin walked in the door, not only to speak but also to listen. In that context, Udin's simple presence in the community house was a vocal sign. When I asked him why he was here when the "action" was beginning across the river, his reply was straightforward: "Here is a place we can do something positive."

On this night, the councilman's words and presence also introduced a broadly situated representation of curfew not simply as a concept but as a social activity, located not only in the history of the civil rights struggle but also in the context of life in urban neighborhoods. Represented as such an activity, the curfew was inseparable from the probable consequences it held for black men who had any engagement with the legal system. Although Udin could have easily given an ACLU legal reading or a political policy statement on curfew, he chose to talk out of his situated knowledge as an urban black man; he shared a representation that cast young men as personal agents with intentions and emotions, engaged in actions with implications.

When the director of the proposed curfew detention center rose to reply, she appeared to be walking into this discussion from a deeply different narrative. In her account, the curfew was a socially concerned activity to save young children. Her words sketched a problem space that seemed to bear no relation to the activity articulated by the teens or councilman. She described (and justified) the curfew solely in terms of an image of ten- to twelve-year-old children who, she envisioned, would be found on the street at midnight, afraid or unable to go home, who would find food, games, counseling, and social support in the educational environment of the curfew center. This possible scenario, and no doubt legitimate concern, had not entered discussions at the Community Literacy Center. At the same time, as it became painfully clear, her narrowly situated representation of what this social policy meant completely failed to grapple with the practical and symbolic consequences of the curfew as a racialized teenage policy and as a police-controlled institutionalized activity. Her representation failed to account for a powerful and culturally shaped rival reading of curfew as a human activity, shaped by actors with a history and intentions not dreamed of in her policy.

Juxtaposing her mental movie with the situated representations of Udin and the teens posed the problem to this group in an unanticipated way. In a community conversation, cross talk between individuals is not about resolving their personal differences, much less winning a debate on positions. It is about the opportunity for each of the participants in the room (speaking or silent) to transform their own understanding in response to compelling and diversely situated rivals—giving what they can and taking what they need from this cross talk to build a more reflectively negotiated meaning for themselves and their situation.[9]

But strong statements and stark differences can also shut down transformation by cutting off dialogue or sparking polarized debate. So when a black parent angrily asserted his right to regulate his own child, the teens calmly moderated the dialogue by welcoming his contribution and asking for a rival to this idea from the speaker himself or others. Their invitation to collaborative cross talk drew out a more tentative participant, speaking this time for single mothers who in fact welcomed the curfew. Afraid of "losing their son to the streets" and unable to buck the tide of peer pressure on their child, they welcomed the support offered by a general curfew on all youth. For those of us easily drawn to the talk of civil rights, this situated knowledge once again qualified our image of a curfew, locating it in the dynamics of urban parenting and yet another set of possible outcomes. In this intercultural inquiry, the cross talk that revealed these divergent understandings qualified and conditionalized the meaning of curfew. But it didn't eliminate the conflict.

Constructive Conflict in Talking across Difference

There are times when I have regretted framing my account of negotiated meaning making around the notion of *conflict*. Others (those who are not intentionally advocating a discourse of disruption) have also tried to qualify its bad-natured overtones. *Contradiction*—the term activity theorists use—is a kinder, gentler concept. And indeed, the generative conflicts I observed in the writers described earlier (1994) did not escalate into adversarial confrontations among the multiple voices those writers were wrestling with.

However, I remain attached to the term because it was when a contradiction rose to consciousness (if even momentarily) and became a conflict—a problem for *somebody*—that it also became the prologue to struggle and a negotiation that produced new meaning. A meaning, I hasten to add that was often a tentative, revisable, best stab but was, nevertheless, a meaning that could guide to action. In this intercultural inquiry, I believe we can learn something about the generative side of this conflictual process by looking at the play of its hybrid discourse and at the reflections of students.

A Hybrid Discourse

One of the defining features of an intercultural inquiry is the mix of expectations, conventions, and rhetorical traditions people bring to it. The rough-and-tumble style of a community organizing meeting, for instance, thrives on adversarial argumentation that would be deemed inappropriate in the rational decorum of an academic policy discussion.[10] Against a backdrop of loaded expectations, a community problem-solving dialogue and its supporting texts create what we have described as a "hybrid discourse" (Flower, 1997a; Peck, Flower, and Higgins, 1995). More precisely, they create an enfranchising space, which invites hybrid discourse. In the name of inquiry and prophetic social justice, the teen writers and adult audience members alike are asked to participate in a deliberate mix of literate practices. The powerful moves of narrative, dramatization, and expressive, personal statement coexist almost seamlessly with the systematic thinking of problem analysis, decision making, and rival hypothesis thinking, which are, in turn, linked to strategies for writing and dialogue shaped by composition research and a reader-based rhetoric. Frank, for instance, chose to conclude his text by switching from the playscript written in slang to a highly analytical text move based on the options-and-outcomes strategy. This decision-making strategy not only generates "multiple, competing and complementary options . . . it subjects these options to the test of local knowledge—it uses teenage expertise to play out probable outcomes under real conditions. Action plans are then judged, not by good intentions, but by predicted outcomes" (Flower and Flach, 1996). Frank outlined three sets of possible outcomes from this event (for police, teenagers, and policy), using his teen expertise to judge the probabilities. As this excerpt from his conclusion shows, Frank has not lost his grip on reality.

Options and Outcomes for Dennis and Shawn

OPTION: Dennis and Shawn could get in the car with no questions asked.
OUTCOME: The Cops would never grab them.
OUTCOME: The cops would push them in the car anyway.

The title page of the document produced for the community conversation (see fig 7.1) is another mixed genre. The administrative talk of the original policy is translated into plain language in order to spotlight problematic issues: how, for instance, will police "identify" a "potential curfew violator" for interrogation on the street? The text design—with its arrows and script-like font—reanimates in text the social goals of the Community Conversation;

it turns a static official pronouncement into a dialogue by posing questions that the downtown authors of the text didn't consider, from a point of view they failed to solicit.

A less obvious but deeply motivated feature of this dialogue and its texts is also the shift from a discourse of policy and principles to what Dewey (1929/1988) might have called a discourse of consequences. Frank's conclusion (like Sala Udin's advice, Andre's story-behind-the-story, and activity theory) sees ideas as actions, taken in a particular time and place, that have consequences. And the problem the dialogue addresses is imagining consequences that lie outside one's own cultural experience.

Another strength of a hybrid discourse is that it is not dominated by *either* an elite or vernacular discourse, by the talk of school or street. The teenagers and some audience members also move back and forth between Standard English and African American Vernacular English, sometimes for rhetorical effect, sometimes as everyday speech. The mix of genres and languages is itself a statement about the nature of a genuine community/ university/civic collaboration. The problems that motivate this dialogue can only be understood if we embrace multiple—often contradictory and competing—perspectives. Not only must people feel authorized to speak in the languages they bring to the problem, these diverse perspectives must also be recognized as inseparable from their distinctive modes of representation. The melded genres, the shifting linguistic registers, the play with and against multiple conventions bring the expertise of youth and the situated knowledge of urban residents into intimate and authoritative contact with adult and mainstream structures of power.

However, it would miss the point to focus merely on dialect and discourse conventions. The force of this "special voice," as Prendergast (1998) called it, was not just to validate varieties of language or oral-versus-written styles but to validate diverse people—to acknowledge the intentions and values they bring to this issue and to uncover the complex representations of reality that they hold. It was the activity of enfranchising intercultural interpretations—multiple ways of knowing, strong rivals, and situated knowledges— that opened the possibility for new negotiated understandings.

Indications of Transformed Understanding

Though it would be nice to say that in the wake of this event, the curfew policy was changed, the police reformed, and the teens became literate activists, social change doesn't seem to happen that way. The goal of this intercultural inquiry was a transformed actionable understanding. But it is hard to know if this community conversation on curfew became a pearlescent grain of

Fig. 7.1 Title page of the curfew newsletter of the Community Literacy Center

Raising the Curtain on Curfew

CURFEW POLICY: A Plain-English Version

On the Street

The Curfew Policy puts Pittsburgh Police in charge of enforcing curfew. First, a police officer will use the following criteria to identify a "potential curfew violator":

- observation and experience assessing people's ages, including personal attributes and conduct.
- responses to such questions as, "How old are you?" and "May I see some identification?"
- commentary from other people who may be present.
- the officer's personal knowledge.

Next, the officer tells the teen that he or she is violating curfew and should go home. If the teen refuses to go home or is seen violating curfew a second time that night, the officer next "cites" the teen. (This means that information that the teen has broken curfew will be noted on that teen's record.) Then the officer will take the teen to the Curfew Facility.

At the Curfew Facility

At the Curfew Facility, the teen is turned over to the custody of the personnel operating the facility. After getting some information from the police and the teen, the Curfew Facility Personnel next call the teen's parent or guardian. If the parent comes to the facility for the teen, the teen and parent can go home just as soon as they schedule a date for a hearing in front of the Magistrate.

However, if the parent refuses to come to the facility or if the Personnel can't reach a parent or guardian (and so conclude that the teen has no supervision at home), then the Curfew Facility Personnel will contact the Allegheny County Children and Youth Services officials. Any teens remaining in the Curfew Facility when it closes at 6:00 a.m. will be turned over to CYS officials or, in some cases, to school officials.

All of this assumes the teen has done nothing more than violate curfew. However, if the teen is found with a weapon or with drugs, or has an outstanding arrest warrant or is on probation, the officer will apprehend the teen and take him or her to Shuman Detention Center.

About the Curfew Facility: The Curfew Facility will be a special type of "emergency juvenile shelter" licensed by Pennsylvania's Department of Public Welfare. At the facility, doors will be locked so no one can come in. Although they won't be locked on the inside (that would be against the law), teens who try to escape will be confined again and cited for violating another curfew. Police officers and metal detectors will provide security for the facility.

What problems might there be with trying to identify a "potential curfew violator"?

What would it take for teens and police to achieve mutual respect?

What might be some consequences of contacting CYS?

What might actually happen at the curfew facility?

What are some alternatives to the city's curfew policy?

THE COMMUNITY LITERACY CENTER

A Collaboration of the Community House and the Center
for the Study of Writing and Literacy at Carnegie Mellon University

sand in the oysters of any of the participants. The director of the police academy, struggling with a crop of urban-ignorant recruits, did ask for copies of *Raising the Curtain on Curfew.* Some neighborhood officers joined in a subsequent CLC project. But it was a mentor's writing that lets us see some indication of the realistically indirect way generative conflict might help change understanding.

In the two weeks following the Conversation, the mentors reconvened as a college class to present their own inquiries on a problem that mattered to them. In the spirit of intercultural inquiry, their own inquiries needed to bring voices and data sources to the table, in a final paper that required them to

> collect interpretations and analysis from at least three different sources/participants and at least three different kinds of data. If, for instance, you are a mentor conducting an inquiry that involves teenage writers, imagine yourself inviting a number of people and/or voices to the table to discuss your question with you. (Flower, 1998, p. 420)

The first thing to notice is that the inquiry we will examine makes no mention of curfew. It was triggered, mentor Karen Pierce writes, by Ken Harvey, the kid in Mike Rose's *Lives on the Boundary*, who asserts, "(with studied, minimal affect), 'I just wanna be average.'" Pierce says, "Ken's behavior as a student angered and frustrated me, clashing with my own persistence in institutionalized education" (qtd. in Flower, 1998, p. 422). She notes that her personal investment in this question was also prompted by the equally disengaged style of Delmar, the teenage writer she was mentoring, who melted out of the program shortly before the end.

But the problem that she invited Delmar to help her understand is, however, deeply tied to the threats the teens perceived in the proposed curfew and the stance Councilman Udin proposed—stay clear of the system.

> Through my interactions with Delmar at the CLC, I began to get a deeper sense of the contingent realities involved in one student's academic life. Early in our time together, Delmar, explaining street-smart strategies, commented that a good way of staying out of trouble with the police is to seem like everyone else. By stressing the importance of not sticking out or drawing attention to himself on Pittsburgh streets Delmar illustrated a non-academic facet to just being average. He reasoned the more average he could look on the street, the less threatened he would feel. In this context, then, being average seems a positive reaction to life circumstances. (qtd. in Flower, 1998, p. 423)

For Karen, the outcome of this community problem-solving dialogue on curfew was that it led her to reconsider the logic of teenagers' relationship to dominant institutions, such as, school—an institution that *she* understood and cared about, to which she had tied her own identity. Out of the dialogue, her subsequent taped discussions with Delmar and two other teenagers, and reading two books on education, Karen describes her movement to a negotiated meaning.

> I was prompted to question my critique of academic averageness, and began to see dangerous glimpses of classist, elitist presumptions in my attitude. Perhaps my notions of averageness as a merely adequate non-exemplary mode of being in the world did not encompass the "stories-behind-the-story" of those who seem average to me. Further, maybe those who seem average to me are seen as greater-than-average in other contexts by other people. Academia is just one setting in which averageness can play a role. Perhaps those who seem academically average are socially outstanding. Or perhaps not. I began to sense the complexities involved in considering averageness and was ready to pursue an investigation of them. (qtd. in Flower, 1998, p. 422)

Intercultural rhetoric operates in a force field of contradictory agendas and conflicting voices. The intercultural inquiry described here is a literate practice that tries to elicit real differences without polarizing people and to negotiate conflict without silencing it. It places its bets on multiple ways of representing what people know. Its hybrid discourse and shared situated knowledge can translate ideas into actions and outcomes and in doing so challenge and transform understanding. But ultimately, I am convinced, talking across difference depends on an ability to listen, to question, and to stand "ready to pursue" the complexities of other people's reading of the world.

8 *Taking Rhetorical Agency*

Cornel West calls his readers to affirm the agency and capability of the powerless—of the socially disenfranchised people that we tend to represent as victims, clients, or objects of someone else's oppression or our charity.

> The most significant theme of the new cultural politics of difference is the agency, capacity and ability of human beings who have been culturally degraded, politically oppressed and economically exploited by bourgeois liberal and communist illiberal status quos. This theme neither romanticizes nor idealizes marginalized peoples. Rather it accentuates their humanity and tries to attenuate the institutional constraints on their life-chances for surviving and thriving. (1993, p. 29)

It seems contradictory: how do we acknowledge the reality of "degraded, oppressed, or exploited" people—who are clearly not the masters of their own fate—and still assert the presence of "agency, capacity and ability"?

> (T)he new cultural politics of difference affirms the perennial quest for the precious ideals of individuality and democracy by digging deep into the depths of human particularities and social specificities in order to construct new kinds of connections, affinities and communities across empire, nation, region, race, gender, age and sexual orientation. (West, 1993, p. 29)

West's assertion is a classic statement of prophetic pragmatism—an unflinching critique of injustice driven by the prophet's sustaining vision of an alternative reality based on love and justice and the pragmatist's unflagging search for the options and alternatives that allow transformative praxis. It asks us to walk into a contested space and do our work in the midst of conflict and contradiction. But just what is this "agency" of the powerless? And how could the privileged ever contribute to representing it without co-opting it? How could they (we) do so in a way that makes a difference within the activities and institutions that deny agency?

What Counts as Agency?

A confrontation over a teen-authored Community Learning Center publication suggests some conflicting notions of what should count as agency in everyday life. The teens in Raymond's group were trying to write about drugs—to other teens from a teenager's point of view.[1] This was no easy task combining straight talk from rival points of view pro and con with a text teens would read. Raymond was working on an ambitious plan that included a playscript, a flashback, and a dialogue with the reader. Two weeks from completion, when his mentor was called to jury duty and a sudden summer-job opportunity took Raymond away from the project, Raymond resisted the temptation to simplify his task and came in alone after his job to finish the text. He didn't get to join the final editing session, but the published document (which used the text as he had written and formatted it) celebrated Raymond's impressive piece of work despite its rough edges.[2] The text started out with the dramatis personae: John, a friend on drugs, and Writer Raymond's alter ego, a character called Ray (see fig. 8.1) (Musgrove, 1992). Across the page was a picture of a self-confident young man, dark skinned, dark shirt, dark glasses, with the byline he had chosen: "Raymond Musgrove, Playwrite."

We were delighted when Raymond's English teacher came to the Community Conversation. Seeing these self-confident, articulate, published *writers* standing up, initiating a dialogue with adults and the neighborhood alternately pleased and shocked teachers; it revealed capacities they had not seen in their classrooms. We had seen the Pygmalion effect follow such events: teachers' expectations and encouragement went up and so did the students' self-esteem and performance. Publicly representing these teenagers as rhetorical agents, local knowledge experts, and decision makers influenced both the teenagers and the authority figures around them. But not always in a way we intended. Shortly after the Conversation, the word came back to us. Raymond's English teacher was angry. Raymond's unedited text, with its mix of unconventional punctuation and dialogue, Black English Vernacular, and garden-variety errors of grammar and spelling was proof enough of her contention: we had puffed him up. It seems he now thought he was a "writer." And this had made her job—of showing him that he indeed was not—twice as difficult.

The most important debates over grand abstractions like agency are conducted in quite local fields of action with their own specific terms of engagement. In the playing field of literacy studies, rhetoric, and composition

Fig. 8.1 Raymond Musgrove's column from *Let's Talk about Drugs*

A Teenager That Needs Help but Don't Know How To Face It

by Raymond Musgrove

JOHN a boy who uses crack that he thinks that the problem in his life would be solve.
RAY a teenager who care about other people like John.

(Boy name John Kennedy in a locker-room sitting on a wooden bench then out in the open John pulls out a bag of white powder which we know as cocaine. As soon as John was about to snort the cocaine, one of the school football coaches comes in, and when the coach saw what was about to happen, he quickly jump at John saying stop and stared at John. Well, as for John, he was kind of in a shock at the moment. As the coach gave him the facts about drugs, John just turned his back. And when the coach got done preaching as we teenagers may say he whip this on John, "If you don't get no help for your drug problem you'll be off the team faster than you got on it." As John coach goes toward the exit John sits on the bench speechless.)

Scene I

(Ray, one of John friends, well, he not just his friend he is best-friend who likes to help others who's overhears the shouting down the hall of John's football coach so he decides to give John a little visit.)

Ray: A, John. What this I overhear about you using drugs
John: What is it to you? What do you care.
Ray: Well you are my best friend and I concern about you and if have you had a problem I should know about it.
John: Why are you so concern about me? We're not related or anything and plus where do you get of saying that I have a problem (laughing)?
Ray: Yes I think you have a problem. If you don't know what your problem is I shall state some examples.
John: Yeah, name one if you can.
Ray: Do you remember the time when you were at my house I think it was just last week when you pulled out some white powder called cocaine?
John: So you think you're so hot let me tell you about yourself well I really don't like people telling me what to do and trying to run my life and I don't need none of your pep talk about you trying to help me because all you doing is putting more pressure on me. So if you really want to help me why don't you back off.

(Ray walks off as John tells him to butt out. I guess John doesn't want any help, don't you think.)

Scene II

(Two hours later John is now at home in bedroom he begin to get very tired so he decides to stretch out on his bed a few minutes later John is fully sleep as John begins to dream he begin to dream about when Ray was trying to help him with his problem in the locker-room.)

[JOHN'S DREAM]

Ray: A, John. What this I overhear about you using drugs. Well, you are my best-friend and I concern

about you. And if you have a problem I should know
about it.
(John would like to say something but can't talk. All he
could do is move around. In the moment of time John
begins:) I don't need any help. I don't need any help.
(Then Ray begins to say:) Get up out the bed and look at
yourself in the mirror. Look at yourself. Your body is
starting to get wrinkled and your muscletone is starting
to get very saggy and look at this catch. (Ray throws
John a football and John tries to catch the football, but
his reflexes were not 100%, and plus I don't think he
had the muscle to catch the ball.) John, guess you
didn't take your rock today. Here have one.
(Soon as John tries to reach out to get the rock he begins to
fall forward and he starts to tumble on the the floor.
Then he wakes up from his mysterious dream saying to
himself:) I need help.

Scene III

The next morning John sees Ray at his locker so he
goes over to Ray.)

John: A, Ray, look here for a minute. I was thinking about
what you had said to me about me having a problem. I
finally realize that I had a problem, and you know
what. I want to thank you for pointing out my problem
before it got worst than it already is.
Ray: Since now you are before me, do want some help???
John: I would be glad to get some help because you know
what? Yesterday I had this strangest dream and it
showed me what I was going to look like in the future
if I didn't get off drugs right away. (John begins to
finish telling his story about his dream.)

* * * * *

*What do you think as the reader of this play: What's
going to happen to John after the weeks of treat-
ment? Which one do you think will happen to John
in the future?*

*• Will John forget all about Ray before school out
and start to use drugs all over again?*

*• Will John go to some of his helping classes, then
after a short period of time will he decide to think
that these classes are not for him?*

*• Will John go head and try to get some help so he
won't look like what he would look like in his dream,
and will he try to listen to other people who's trying
to help him instead of ignoring them?*

*If you were wonder what happen to John, well, John
finished his classes of his drug problem. Now he is
going to the twelfth grade. He is now the capt. of the
football team and he is helping others who is having
the same problem that John had.*

teaching, the agency question often becomes: so what does it take to be seen as a *writer*? What counts as rhetorical agency? From one point of view, it is easy to be appalled at Raymond's repressive or authority-conscious teacher and secretly pleased at the CLC's small act of resistance, assertion, and support. The publication, the photo, the public event were strong affirmations of Raymond's standing as a writer and agent in his community's response to drugs.

Yet we must consider a strong rival hypothesis posed by many composition scholars who argue that what minority students like Raymond need most is to learn the strategies of academic discourse—the tricks of this mainstream trade. If the path to empowerment is through the language of power, where does the illusion of agency (in the absence of real material agency) get you? Or as one of my most outspoken black mentors put it, "I mean, this literacy is what you're using to present these texts to a board. But if you keep doing this kind of literacy, you'll never be on a board" (Long, 1994, p. 197).

From this perspective, expressive personal writing may be appropriate for engaging children or building self-esteem in the marginally literate. It is charming when seventh graders proudly read from the author's chair; it can be heartwarming or painfully moving when unlettered project mothers "publish" their one-hundred-word essays in the *Journal of Ordinary People* (whose motto is, "Every person is a philosopher"). But the voice of real-politik comes back to taunt us. Within the institutional context of school, especially college composition, these pretenders to the status of *writer* will soon be found out and renamed. In the words of the formidable dean at the University of California at Los Angeles who dismissed Mike Rose's program for underprepared college students, these are "the truly illiterate among us" (1989, p. 2). The vogue in basic-writing programs for teaching underprepared students to freewrite or gain fluency before control comes in for the same criticism (Delpit, 1986).

In composition studies, this definition of a *writer* as one in control of an elite discourse stands behind the preoccupation with academic discourse and the scholarship devoted to exploring its features, analyzing how to teach it, and studying the students who don't have it. Students qualify as rhetorical agents when they can control such elite discourse. In denying this status to the author of a nonstandard text, we assume we are just being realistic, passing along lessons he will learn soon enough in the school of hard knocks.

The dilemma of how to represent Raymond (as playwright/writer/agent or as unskilled youth/learner/pretender-to-literacy) is hardly new. The problematic agency of the vulnerable is posed by Charles Dickens's David Copperfield, who begins his autobiography wondering, "Whether I shall turn out to be the hero of my own life, or whether that station will be held by anybody else, these pages must show" (1849/1950, p. 1). Our popular if exclusionary notions of what counts as agency are rooted in these high-stakes images of writers, rhetors, and heroes and heroines—individuals in control of their lives, their medium, and their impact on others. When the script calls for an agent or hero/heroine, marginalized teenagers really needn't apply. On the other hand, intercultural inquiry positions people to listen, learn, collaborate, and construct knowledge jointly by asserting the authority and expertise of those marginalized partners. So how do the privileged partners look beyond these social scripts to see a thinker, choice maker, holder of values; how do we become attuned to the agency of Others? Consider some of the familiar images of agency associated with the scripts of individualism and resistance and how they differ from rhetorical agency—and the kind of action we may need to teach ourselves to see.

Agency as Power and Control—*The Script of Isolated Individualism*

In the grand narrative of American individualism, agency belongs to the actor, the hero or heroine—the cowboy, the gangster, the vigilante, the Horatio Alger. He (nearly always, a "he") operates with uncompromised independence. Obstacles exist merely to test his power and be overcome. If he is the underdog, the oppressed, so much the better, for he can respond with a grand gesture of opposition. Barriers exist simply to reveal his acts of iron will, independence, and resistance. The agent/hero is captain of his fate, the master of his soul. This is the heady stuff of novels and movies.[3]

However, for everyday use, within institutions like the office or classroom, agency depends on one's power to control or least influence external realities—to be a mover and shaker—or at least to attempt to do so out of conscious, willed choice. We "take agency"—we wrest the microphone or take the floor or wield the power for the pen—as an act of power and intentionality in the face of opposition. But here's the catch—action without the perception of control doesn't seem to count. The emotional outbursts of women, defiant teenagers, or angry workers are easily dismissed as mere reactions. The hero may not overcome the world, but he acts with the certainty of masterful self-control.

This grand narrative of individualism is both invoked and denied in the CLC publication. The sober pose of a broad-shouldered, young black man in shades atop the caption, "Raymond Musgrove, Playwrite," is a gesture of such agency—a playfully defiant assertion of status and authority. But the gesture is quickly undercut in mainstream eyes by the "uncontrolled" prose that follows.

Ironically, the agency of Raymond was also dismissed by another group of readers because his prose was not "black" or "street" or unconventional enough. Because he appropriates some of the tools (but not all the conventions) of an essay and a playscript, because slang and Black English Vernacular is mixed with standard schooled talk, without the insider talk of "real" drug users, his writing can be dismissed as not sufficiently "authentic." That is, it does not fit the image of either a writer or an authentically resistant homeboy. Discourse conventions, James Gee would argue, are designed to do just this—to sort out the insiders from the pretenders (1989). They lead us to represent people in terms of the discourses they *don't* exhibit or control, in terms of deficits rather than intentions and actions. And in this case, Raymond fails to exhibit the markers of individualism and power associated with black-identity politics.

This is not to say that speaking the discourse of an "authentic" oppressed individual would work for him in the end either. As feminists discovered, women who spoke with the authority of their experience and passion were represented as being merely and only voices of emotion. Just as expressive writing was marginalized in composition circles by the juggernaut of academic discourse, the voice of emotive authenticity can be easily dismissed as a marker of agency. Our schemas can account for willful assertion by attributing it to children or the naïve, simple native. Though both exhibit will, they are denied the status of reflective reasoned actors, of agents.

The public discourse surrounding poverty and welfare reform is a vivid case in point in its willingness to subordinate and objectify "needy" clients as the problem and to vilify recipients as "welfare queens" but reluctance to entertain their voices and perspectives. Lorraine Higgins and Lisa Brush's (2006) richly elaborated study of women trying to enter this debate defines this denial of rhetorical agency in terms of classical ethos.

> *Ethos*, as a strategy of persuasion, refers to a speaker's perceived reputation—her prudence, virtue, and demonstration of moral purpose through action, in short, her *character* (*Rhetoric* III. xvi. 8). Establishing *ethos* is particularly difficult for welfare recipients, however, because dominant discourses impugn their character as a means of dismissing their perspectives and justifying punitive policies. In establishing *ethos* through their rhetoric, welfare recipients have to challenge dominant representations of themselves. They can only do so by connecting with the substantive and moralistic categories of the dominant discourse, but they have to do so without reiterating its stigmatizing terms. (p. 698)

The rhetorical situation creates a double bind for these speakers. Not only are they without "standing" but (as we saw in the community conversations around curfew) they must also connect with the dominant discourse to be recognized, even though their expert, situated knowledge is best expressed in the easily dismissed discourse of narrative.

It seems that the cultural narrative of individualism (even if one has an "authentic" identity) is unlikely to legitimate a marginalized speaker and writer. With its focus on willpower, testosterone, independence, and control, this script is unlikely to cast Raymond as the hero of his own life. Moreover, this litmus test for agency has a limitation for understanding agency as a literate act. When it sets up its simple dichotomy that separates the agent from his opposing forces, it fails to acknowledge that the conflicting values, assumptions, goals, and ideologies a writer must confront are not always "out there." They are often inside as well, in the complexities in one's own thinking and feelings called into confrontation by the effort of understanding. As I suggest shortly, this familiar model of agency fails to account for the deliberative actions of everyday people attempting to make meaning in the face of genuine internal and external conflict.

Agency as Resistance—The Script of Ideology

The image of agency that poses the strongest counter to individualism is another grand narrative built around ideology. In the popular account, the "author's chair" is usurped by the figure of Discourse and/or Ideology. Critical theory dramatizes this shift with Michel Foucault's succinct obituary for the author who "does not exist" (1977). In its simplified form, this image turns the script of individualism on its head: the agent/author figure is replaced by social forces, material realities, and power relations that coalesce in the construction of ideologies. These, in turn, shape the meanings that speak *through* the writer. Individuals, authors, actors, and agents are rewritten as subjected subjects. Writers either appropriate or are appropriated by the discourse, which circulates as knowledge. Agency in this script is reduced from action *for* to acts of defense *against.*[4]

Critical theorists struggling with the deterministic implications of this position would rescue agency by relocating it in the language of resistance. In the foreword to such an effort by cultural critic Paul Smith, John Mowitt notes, "Agency, as the activating dynamic of political resistance has been thrown out of theory with the working class" (Mowitt, 1988, p. xi). Such a decisive move is justified by the assumption that the term *individual* refers to the "illusion of whole and coherent personal organization, . . . a term ideologically designed to give the false impression that human beings are free and self-determining" (pp. xxv–xxvii). It is not clear exactly who takes this naïvely extreme position. Nevertheless, the alternative for Smith is to see human agents or "subjects" as the shifting intersection of multiple, provisional, and often competing subject positions invoked by discourses of race, gender, and class. This conflict can then be "theorized as society's perpetual production of resistance to itself" (Mowitt, 1988, p. xv).

Smith's attempt to theorize a justification of agency within the discourse of critical theory is a thoughtful theoretical in-game that, in the end, produces a rather anemic vision of agency and human action.[5] Not only is agency limited to a process of resistance, it is also mounted not by a human subject but by competing ideologies that appear to have assumed the Author's chair. This is not an agency of constructive or ethical acts. Perhaps more disturbing, the image of the human agent that does emerge in this picture seems to bear a much closer resemblance to cultural critics like Smith, Julia Kristeva, or Roland Barthes—someone engaged in the elite discourse of critical theorizing—than to any of the everyday people in West's account.[6] As Lester Faigley points out, postmodern theory has failed to produce a theory of agency that can move from critique to political action (1992, p. 39). My concern is more narrowly focused on what our theories lead us to see. Exchanging the shopworn schema of the autonomous individual for one that dramatizes the play of discourse and ideology may end up blinding us to the presence of actual acts of rhetorical agency *within* a constraining and contingent world.

Another line of approach from rhetorical criticism invites us to embed rather than eliminate the individual. Dilip Gaonkar critiques the humanist paradigm for its assumption that "the agency of rhetoric is always reducible to the conscious and strategic thinking of the rhetor" (1993, p. 275). For example, a study of Charles Darwin's *Origin of the Species* built on this "agent-centered model of 'intentional persuasion'" would assume that Darwin's use of religious metaphor cleverly anticipates a skeptical audience response. By contrast, in Gaonkar's "intertextual" reading, the text reflects *not only* an author's own conflicted and changing understanding of the implications of his science *but also* the hand of available social and linguistic resources (that are at times in conflict with one another).[7] This image of what I would call an "embedded agency" offers a more balanced way to analyze *texts* in their social and ideological context. It is less helpful, however, for understanding, much less supporting, the rhetorical agency of *writers*—especially noncanonical ones.

For theorists committed not only to theory but also to change, the various scripts of ideology create a genuine dilemma. When critical theory tries to talk about colonialism, for instance, it finds itself in what Henry Louis Gates describes as a double bind.

> You can empower discursively the native, and open yourself to charges of downplaying the epistemic (and literal) violence of colonialism; or play up the absolute nature of colonial domination, and be open to charges of negating the subjectivity and agency of the colonized, thus textually replicating the repressive operations of colonialism. (1991, p. 662)

For example, the inner-city women Ellen Cushman (1998) describes maneuver through the asymmetrical power relations of a city bureaucracy, both using and being controlled by the institutional languages that control welfare and housing for the poor. When a gatekeeper bureaucrat simply assumes that Raejone can't read and takes over reading the form, Raejone describes it as, "The whole time I be thinking to myself, 'What? 'Cause I'm poor, I can't read, you f——ing bitch?" When the caseworker then fills in optional information on race without asking consent, all Raejone can do is assert her intelligence by drawing attention to the fine print that states her right to choose, challenging the caseworker's procedure, and demanding an explanation for what use that racial information would be put to. After the encounter, Raejone complains bitterly, "its an everyday fight for us to get simple respect" (p. 158). Does this limited, compromised rhetorical action constitute agency? Or what about the women who seek out Ellen's help to craft a phone script in "White English" for apartment hunting because "that's what landlords want to hear." "It ain't," Lucy says, "that *I* think White is more respectable than Black. But I think they going to think that way" (p. 85).

Cushman is acutely aware that her study of the "struggle and the tools" of poor women has revealed few indicators of power, control, or the resistance identified with theories of critical consciousness. But she locates the problem not in the women but in the markers *we* look for.

> Critical theories have too narrowly defined what counts as critical consciousness. Because many scholars believe that critical awareness leads to unified social movements, sweeping structural changes, or radical shifts in consciousness, they disregard other forms of social and linguist agency found at the point where power is applied daily. (1998, p. xx)

An anonymous reviewer of Cushman's book manuscript illustrated this point, asserting, "Critical consciousness signifies an awareness of the structural nature of oppression which leads to collective action to challenge the status quo." Cushman acknowledges that women she studied showed little interest in this standard of collective action.

> But the problem here isn't with the community members' lack of political awareness and savvy—the problem is with this definition . . . which fails to reflect social realities where critical consciousness does not always lead to collective action nor to unified class struggle. (1998, p. xx)

In opening up "the possibility of seeing and appreciating the nuances of daily political struggles," Cushman's accounts show us "how individuals can both accommodate and undermine, both placate and rebuff, both obey and challenge while they negotiate constraining social structures" (1998, pp. xx–xxi).

Recognizing Agency in Others

Teaching Ourselves to See

Acknowledging agency in the actions of someone else is not the automatic outcome of political correctness, liberal beliefs, or goodwill, especially if that someone is perceived to be nonauthoritative—low in the status/power hierarchy, a subordinate, less educated, a basic writer, a youth. Of course, the readers who discounted the authority of Raymond's nonstandard or nonstreet and unedited prose may present a special case. So when Susan Lawrence (1996) wanted to study interpretive strategies college readers might bring to community literacy texts and to intercultural readings more generally, she used texts that included the cogently argued, Standard English account of Shirley Lyle's response to police harassment discussed in chapter 2.

Lawrence asked eight paid students, unconnected with community-literacy projects and representing a spread in age, gender, and discipline, to think aloud as they read the text, which included occasional prompts to report, "How do you interpret the text at this point?"[8] The four widely used patterns of sense making Lawrence observed reveal how readers represented not only the text but also their relationship to and image of its author. Faced with an unfamiliar text by an unknown teenage author, the default strategy of one group of readers was to treat it as a writing sample. Homing in on text mechanics and ignoring main points, readers represented it as a "correctable" text. The writer they constructed was presumed to be in control of neither the text nor its meanings. In an apparent contrast, other readers saw it as a sample of creative writing, focusing on its literary moves, which "set up the background; it's a classic introduction," and even "We see the introduction of the savior element, the epic circle's gone fully around." Like error-focused reading, this, too, fails to engage the writer's claims. "Rather than stunting interpretive efforts," Lawrence notes, "this one encourages it, . . . [but] it, too, has complex consequences if the goal is authentic intercultural engagement" (p. 11).

A second interpretive move she called the "goodwill" strategies shows why. Some readers relied on empathizing moves, seeing the writer as a person "just like me" or

> just a regular kind of teenager who's going through regular kinds of experiences, experimenting with taboo things. . . . yeah, I can identify with this, I remember as a teenager going through this, I remember drinking, out in a field with my friends, and getting caught, so you know. (p. 14)

The assumption of identity can lay the ground for a strong intercultural relationship, but do the experiences of suburban, white, college students match Shirley's vision of "being hassled by authority figures"? Lawrence argues, "To read someone else's experience through one's own may confound crucial distinctions between experiences; in this case that distinction is racism" (1996, p. 14).

The flip side of empathy was a distancing move, which acknowledged a potential gulf between experiences—but went on to elaborate by importing a schema of the Other in which the author, Shirley, becomes someone "who has to figure out where their next meal's going to come from" in contrast to "someone who lives a happy life."

> Although [this reader] sees some of the message clearly, there is no indication in Shirley's text that she lives in a not-so-nice-home, or that her family cannot put food on the table. . . . When sympathy moves come into play they go hand-in-hand with schemas that call up stereotypes—in the service of understanding a distant reality. . . . [They also set] up a particular relationship between reader and writer. The reader/ the sympathizer has the authority to construct the writer/the other as needy. The power relationship that comes with the territory, then, is one in which the sympathized-with is pitiable and without resources, and the sympathizer is secure, privileged—and distant. (p. 16)

Lawrence makes it clear that she does not exclude herself from "the group of practitioners who put interpretive moves from elite discourses into play." What matters is that these strategies can "hinder engagement at two critical junctures: first, they allowed readers to avoid the writers' main points, and second, they allowed readers to build representations that did not acknowledge the writers' agency" (p. 18).

The challenge here is to read against the grain of our own, inevitably present, easily activated, interpretative schemas. How can we uncover the interpretive agency of a nonauthoritative writer—to see the *argument* they are making, to see an alternative experiential *reality* they may offer, and more fundamentally to see them as the bona fide, authoritative *interpreter* of their own and their community's lived experience?

Why Does This Matter?

One may, of course, ask, why does this matter? When West asserts that the "agency, capacity and ability" of marginalized people is the "most significant theme of the new politics of difference," he is speaking as a black philosopher and cultural critic addressing other "culture workers" (1993, p. 29). But is learning to see and represent this agency *really* the job of community-literacy educators, mentors, community partners, or privileged activists? Moreover, evidence of rhetorical agency (i.e., of meaning making that deals with conflict, deliberates, builds negotiated understandings, or makes value-based decisions) may be difficult to observe in the actions of people who are so patently not in control of their lives and situation or are not mobilized in collective resistance. Why should the privileged partners (the university mentors, teachers, or researchers) go to the effort of uncovering, acknowledging, and representing these veiled and discounted indications of agency in others?

Perhaps the most fundamental reason is that *teaching ourselves to see and affirm* the deep springs of agency in others is a prerequisite to dialogue. Martin Buber calls this entering into an I/Thou (rather than in I/It) relationship with another person (1958). But such affirmation is also central to public discourse in scripts as different as those of Paulo Freire and Jürgen Habermas.[9] Freire's Christian, Marxist-based dialogue calls for open access to the public sphere in relations that are free from subordination or domination. Even teachers are partners in a joint inquiry with their students (1970/1985). Habermas (1962/1989), on the other hand, is preoccupied with the quality of the dialogue, not access. Nevertheless, in his ideal of communicative action, differences in status and power are bracketed—respecting the argument, indifferent to the arguer—in order for people to reach an unconstrained understanding shaped by reason, not force.

Discerning these indications of rhetorical agency matters on another level because we read them as signs of something even more important—as the outward indications of an activated inner life. They are the evidence of the deliberative consciousness, the heightened awareness, and the deep interiority we attribute to ourselves. And on the basis of these signs, we attribute this same sort of complex, valuing, decision-making inner life to others.

So what happens when the marginalized, the vulnerable, the young, the poor, or the powerless fail to exhibit the signs of will and control that count for agency? What happens when these unauthorized Others are represented in our texts and our minds as victims, patients, or clients, as failed learners or illiterates instead of agents? One result is that we become less and less likely to attribute a significant inner life to people who fail to flash the proper signs. Even when we sincerely and staunchly assert the equality and humanity of excluded Others in principle, our representations of writers like Raymond may undercut such claims. Representations that depend on elite standards of competence and control or of political consciousness and resistance won't pick up the subtler signals of awareness, deliberation, and choice. They may simply obliterate the fact that the production of tangled grammar can coexist with a reflective life of the mind. We fail to see Raymond as a full-fledged agent—that is, someone to whom we ascribe a deliberative inner life, whose choices we respect as choices, capable of being the hero of his own life.

Mike Rose saw this blindness at work in the emerging politics and pedagogy of remediation, in what he called

> the disturbing tendency to perceive the poor as *different* in some basic way from the middle and upper classes—the difference now being located in the nature of the way they think and use language. . . . They lack a logical language or reason in ways that limit intellectual achievement, or, somehow, process information dysfunctionally. . . . We seem to have a need as a society to explain poor performance by reading deep into the basic stuff of those designated as others: into their souls, or into the deep recesses of their minds, or into the very ligature of their language. (1989, pp. 221–22)

The grand narratives of individual action and collective resistance can blind us to the distinctive forms "agency, capacity, and ability" may take in nonheroic, ideologically enmeshed lives within the press of limiting situations. With Ellen Cushman, Lorraine Higgins, Lisa Brush, and Glynda Hull, I want to argue that when we fail to see the markers of agency within a Raymond or Lucy, the problem may not be in them but in us and the indicators we are looking for. Affirming others can mean teaching ourselves to see and represent what the popular scripts deny.

Agency as Dialogic Action—A Philosophical Script

In trying to imagine a more expansive and inclusive notion of agency, various theoretical and philosophical discussions have focused on *dialogicality* as way to capture the responsive and interactive nature of human action.

Mikhail Bakhtin's insight into intensely dialogic orientation of language, utterances, and thought argues that the "word" always emerges from prior discourse. It finds its object "already as it were overlain with qualifications, open to dispute, changed with value ... of alien words that have already been spoken about it. It is entangled, shot through with shared thoughts, points of view, alien value judgments and accents" (1981, p. 276). In addition, "the word in living conversation is directly, blatantly, oriented toward a future answer-word: it provokes an answer, anticipates it and structures itself in the answer's direction" (p. 280). This is not to dismiss the role of intentional action: "The word in language is half someone else's. It becomes one's own only when the speaker populates it with his own intention, his own accent, when he appropriates the word, adapting it to his own semantic and expressive intention" (p. 293).

What would it mean to take agency if agency is intentional but not independent? If it were not merely an action but a transaction in "an elastic environment of other, alien words" (Bakhtin, 1981, p. 276)? What if you are a marginalized speaker in an elite discourse where those words "are already populated with the social intentions of others [and the speaker must compel] them to serve his own intentions, to serve a second master" (p. 300)? The answers, as both Bakhtin and Lev S. Vygotsky suggest, will be found in looking at socially situated action, including the discourses and material conditions that mediate it.[10] Community literacy as one such site allows us to see a particular kind of rhetorical agency in action. But before we turn to that close examination, I want to put it in the context of three recent theoretical discussions of agency that use a dialogic framework to reveal its embedded, responsive, and reflective nature.

The Embedded Agent

Contemporary rhetoric needs to make good on its traditional promise: to offer a credible art of performance and pedagogy. But to do so it needs a working theory of agency, which neither the illusions of humanistic individualism nor the postmodern erasure of that individual can supply. Some contemporary scholars move out of this dichotomy by shifting attention from the intentional, expressive agent/rhetor to the action—that is, to the situated rhetorical performance itself and its relation to an enabling cloud of contingencies.[11] In this image, an act of rhetorical agency can not be separated from the necessary material conditions, such as, time, place, people, or topic, that allow a speaker to occupy what is called an agentive space. And unlike images preoccupied with an individual's intention or skill, it attends to the consequences of rhetorical action. A performative model acknowledges both the dancer and the dance, asserting the relationship between social, cultural, material, and individual forces by which an "embedded agency" shapes rhetorical action.

However, a difficult question remains, to which we return shortly. Studies of performance make it clear that those agentive spaces for enacting rhetorical agency are normally opened up by those with cultural capital to others like themselves, that is, to speakers who play by mainstream rules and by its conventions of literate performance (which include the gender and class of the performer). Can these mainstream accounts of socially situated actor/ rhetors resolve the problem Cushman and Lawrence raise? Will these accounts prompt us to see, much less appreciate, a more indirect, nonstandard performance—one that doesn't fit our expectations of conventional discourse or outcomes? Is the agentive space of the author's chair to be limited to what we think of as the socially authorized speaker?

Rhetoric is not alone in seeking more expansive accounts that can speak of individual action and communal connectedness in the same breath. In philosophy and theology, Charles Taylor and H. Richard Niebuhr place rhetoric (in the form of interpretation and dialogue) at the heart of their visions of moral agency. They help us see rhetorical agency in the context of social ethics of the sort both Rose and West raised earlier.

The Agent as Reflective Meaning Maker

In his philosophical inquiry "What Is Human Agency?" Charles Taylor asks what it means to be a fully human agent in a world that does not bend to our will. In his scenario, the old-fashioned hero of individualism may be no different from any other creature, merely acting to achieve his desires, based on a utilitarian calculation of costs and benefits. The mark of a responsible human agent, on the other hand, is the capacity to "evaluate" desires, to reflect on "the qualitative worth of different desires," with "such categories as higher and lower, virtuous and vicious, more and less fulfilling, more and less refined, profound and superficial, noble and base" (1985a, p. 16). This kind of "reflective self-evaluation" demands what Taylor calls a "vocabulary of worth" that lets us be articulate about our choices and in deliberation with others (1985a, p. 24).

Should the college teacher, in Taylor's example, pack up to take a job in Nepal (and a leap into the unknown) in order to renew his sources of creativity, to win rejuvenation by courage and decisive action? Or is it better to hang in, honor standing loyalties, accepting that nothing in life is won without discipline? The answer depends on the difficult job of weighing the worth of these desires, not according to a simple calculation of benefits or a set of received values but according to their worth to the agent.

> The question at issue concerns which is the truer, more authentic, more illusion-free interpretation [of the situation], and which on the other hand involves a distortion of the meaning things have for me. (1985a, p. 27)

Such questions are also choices about identity. In choosing to be daring or disciplined, to seek or to stand firm, we are identifying ourselves with "the kind of life and the kind of subject that these desires properly belong to" (p. 25).

What I find so compelling in Taylor's image of agency is his sense of how difficult it is to articulate a vocabulary of worth and to make such reflective deliberative choices.

> There are more or less adequate, more or less truthful, more self-clairvoyant or self-deluding interpretations. . . . [A]n articulation can be wrong. . . . a distortion of the reality concerned. . . . Our attempts to formulate what we hold important must, like descriptions, strive to be faithful to something. But what they strive to be faithful to is not an independent object with a fixed degree and manner of evidence, but rather a largely inarticulate sense of what is of decisive importance (p. 38). . . . Moral agency . . . requires some kind of reflexive awareness of the standards one is living by (or failing to live by). (1985a, p. 103)

So what is this philosophical image of agency? Taylor rejects an "unproblematic" view of the agent as a goal-directed actor whose humanity demands our respect because of "his power to make a life-plan and act upon it" (1985a, p. 104). The marker of agency is not action, control, or even choice. Rather, it is the indication of engagement in this *deliberative, interpretative, constructive encounter* with a "largely inarticulate sense of what is of decisive importance" (p. 38).

> Agents are people for whom things matter, who are subjects of significance. . . . [I]n our interpretation of [their] personal capacities the centre is no longer the power to plan, but rather the openness to certain matters of significance. This is now what is essential to personal agency. (pp. 104–5)

In the attempt to articulate what matters, we remain open to "radical evaluation" (pp. 41–42). And through articulation what we strive to create is not consensus but common meanings, which are the basis of community (1985b, p. 39).

The Agent as an Interpreting Responder

Like Taylor, H. Richard Niebuhr describes an agent as a "being in charge of his conduct" (rather than other people's actions). And he, too, finds something missing in two dominant, traditional images of the human agent. One he calls *man-the-maker* (who acting for an end or goal and seeking the good or ideal fashions both things and himself) and the other *man-the-citizen* (who living under the law and adhering to the socially legislated right finds selfhood in community) (1963, pp. 48–54). In *The Responsible Self*, Niebuhr argues for an alternative, interactional image of moral agency in *man-the-responder* (who, engaging in dialogue, acts in response to action upon him, defining himself by the nature of his responses) (p. 56). For Niebuhr, "the symbol of responsibility contains, as it were, hidden references, allusions, and similes which are in the depths of our mind as we grope for understanding of ourselves and toward definition of ourselves in action" (p. 48).

The script of response as he describes it highlights two critical events: First, our actions are an answer to action upon us (this is not about an isolated individual); however, they do so "in accordance with our *interpretation* of such action" (p. 57; italics added). Mere reactions are not the work of moral agency. Secondly, the action of response is dialogic in Bakhtin's sense. It is taken, Niebuhr says,

> as anticipation of further response . . . of answers to our answers. An agent's action is like a statement in a dialogue; . . . it anticipates objections, confirmations, and corrections. . . . Responsibility lies in the agent who stays with his action, who accepts the consequences of the form of reactions and looks forward in a present deed to the continued interaction. . . . [A]nd all of this is in a continuing community of agents. (1963, pp. 61–65)

Niebuhr's and Taylor's visions of the agent as a responsive, responsible, choice maker depict, to my mind, actively rhetorical beings. Moreover, they offer some striking parallels to the rhetorical practice of community literacy and its version of rhetorical agency. In these scripts, what counts for agency is not merely interpretation or self-expression but an act of *negotiated* interpretation and understanding that *has chosen to respond* to multiple voices—including those of history, context, values, and imagined outcomes.[12] Moreover, these rhetorical agents are prepared to *go public*, to engage in a dialogue that listens, speaks, and expects a response to which they are prepared to respond. Even though Taylor focuses on the choices and criteria of worth agents use to make decisions, he and Niebuhr offer a vivid picture of a conflictual, constructive process of meaning making around matters of significance—a process that is personal *and* community based.

Rhetorical Agency in Community Literacy

Community literacy allows us to observe a related but distinctive process that I have been calling *rhetorical agency*, which operates as *a performative public practice of interpretation and dialogue.* Shaped by its roots in rhetoric and prophetic pragmatism, community literacy has much in common with the performative process described by contemporary rhetoricians and the reflective processes found in Taylor and Niebuhr. However, like the praxis of action/reflection in Freire (1970/1985), community literacy is continually and centrally concerned with the problem of difference.

Our standard ways of talking about agency as the work of an "authorized" speaker, standing in an "agentive space" dealing with a "subject of signifi-cance" might seem to rope off the Author's Chair as a reserved place, if not for Taylor's philosophers, at least for speakers with some sort of conventional "standing." Community literacy, on the other hand, foregrounds everyday people, engaged in a collaborative, intercultural inquiry into matters of lived significance. Consider problems such as respect (and how to demand it from those in authority), a city curfew policy, or street drugs. The understand-ings people construct around these issues call for deliberation based on a vocabulary of worth that articulates *different* ways of valuing.

Community literacy makes a distinctive contribution to our thinking about agency and rhetoric by demonstrating that rhetorical agency can be the work of *everyday people.* Such people may indeed stand outside the discourses of privilege or power. But they are nevertheless carrying out the demand-ing work of discovery and change that is at the heart of rhetoric. The teens, tenants, mothers, low-wage workers, and college students of community literacy take *rhetorical* agency not just by speaking up but by *acts of engaged interpretation and public dialogue carried out in the service of personal and social transformation.*

Such agency differs from images found in mythic narratives and our scholarly portraits of rhetors from Cicero to Darwin to Sojourner Truth. The people of community literacy (from teens to tenants to college teachers) are not the movers and shakers who wrest the spotlight to galvanize radical social/intellectual change; nor are they the civic/corporate/scholarly "suits" whose social standing gives them a hearing, a readymade agentive space. And they are certainly not lonesome, individual voices in the wilderness.

Just as one swallow does not make a spring, one activist with an agenda (no matter how outspoken) does not achieve rhetorical agency in isolation. Agency exists in *relation* to forces that open up a space and time for action, to the conditions that give a hearing, and to the conventions and contin-gencies that shape a performance—over which the rhetor may have little control. The performance (or enactment) of rhetorical agency is in effect the *orchestration* of multiple elements and forces, which include the presence of a forum like the Community House, a body of people willing to become a public, and a collaborative process that can turn the intentions of multiple speakers into a public idea. Speakers like Raymond, Shirley, and Andre are not independent players in the script of their own rhetorical performance. *Rhetorical* agency, unlike an expressive act of will, is intensely relational; it is both internally and publicly dialogic.

Nevertheless—and this I will argue is crucial—these individual speakers can be the heroes and authors in their own story. Traditional, individualist humanism has celebrated the rhetor with Quintilian's image of "a good man speaking well." Community literacy, you might say, rewrites the script in decidedly relational terms as "an everyday person *rising* to reflective *engagement* over issues of shared concern." Rhetorical agency is an interdependent, not an independent action—however, choosing and rising to take it is a *significant* and a *personal* choice. In the same sense, our theories need to affirm both the personal *and* the public and both the individual *and* the collective aspects of a rhetorical action.

For the individual in this story, the script for attempting to take rhetorical agency within community literacy is remarkably demanding. Unlike the scripts based on power, control, or resistance, which might allow one simply to express, resist, or advocate a received position, this kind of rhetorical agency begins in engagement with contested issues and ideas in order to inquire, seek rivals, and construct a more expansive and shared intercultural understanding. Agency starts with the intellectual (and emotional) work of *engaged interpretation*, interpreting and responding to competing voices and forces in your community. In this script, one takes rhetorical agency (as an internal, yet social act) by building a negotiated understanding—that is, by rising to the level of personal meaning making and engaged interpretation that attempts to embrace complexity, contradiction, and difference in the voices of others.[13] Like Taylor's reflective deliberator, the writer as *rhetorical* agent goes beyond self-expression into a reflective engagement with contested meanings that have a shared and public significance.

It is this collaborative but also individual, intellectual, and ethical work of engagement that that gives the everyday person a claim to standing as a rhetorical agent. But such standing is only realized if one rises to the second, often intimidating requirement of rhetorical agency—*the act of going public*. This more visible aspect of rhetorical agency is the writer's attempt to engage in actual dialogue with a community in search of more transformative and transforming understandings. With these two acts, even the politically voiceless and economically powerless carry out the essential work of rhetoric—the dialogic work of discovery and change. Finally, as discussed in the next chapter, this script of rhetorical agency also offers a distinctive role for people of privilege, in which one affirms the agency of *others* by seeing, developing, and documenting it.

Engaged Interpretation: Building a Negotiated Understanding

Rhetorical agency starts with interpretation under pressure. The story of Raymond Musgrove, playwright, documents a revealing set of demands, values, choices, and negotiations.[14] First, Raymond is *not* the streetwise brotha' some readers wanted but a teenager trying to grow up on streets where danger and drugs are omnipresent, live options. He is not trying to speak as a gang member or drug-savvy insider but is trying to speak from where he stands to his peers to "help other teens think twice about using drugs." If mainstream readers get sidetracked by the stern demands of grammar, his peers were convinced that what mattered (i.e., the only way to get through to other teens) was imaginative, performative arguments that brought possibilities to life (and in some cases scared the daylights out of you). In response to the expanded array of voices/choices/forces Raymond chose to entertain, his text (see fig. 8.1) is also one of the longest and most rhetorically complex in the CLC booklet. It moves from a narrative in which the coach discovers John using drugs, to a scene 1 dialogue in which John angrily brushes off Ray's concerned attempt to get him to confront the problem. Scene 2 is a dream sequence in which John sees the consequences of his habit, and scene 3 is a reconciliation of the friends and John's recognition that he needs to get help. Then, in a surprising turn, the text moves from a playscript to an italicized direct address to the audience.

> *What do you think as the reader of this play: What's going to happen to John after the weeks of treatment? Which one do you think will happen to John in the future?*

The series of options starts with a reality statement: "Will John forget all about Ray before school out and start to use drugs all over again?" It ends with a clean John, now the twelfth-grade football captain and helping others. But the other possibilities and John's initial resistance stand as part of the reality.

What is most interesting about this elaborate rhetorical performance (with its mix of narrative, drama, flashbacks, gothic dream effects, teen talk, rival hypotheses, and dialogue with the reader) is the series of choices behind its production. And the fact it even exists.

Early on, at his mentor's encouragement, Raymond plunged into vigorously rivaling each move in his moral tale: "This chore of developing the characters' rival arguments was difficult and time-consuming, requiring Ray to painstakingly perform each character's lines as he generated them—all the while keeping in mind the global development of the play" (Flower, Long, & Higgins, 2000, p. 282). His complex plan often seemed "just too hard," and when the resistant John keeps throwing rivals and counter arguments back to Ray (the character) like rhetorical hardballs he must return, Raymond (the writer) struggles: "It's hard for me to get all that together in my head," he tells his mentor (p. 283). In short, Raymond has given himself what would be a challenging task for any writer.

The more remarkable part of the story comes in the final sessions. Just before the writers were about to edit, Raymond's mentor left for jury duty, and Raymond was chosen for a desirable precollege summer job. With his mentor's encouragement, he chose to stick to his plan, working at the computer with material from a taped planning session, writing all afternoon on his own and coming in before going to work to finish the piece by the deadline—three scenes, epilogue and all. Although some much-needed editing got short shrift, Raymond made significant and difficult choices, in the face of a demanding, self-designed rhetorical task with multiple, competing goals.

I think of Raymond as a significant example of the rhetorical agency that arises in the midst of negotiated meaning making—in part because he *doesn't* fully succeed in overcoming all difficulties, controlling his medium, exhibiting unruffled will, or achieving uncompromised success. What he does do is to persist in an engagement with multiple voices in order to tell the complex "truths" of "facing it"—trying to negotiate their meanings as he articulates his understanding. Although the apparent happy ending of his script displeased some readers, it was not a default choice. It was a deliberate assertion of possibility—perhaps the best he could frame at this time—in the face of some strong and competing rivals he had worked to consider. In short, he chose to approach a matter of significance as a dialogic agent and maker.

Going Public: Dialogue in Search of Transformation

This initial act of rhetorical agency, which gives Raymond the right to the Author's Chair, is the grounding for that second moment when a writer like Shirley rises from her chair to engage in public dialogue with her community. Once again, I want to be attuned not only to the big gestures of public performance but to the more subtle, local indicators—to those moments in which writers and speakers attempt to create a community dialogue, in which they listen, respond, and draw others, in one way or another, toward a transformative understanding. This is not an easy form of rhetorical agency to achieve under any circumstances. It requires nurturing, no matter who you are. But if such acts of agency do not use the discourse moves we recognize from academic or professional talk, or if they are of necessity indirect or culturally coded, maybe the first step university partners must take is to become attuned to the acts of rhetorical agency already around us. And the second is as rhetors in our own right to more publicly articulate and affirm what we see.

Raymond struggled so long with this piece because he was attempting to imagine the potential responses of his teen readers who, like John, might respond with reasonable skepticism and cynical dismissal but also unspoken hopes for a different future. The scripted dialogue is not just a textual hat rack for personal expression or a familiar just-say-no argument but part of a genuine engagement with a problem and with his imagined readers. The text is dialogic on many levels—in its dramatized discussion, in Raymond's effort to anticipate readers' responses, and in its willingness to give unpersuaded readers an actual voice in the text, making himself vulnerable and responsive to their reading of this shared problem.

This text is a public act of transformative rhetoric on a series of levels in addition to its publication and presentation in a Community Conversation. Acknowledging uncertainty, Raymond, nevertheless, positions himself in the text as an agent of change, speaking to his peers about the fragile possibilities for transformation he sees for John. The text most obviously dramatizes the action of John, who, in the end, rises to Taylor's deliberative engagement with what is significant in his own life. But perhaps more important, it enacts the transformation of a teenager (in Ray, the character) who becomes a rhetorical agent for change, who confronts his resistant friend at the locker and dares to speak about issues of significance.

What Counts as Transformative Action?

It is possible in these terms to make a good case for Raymond as a rhetorical agent—as a reflective meaning maker in a public dialogue with others on issues of significance. Yet, some might still ask, is that really good enough? How might we talk about (much less track) its transformative potential? To begin with, this act of public rhetoric is marked by its vulnerability. It is vulnerable to the uncertainty that accompanies its vision of possibility, to the possibility of laughter or rejection from teenage peers, and to our equally easy dismissal of this little error-ridden essay as an act of real agency or public rhetoric. Rhetoric, with a tradition to uphold, has its own canonical version of the individualistic hero. This rhetor is the charismatic speaker who moves the crowd to awe, pity, agreement, or even action—to change their hearts, to strap on their six-guns, or to head to the polls. If rhetorical agents are recognized only by power and impact, Raymond does not measure up. Nor is he likely to. The public sphere of modern stratified societies is often marked, Ralph Cintron argues, by its "unremitting enforcement of powerlessness upon those [like the Chicago gang members he studied] whose actions speak of a need for power" (1997, p. 194). The root of exclusion is fear: "Locate the anxiety of the public sphere, and one will have located the limit for engaging in rational discourse and, hence, for constructing a participatory democracy" (p. 195).

Raymond fares little better in rhetoric's more elite scripts, which describe the discourse of the public sphere and its legitimate members. As Habermas describes the ideal public sphere, speakers win warranted assent from their peers not by appealing to their emotions or self-interest but by building a logical argument, grounded on universal principles (1962/1989). Assent is won by the power of the "best" argument built on premises and evidence others cannot deny. Yet, as our study of Raymond and his group quickly discovered, evidence and logic were not the strategies of choice for these urban teens. They knew their audience and chose to speak to them in a discourse of performance. Attuned to the power of statistics, for instance, they exaggerated and even offered to make up evidence for effect! But, most of all, they performed their ideas. They enacted arguments in plays, narratives, and scripted dialogues, and they gave dramatic life to the *possible* (usually horrific) outcomes of drugs.[15] Rather than logical force, they strove for what Kenneth Burke (1950) would call *identification*. Identification presumes that you persuade others by talking their language, by speech, gesture, attitudes, or ideas that *identify* your ways with theirs. This performative logic, far from silencing dissent, also gave voice to the resistant responses of the unpersuaded and their unsupported claims—rivals that an authoritative argument would have swept aside.

It seems unlikely that the elite tradition of disputation and logical truth-seeking associated with Plato's dialectic would see much transformative potential in Raymond's rhetoric. However, a counter rhetorical tradition, given new shape by writers such as Janet Atwill, Susan Jarrett, and Gerard Hauser, values a different set of actions.[16] Plato's model of knowledge-making as philosophical inquiry, Atwill argues, has indeed shaped and dominated the thinking of liberal humanism, urging us to equate knowledge with the acquisition of selected bodies of information, rather than with the cultivation of an art or techne of discourse (1998). As the mark of an elite, leisured class of gentlemen, Plato's philosophical practice held itself above participation in the rowdy democratic politics of Athens and gave us an art of discourse shot through with restrictive, class-based, gendered, and ethnic assumptions about who participates and why. (And now, of course, we urge the learners marginalized by this culturally marked image of liberal education to aspire to and value *its* art above their own cultural practices.)

Traditional humanism's reading of both Plato and Aristotle not only discredited the sophists but also, more important, blinded us to the significance of the sophist's "alternative, situated standards of knowledge and value" (Atwill, 1998, p. 11). For example, Isocrates saw the path to wisdom leading not through philosophical reflection but through deliberation, shaped by the practice of *logōn technē,* or art of discourse. Like community literacy, it supported an art of exploring rival perspectives that was at once a public act and an interpretive, internal one.

> For the same arguments which we use in persuading others when we speak in public, we employ also when we deliberate [bouleuomenoi] in our own thoughts; and, while we call eloquent those who are able to speak before a crowd, we regard as sage those who most skillfully debate problems in their own minds (*Antid.* 256–57). (Isocrates qtd. in Atwill, pp. 27–28)

The goal of this tradition, Atwill argues, was not universal truth-seeking but social and political intervention. While the speaker of humanism succeeds by conforming to a normative ideal of the rhetor (as a man of *virtue*—breeding, elegance, taste, and discourse knowledge), the rhetor of Isocrates and Cicero is driven to achieve esteem and honor from his community (not the gods) within a situated discursive exchange. His art or techne is a power and a set of transferable strategies (p. 7). It draws on what Aristotle called *productive* knowledge—the capacity to articulate and intervene rather than represent what was already known. It works from the impetus attributed to Prometheus to test and transform, to disrupt patterns of power and limitation, to invent new paths, and to shape new realities with the rhetor's art (pp. 2, 66–69).[17] In his intentionally situated way, Raymond was working to challenge and disrupt the community patterns John (and other teens in this booklet) took for granted, to experiment with multiple rhetorical strategies (from drama to reflection and rivaling), and to articulate a vision of possibility and change.

This transformative rhetoric, designed to intervene in the affairs of one's community, stands in the tradition of that distinctive techne or art of discourse championed by the Elder Sophists, as Susan Jarratt describes it (1991). Not limited to the "frozen perfection of Aristotelian logic" and its causal arguments, sophistic rhetoric explored problems through narrative and argued by juxtaposing antithetical interpretations, exposing the complexity of the evidence in order to gain greater explanatory power (pp. 4, 19). Unlike a Socratic dialogue guided by a master in search of a universal truth, this rhetoric was the starting point for negotiating a useful course of action (pp. 49–50). It used its art self-consciously to draw out the complexity of a problem and to draw its audience into a process of deliberation and revaluation. Within these counter traditions, associated with deliberative discourse, sophistic rhetoric, and the vernacular public sphere, Raymond does indeed achieve rhetorical standing. Here the markers of transformative potential are not elite status or its discourse; rather, they include the disruption of conventional patterns of power, the creation of starting points for negotiating useful action, and the call that draws others into new forms of deliberation.

A final critical marker is the ability to put new representations of reality into circulation. This idea is central to counterpublic theory (the subject of the next chapter). But if John Trimbur (2000) is right, Marx's notion of circulation (the term Marx coined) gives us a new way to see the contribution of community discourse. An analysis that looks at the entire process of creation, production, and delivery suggests that Raymond and this fourteen-page newsletter were putting more than arguments into circulation.

The same week *Let's Talk about Sex Drugs* came out, all the faculty and staff at my institution received an eight-page booklet (oddly similar to the CLC's) on drug abuse under the signature of the university president. It, however, began with a cost-benefit analysis of drug use in the context of "pleasure-enhancing activities" of "mankind" and their deleterious consequences. It then supplied scientific information about drugs, including medical terms and long lists of probable health risks, followed by extensive legalistic tables on university, state, and federal sanctions and penalties for drug abuse, concluding with a synopsis of assistance programs. So how do we assess the value of this document compared, say, to *Let's Talk*? The commodity value of such a document, Trimbur (2000) argues, lies partly its usefulness to potential readers in need of such information (i.e., its *use value)*. But value also lies in what the various people in the production process (from the writers, the researchers quoted, and the human-resources office credited with producing it, to the university president displaying his authority and values in authorizing it, and so on) get from the labor of contributing to the process (i.e., its *exchange value* for them). The worth of such labor is calculated by the researcher, for instance, in terms of citations, research grants, visibility, or promotion.

Comparing the university and community "modes of production" suggests a new aspect of the transformative work of *Let's Talk*. This wider analysis of creation, production, and delivery, Trimbur argues, reveals how documents, like the university booklet with its high *exchange* but rather low *use* value, work to preserve hierarchical social relations and the status quo. The production decisions surrounding *Let's Talk*, by contrast, were typically based on *use* value. Both groups, for instance, had to make decisions surrounding "delivery." But note the social relations each mode of production called up or reproduced. Before the teens settled on the newspaper-styled booklet, they considered creating fliers and posters to tack up on "hot" corners or around convenience stores. And they had debated the price of "being useful"—that is, the hazard and discomfort of trying to hand out such a text in such places. Printing their document required gratis contributions and foundation grants, reestablishing those institutions' connection to the public good. And the text was hand distributed as part of a live community conversation that authorized the teens as experts, then handed out to selected classes at school, and thence distributed through a Web site. When we compare this to the process of the university publication, we see that the social machinery that authorizes a university document and reinforces elite, institutional social relations is also reinscribing distinctive patterns of authority and power. And here is Trimbur's point: this "process of production determines—and distributes [not only a message but also] a hierarchy of knowledge and information that is tied to the cultural authorization of expertise, professionalism, and respectability" (2000, p. 210). Moreover, what is getting distributed by "different types of reading matter is the productive means to name the world, to give it shape and coherent meaning" (p. 209). By illuminating the process of production and circulation behind these two texts, Trimbur urges a critical question: how is the institutional process itself articulating and authorizing a resistant, exclusionary meaning of "professional expertise"? Secondly, he is pointing to some criteria that would give (unauthorized) rhetorical agents like these teens standing as transformative rhetors. That is, does their process offer the ability to "problematize expertise," to imagine an "alternative basis" for authority, or to a model a way to produce not only exchange value (i.e., using writing to build a rep or a resume) but also to produce socially useful knowledge that answers questions the users themselves have posed (pp. 214–15)? Such a techne would help create what Carolyn Rude (2004) calls "an expanded concept of rhetorical delivery."[18] And its value would lie in the effort "to redistribute the means of production in order to increase public participation" in the work of knowledge-making (p. 216).

Is community literacy, then, the work of *rhetorical agents*? If we only allow acts of eloquent public advocacy or rational argument demanding warranted assent to count for rhetorical agency, then Raymond's process of deliberation, meaning making, and dialogue will fly beneath our radar. But I would argue that in a rhetorical reading of this text, agency emerges in a vigorous and significant form. It appears first in the engagement with conflict (this is not the agency of unfettered expression), secondly, in acts of negotiation with conflicting forces from within and without, and, finally, in attempts to enter a genuine dialogue not geared to win a debate or mount an argument so much as open a door to inquiry and the delicate possibility of transformation. Its agency depends on both personal action and the social, collaborative work of a counterpublic. The danger is in overlooking the unconventional or untrumpeted forms of rhetorical agency that emerge in the work of thinkers, teachers, learners, and strugglers alike, who are willing to acknowledge and engage in generative inquiry amid conflict. The agency of negotiated meaning making and public dialogue is often the work of unheroic acts, of qualified successes, of inevitably conditional achievements. It is based on the mixed motives and conflicting desires of what West calls everyday people—people in which I include myself, other learners, and marginalized speakers and writers like Raymond.

Affirming a Contested Agency

I want to propose a paradox. People who stand within circles of privilege (like myself and many readers of this book) may also be standing in need of empowerment. What we need in this case is not a space to express our identity or the power to resist pressures upon it but the capacity to speak publicly for something of value in a committed but critical way. By critical, I mean taking an experimental stance to our own knowing (including our beliefs and values), engaging in an inquiry about what they mean in practice, and remaining open to transformation. And yet, many of us are nervous about speaking for rather than against something and suspicious of those who do. With good reason. Commitment can slide from the hilltop of inquiry down into the pits of certainty and rigidity; it can signal a willed blindness to the disturbingly tangled reality of problems for which there are "no right answers." Or affirmation may sound like a naïve optimism that would make us look foolish in the withering and invulnerable gaze of cynicism. Moreover, we tell ourselves, isn't a public rhetoric of affirmation and commitment best left to the likes of a Ralph Waldo Emerson, John Dewey, Martin Luther King Jr., Paulo Freire, or Cornel West, whose sweeping, elegant, or profound analyses of the world give them the sense of personal agency, authority, or political power one seems to need?

If it is true that the privileged (as scholars, teachers, students, citizens) do sometimes stand in the need of the empowerment to affirm, here is a more welcome paradox. In community literacy, the privileged become empowered to speak by becoming able to speak for the hidden agency of marginalized, silenced, or disempowered others. We need to be precise here; this "speaking for" does not mean "speaking in place of" others; it is not a matter of theorizing about or asserting bold claims. It is the caring, patiently precise, and writerly work of drawing out, documenting, and giving visibility and presence to the agency of someone else (in their own eyes and the eyes of others) when that person is presumed to lack such capacity, insight, or expertise. In this rhetoric of engagement, students and educators become rhetorical agents by seeing, supporting, and giving a public presence to the agency, capacity, ability, and insight of community partners. Such engagement takes different forms, from supporting to documenting to public fashioning. This chapter documents a form that emerged from the Community Literacy Center experiment, but it stands in the company of work by writers with different theoretical groundings but a similarly motivated sense of the urgency of public talk. Some of the most significant images of possibility for me have been found in Shirley Brice Heath's community-development documentaries, Glynda Hull's multimodal digital storytelling, Ellen Cushman's praxis of new media, Jeffrey Grabill's technological and organizational intervention, Ira Shor's academic activism, Eli Goldblatt's New City Community Press, and David Coogan's materialist portraits of civic dialogue. They are part of a growing number of teachers and scholars turning to the public and civic possibilities of rhetoric and composition.

Nurturing Rhetorical Agency in Everyday Life

Learning to take rhetorical action needs sponsors, especially if your schooling envisions more passive roles for you. Raymond was called by his mentors to take a new kind of rhetorical agency in the supportive publics of the Community House. But sometimes one must initiate dialogue and invent a new path in more socially charged situations. When Amanda Young brought her interest in medical communication to a community literacy project, she discovered "a disturbing tendency among [these] adolescent girls to attribute responsibility for their reproductive health to someone else: their mothers, their boyfriends, or, in a distressing number of cases, a relative or family friend who had molested them" (2000, p. 39). She developed an interactive computer program called *What's Your Plan?* that used the strategies of community literacy to support girls in making decisions about sexual relationships, health, abstinence, and contraception (1999). When girls open the program's multimedia magazine (*Teen Scene: Dice or Dialogue?*), they find themselves in a heart-to-heart talk between Brandy and Tyrone about their relationship and choices around abstinence and sexual activity. It's a touchy topic that raises the question of who is in control. Posing a choice of leaving things to chance (i.e., the dice) or engaging in dialogue, the program draws out girls' knowledge of myths and facts about reproductive health (such as, the assumption you won't get pregnant if you are overweight or it's your first time) and lets them explore alternative methods. It collects the user's responses and helps her use them to draft her own personal plan based on what she values.

Young's study follows a group of teenaged Planned Parenthood Peer Helpers, analyzing changes in their rhetoric of agency as they work with the program. A revealing problem arises when strong intentions are combined with weak plans. Some girls exhibit what Young defines as a "strong agency" that faces up to conflicts in goals and values and asserts, as this writer did,

> Just tell him straight, you're not going to have sex 'til you're married and that was a decision that you made for yourself. HE'S JUST GOING TO HAVE TO DEAL WITH THE FACT. (2000, p. 147)

Yet, Bria, a peer helper whom we learn sets a high value on her virginity, "actually suggests that she wants to hide from guys the very thing that she values most about herself: 'I would never tell my boyfriend that I'm waiting for marriage because that would probably turn him off'" (p. 200). As Bria talks and writes her way through the program, she explains and elaborates scenarios with her mentor, figuring out what she would actually *do* "if . . ." and trying to explain her own decisions to herself. We can see her working through issues of her own identity.

> I'm not going to lose my virginity to someone that has other chicks on the side. I have so much more respect for myself. I want someone to treasure me. He [a boyfriend she recently broke up with] missed out because he wanted to be a little player. He was doing me a disservice. [But] I really do miss him. . . . You wish there was some compromise, but there is no compromising yourself. It's like it gets to that point where you are really struggling inside. (p. 157)

Through the course of Bria's on-line dialogue with the scripted digital actors in *What's Your Plan* and live dialogue with her mentor and friends, we see this young woman working toward a more reflective, "strong" rhetoric of agency that lets her not only articulate her own goals (those firm but abstract intentions) but also test her knowledge, explore conflicts and dilemmas, confront implications, and imagine very personal, negotiated plans of action. As one astute teenager put it, "I don't want to be a thirty-year-old virgin, but I don't want to be a seventeen-year-old mother either" (p. 169). And as philosopher Charles Taylor put it, the self-reflection and dialogue of a responsible agent depends on an articulate "vocabulary of worth" (1985a, p. 24). Bria later reports how ideas rehearsed in this virtual rhetorical setting do in fact reappear when she is on a date.

Young's research with people dealing with sexual health and chronic illness shows how they develop this "rhetoric of agency" as a discursive tool kit for sorting out values, engaging in dialogue, taking alternative perspectives, and making personal decisions (A. Young & Flower, 2002). Notice how this form of agency is both a strategic capacity and a collaborative process for taking control of decisions in even these intimate and intensely personal areas of physical and psychological health.

As teenagers like Bria mature, they all too frequently become the women Lorraine Higgins met in her CLC project at Pittsburgh's urban Rainbow Health Center—the angry, discouraged, or silenced clients of traditional public health care. The booklet these women wrote (called *Getting to Know You: A Dialogue for Community Health*) was addressed in part to women like themselves. Its personal problem narratives range from stories of physicians' dismissive (and inaccurate) diagnoses to unfounded charges of medical neglect leveled at a mother whose explanation the medical staff never bothered to solicit. Each problem narrative leads to a "Dialogue" with the rival perspectives of doctors, family members, nurses, and patients, ending with a what-if discussion of better options for all participants. In the preface to their document, the women urge and model rhetorical agency in encounters with the authority of the health care system.

Taking Control: A Note to Female Patients

Women often have a hard time talking and relating to doctors and vice-versa. In fact, some of us (admit it) get so frustrated that we avoid going to a clinic until it is absolutely necessary, and by then it may be too late. . . . The women who have written this book for you are very much aware of the factors that prevent us from getting good care. . . . [We] know that being on medical assistance and feeling insecure about ourselves because we have not gone beyond high school prevents us from speaking up and being assertive about what is wrong with us and what is best for our health. This booklet is about taking control of our health. (qtd. in Higgins & Chalich, 1996, p. 2)

But as the title itself suggests, *Getting to Know You* was also addressed to the larger pubic of health-care providers and would actually be used in training medical students. Taking rhetorical agency with professionals who had already demonstrated a failure to "know you" would require more than assertive narratives.

Crafting a narrative to *interpret* a problem in the service of joint *inquiry* is no easy job to begin with. But Higgins and Lisa Brush define the even more daunting challenge in a similar project with women on welfare.

To participate in public debate, people on the margins . . . must engage others and make themselves understood as relevant interlocutors across constituencies. . . . They must connect enough with the rhetoric of others to be intelligible and persuasive, yet they must rebut rather than reproduce commonsense understandings. (2006, pp. 695–96)

Given pervasive images of the welfare queen and the mother who neglects her child's health care, these writers must construct a counter ethos in their own texts. And to do so, Higgins and Brush argue, meant learning to avoid the powerful default schemas of both popular hero and victim narratives, each of which might erode their credibility and mask the complexity of their lives and decisions. For these women responding to welfare policy, taking rhetorical agency meant transforming the knowledge of experience into realistically complex problem narratives.[1] The assertive rhetoric of "taking control" in the Rainbow Clinic introduction is replaced by a self-conscious commitment to "writing the wrongs of welfare," in which the practices of community literacy lay a foundation for an effective public voice.

In these three cases, the strategic practice of community literacy has found its way into a report to policy makers as well as into everyday, emotionally charged, sometimes frightfully significant dialogues with lovers and doctors. These rhetorical agents can't just feel empowered to "assert and run"; they have an investment in staying in this dialogue and transforming it. As university partners, Young and Higgins nurture agency by offering rhetorical, literate tools for interpreting the situations, setting personal goals, planning, and anticipating dialogue—and in doing so, for coming to see oneself as an empowered thinker, planner, writer, and agent.

Giving a Public Presence to the Agency of Others

Educators and students are comfortable with this teaching, nurturing role. But what about the other, authoritative voices—the doctors, policy makers, vice principals, superintendents—in these dialogues? Can we help create a public dialogue in which people with authority to act also acknowledge and listen to the insights of Others? I believe a rhetorically focused community literacy has a unique capacity to scaffold local public deliberation and to challenge, even reinvent that public's expectations.

CLC projects had traditionally culminated in public Community Conversations. This became the germ of a new sort of dialogue that started with broadly shared public and economic concerns. Defined in the language of downtown institutions, these were problems in which the "suits" already had a strong investment. Under the aegis of the university, the Carnegie Mellon Community Think Tank began in 1999 to convene a series of intercultural, problem-solving dialogues in which authorized, professional expertise sat down with the situated knowledge of community expertise and deliberated over options.[2] The first series of Community Think Tanks were in response to welfare-reform policies that were pushing underprepared workers into equally underprepared city businesses. Dialogues called "Negotiating the Culture of Work and Technology" started with the problem case of Melissa, a low-income, single mother trying to move beyond welfare. As she enters her first real job, Melissa, her supervisor, and peers confront problems with communication, skills, training, networks of support, and respect. The Think Tank drew participants from business, regional development, social services, education, and the urban community, eventually eliciting rival hypotheses and options for action from over 450 participants, speaking from the diverse perspectives of management, employees, and their communities of support.

In a typical Think Tank session focused on Melissa's case, twenty people work at small tables. They see a scenario from her story dramatized in familiar CLC fashion. Prompted by a briefing book and a facilitator, they began their inquiry into "What is the problem here?" seeking the rival interpretations and the story-behind-the-story from one another. Then, in response to a series of dilemmas posed in the briefing book, they are asked, "What are the options for action—and the likely outcomes of that choice?" The Think Tank process asks people to craft a new understanding, transformed by the play of competing/complementing perspectives *and* the normally untapped resources of community expertise.

Over the course of Melissa's problem scenario, she will face a series of decisions. At the decision point examined here, Melissa is enthused at the prospect of a long-awaited "good job" at the University Medical Corp. and headed for her beginning placement in the hospital's admissions office. However, the brief, intense orientation process has left her dazed with technological information overload. Experience tells us that problems loom on the horizon—problems that start with hiring employees who are unprepared for the culture of work into institutions equally unprepared to support their success. As the comments of Think Tank participants documented in figure 9.1 suggest, people interpret the underlying problem here in different ways.[3]

In response to the dilemma posed here as decision point 2 in figure 9.2, the Think Tank participants explore options for the preparation of such new employees. The excerpt from the published Think Tank *Findings* in figure 9.2 shows how ideas from this series of discussions were consolidated by the Think Tank team (and foregrounded in the document design) into responses that highlight multiple, situated voices and perspectives.

Fig. 9.1 Think Tank responses to "What is the problem?"

What is going on here? What is the problem, if any?

A minister says:

> There is a lot more to being successful at work than just knowing technology —what about the rest of the culture of work? Does she know how to solve problems, ask questions, and get along with co-workers? I'm not sure Melissa knows what she is getting into.

A community worker says:

> Melissa's expectations are too high, and she is bound to fail. She thinks she has it made, but she doesn't really understand what "real" work is like.

A union member says:

> Melissa may be coming out of several generations of working-class family —but this new working world is no longer manual or physical labor. She is moving into not only a new paradigm for her own personal life, but she doesn't have a role model within her sphere of living —she may not have the family support to help her through tough times in this new kind of workplace.

This excerpt from the *Findings* also suggests how the Think Tank supports rhetorical agency.

- First, in responding to widely acknowledged problems in hiring these workers, the Think Tank is unlike a standard urban community meeting devoted to complaint and blame, or the forums in which administrators "collect" public comment.[4] As an action-oriented discussion, the Think Tank is focused on "decision points" and "options." These are tested and qualified by predicted outcomes—supplied in many cases by the situated knowledge of people who are normally the (unconsulted) recipients of professional decisions.
- The format of this text reflects the way the dialogue at the table itself was scaffolded by the now-familiar community-literacy practices, such as, defining problems from different perspectives, seeking situated knowledge by drawing out stories-behind-the-story, inviting rivals, and testing options against possible outcomes to build a more negotiated intercultural understanding.
- The text models a dialogue in which the insights from academic research,[5] community-support networks, professional management, and working experience are equally privileged even though (or because) they represent knowledge differently, from diverse, sometimes competing perspectives. However, difference is not allowed to relax into opposition or critique: the dialogue models a discourse that

Fig. 9.2 Think Tank options at decision point #2

Decision Point #2: Hiring

The "standard" training leaves the new employees with information overload and inadequately prepared for independent performance.

Option #1: Melissa is trained in more than technology. The preparation includes a toolbox of strategies that enable her to solve problems, negotiate with her co-workers and supervisor, and manage the extra life demands created by poverty.

A community leader says: If Melissa is able to solve her own problems, . . .[remainder omitted]

Option #2: The welfare-to-work program performs a skill inventory at the end of the program.

A human resources manager says: A skill inventory would let the trainers know the gaps in Melissa's knowledge. They could then retrain her in the areas where she is weak, avoiding problems with Mr. Snyder during those first few days of work.

A welfare recipient says: A skill inventory only measures what the trainers think is important. What about those things outside technology or procedures? Melissa could be lacking in family support, transportation, childcare, problem-solving skills, or even housing. How will a skill inventory assess that?

The welfare recipient's Story Behind the Story: I consider myself well trained for the job market, but there are some problems in my personal life that will affect my work. Sometimes my children are sick or even suspended from school. Sometimes I don't have anything appropriate to wear to work, or sometimes I feel like my co-workers are acting prejudiced to me but I'm afraid to confront them about it. These problems for me cause the most trouble in my own working life.

Academic Contribution

Workplace researchers Kirschenman and Neckerman write that employers can discriminate in many well-hidden ways by requiring text-based literacy tests before being considered for employment. Skill inventories can therefore be seen as ways to weed out employees who would take too much "work" to "fix." The authors argue that because these employees are mostly from the inner-city, skill inventories can be seen as a type of sophisticated discrimination.[*]

---

insists on seeking out rivals in order to craft better options.[6] More importantly, because these voices are in response to each other (one mark of a rhetorical agent), they can actually, at times, build a more qualified, conditionalized, or complex negotiated understanding.

For university partners, public dialogues like this offer an alternative space of engagement. They invite us to move from the familiar roles of teacher, supporter, or nurturer into the role of a *rhetorical researcher* and a *public rhetorician*—whose work is giving a public presence to the expertise and rhetorical agency *of others.*

Becoming a rhetorical investigator starts with role reversal. Recall the students in chapter 4 who were perplexed at what they could possibly do in a project with nursing aides since they felt incompetent to give "advice" (as indeed they were) or powerless to "change conditions" *for* others. These college students were helping develop a Think Tank called "Health Care: The Dilemma of Teamwork, Time, and Turnover," which revolved around a growing local staffing crisis with certified nursing aides (CNAs) and registered nurses in nursing homes and hospitals. As rhetorical researchers, our first job was not to advise but to draw out the silenced voices and to document the unacknowledged expertise of the staff, especially the aides at the bottom of a weighty medical hierarchy. Students learned how to mount an intercultural inquiry into a workplace problem, moving from research, policy statements, and reports into the heart of the matter: to conduct critical incident interviews and hold small-group story-behind-the-story sessions with aides, nurses, supervisors, managers, and other staff. This meant the students had to learn techniques not just for eliciting someone else's situated interpretation of a problem but for hearing what was actually said and documenting it in a way that necessarily interprets and consolidates yet remains true to a perspective one may struggle to understand.

The Think Tank asks students and teachers to move from the role of researcher into public rhetorician—with an ironic twist. We are not called to become the charismatic public speaker, the agent exuding power and control speaking in our own voice. Instead, we invite others into a dialogue; that is, we help create a local public, called up in response to a shared public problem and the promise of intercultural problem solving.[7] Our community partners use their credibility to bring community leaders and everyday people to an event they may approach with experienced skepticism. Our university identity gives us the credentials to bring to the table civic and professional decision makers (who would not come to a neighborhood community conversation). Without being in a position of power to enact change, we can use institutional authority to scaffold an intercultural dialogue (one that gets people actually to play by its unconventional discourse rules). And by publishing documents like the *Findings* in booklets or on Web sites, we use the resources, networks, and authority of the academy to turn a *meeting* into a *public* created by the circulation of a discourse. As community literacy's public rhetoricians, we are able to use institutional authority to give a public presence to the people and perspectives without authority.[8]

Public rhetoricians are accountable to outcomes. But forums for intercultural public deliberation do not, by their nature, lead to legislation or direct institutional change. How do you talk about and track outcomes from a dialogue in which diverse participants merely meet, talk, produce a document, and go back to work? One answer lies in ways *counterpublics*, as *rhetorically* created bodies, work by attempting to realize a vision of the world through address. As Nancy Fraser and Michael Warner argue, counterpublics not only mount claims but they also assert alternative models of public meaning making. They support ways of listening, responding, and case building that challenge the dominant discourse of critical rationality. And they do this through the *circulation* of discourse. Consider some ways circulation works within this local public.

It starts face-to-face. In a typical Think Tank, the people at the table are unlikely to have ever sat down in a sustained discussion with a group like this—much less in a focused problem-solving dialogue. And at the beginning of a session, the Think Tank facilitators can have their hands full, cajoling, humorously badgering participants out of their more comfortable discourses of complaint and blame or prerecorded position statements or advice scripts and into listening to/asking for rivals and taking responsibility to imagine and test options together. But interestingly enough, when people catch on to "the rules" of this discourse game, they appear to appropriate it with some enthusiasm. The experience itself is a powerful argument for intercultural dialogue that makes people self-aware *participants and performers* in a transformed relationship.

How can such a transformation matter? Stepping back to look at the way new forms of social practice emerge, activity theorist Yrjo Engeström argues that the route from knowledge to change is through the "creation of artifacts, production of novel social patterns, and expansive transformation of activity contexts" (1999, p. 27). A "transformation," such as an intercultural dialogue, is "expansive" when it draws people with rival perspectives into communication that lets them reconceptualize the ways they are organized and are interacting around a shared concern (1997, p. 373). The novel social patterns created in such a multivocal event produce what Engeström describes as "a re-orchestration of those voices, of the different viewpoints and approaches of the various participants" (1999, p. 35). The Think Tank changes the social script for dialogue.

This counterpublic circulates its model of an alternative discourse in another form by creating a textual representation of its counter discourse—one that challenges both the conventions of normal policy talk *and* the expected guest list. Think Tanks are a hybrid discourse, in which a focused, well-argued problem analysis is woven from the warp of reasoned argument and research claims and the woof of narrative, reflection, and dialogue that rivals and revises the developing fabric. Recommendations appear in the shape of both a formal executive summary and a rhetorically crafted anecdote. They draw support from the specificity of situated knowledge as well as that of validating standard conventions, such as, the array of credentialed names included as appendix 1, The List of Participants. In this hybrid discourse, stories (behind the story) play a key role but not as vehicles of self-expression or personal testimony. They are developed as tools of inquiry, often used to rival, qualify, or revise an interpretation on the table.

The document design of the published *Findings* tries to reenact the dynamics of this dialogue, representing the play of different voices with names that foreground their diverse social perspectives. The message the text sends out is more than its content—the options for job training, decreasing turnover, or increasing respect in low-wage jobs. It documents not only a body of ideas but also a literate performance; it gives life to frequently marginalized voices and dramatizes the rhetorical agency of those speakers.

The brief excerpt in figure 9.3 comes from decision point 4 on work support for employees like Melissa. At this point in the scenario, having lost a battle with the admission office's confusing computer system, she has mishandled an admission and has once again failed to clock in on time due to unreliable childcare and the two busses she has to catch for work.

In this brief exchange, the Think Tank is doing the work of a local counterpublic on two fronts. First, it has evidently created what Fraser (1990) would describe as a safe place for participants to build arguments and identities. Such a space may have been of slight concern to the human-resource manager at the table. The voice one hears on the session tapes speaks confidently with the agency of her professional authority, apparently comfortable in echoing an HR policy statement that dictates what sort of support is "appropriate." But the welfare-recipient participant, more used to being positioned as "the problem" than the "problem solver," has found a discourse that validates her insight as well. Perhaps more importantly, the material organization of this event (from the equalizing table to the we-take-you-seriously tape recorder to the Think Tank discourse "rules") gives her a metaphorical microphone and place to stand, and she has seized this opportunity to act as a rhetorical agent. Her comment frames an explicit option, supports it with reasons and examples, then projects some additional outcomes (looking "strong") that reveal the employee's motivations (to manage a self-image with the boss) and the possible impact on a manager (who had complained about HR sending him "these people"). The story-behind-the-story takes us deeper into the realities of such employment with a demeaning event. It gives a possible interpretation of the neutral abstraction, "communication" problems (that I can only say my experience would have been unlikely to supply). And it offers an

Fig. 9.3 A Think Tank discussion acting like a counterpublic

Option #3: The company could have a mentor who works full time on an individual basis with new welfare-to-work employees. The mentor could help with technical questions, but also with personal issues like childcare, transportation, and communication.

Academic Contribution

Federal policy analysts argue that there is a disconnection between family, school, community, business, and agencies; this disconnection can lead to failure for inexperienced workers in the system. For example, a young mother who is taking a job training course could ultimately fail to find work if her issues of child care are not addressed.*

A human resources manager says: That's what all human resources departments are for—to help out employees. But I think it is inappropriate for the HR department to intervene in the personal lives of employees—instead, we can refer the employees to family, church, or a CBO.

A welfare recipient says: If Melissa had someone who was working on her behalf, a lot of problems would be avoided. Maybe Melissa doesn't know her rights, or even the bus schedule. This way, she wouldn't have to look silly by asking her boss; instead she'll look strong because she'll be solving her own problems.

The welfare recipient's Story Behind the Story: I had a job once where the supervisor would not let me go on a bathroom break except for lunch. Well, I never found out until after I left—but it is illegal to stop me from using the bathroom! And that was the major reason I quit that job.

---

insight into the employee's reasoning (which probably went undocumented) behind another "failure to hold a job."

From a management point of view, this participant's insight is a substantive contribution that speaks to a live problem. From a rhetorical point of view, this is a counterpublic performance that speaks to an issue at the center of theoretical public-sphere debates—to the struggle for who controls what is an "appropriate" shared public concern. The HR manager has just marginalized a certain form of support as "inappropriate" for this deliberation—as a *private* matter to be handled in the employee's personal life. But, as Fraser argues:

These terms [*private* and *public*] after all, are not simply straightforward designations of societal spheres; they are cultural classifications and rhetorical labels ... deployed to delegitimate some interests, views, and topics and to valorize others. (1990, p. 73)

More to our point,

The rhetoric of domestic privacy seeks to exclude some issues and interests from public debate by personalizing and/or familiarizing them;

it casts these as private-domestic or personal-familial matters in contradistinction to public, political matters. (p. 73)

Fraser's examples include the rhetoric of "economic privacy" in which working conditions (such as, child labor) were a matter between workers and employers, or discussions of wife-battering, which until recently was a domestic issue, not a public one (in the sense that stopping battering is something in which we all have an investment and responsibility).

The welfare recipient has reframed the HR representation of *workplace versus personal* problems (in which an individual needs counseling or family help) into a more inclusive image of *worklife* problems. In her representation, the reality of inexperience, limited resources, and low-wage jobs constitutes a joint problem. One could argue that supporting effective working lives is as essential to local economic development as it is to social justice. In this case, supporting working lives is a rhetorical act; it is a problem representation that puts worklife issues on the table of public deliberation and defines the appropriate public as the whole network of people who are involved.

Counterpublics not only build the identities that allow Melissas to become rhetorical agents, they also set out to change how others respond to those identities and the voices that disrupt the status quo of critical-rational discourse. Counterpublics, Warner argues, exist as a modern form of power, as embodied, poetic-expressive, world-making forces that assert new forms of interaction (2005). When they do their work, they change how we talk with one another as a public. Notice how the academic excerpt in figure 9.3 implies a conclusion not unlike that of the welfare recipient. However, in its discourse of description and analysis, the object of interest is an observed pattern of *disconnection* between support systems (William T. Grant Foundation Commission, (1988). In its representation, women like Melissa may appear as examples but not as decision makers within complex situations and certainly not as rhetorical agents capable of analyzing and interpreting that situation in fresh ways or of entering into a public negotiation of meaning with rival views. The Think Tank asserts the value of an alternative deliberative structure.

In reenacting these intercultural rhetorical performances, the Think Tank does what may be its most important counterpublic work. It not only documents the hidden expertise and the rhetorical agency of everyday and silenced people; it asserts the possibility of transformed understanding. In brief exchanges like this one and extended episodes of negotiation, it models the vigorous, knowledge-generating performance of a transformed discourse.[9]

As writers, document designers, and rhetoricians, we are working in our area of strength—teaching our students and ourselves the art of careful inquiry and listening that can see rhetorical agency in its everyday working clothes, becoming careful documenters of culturally different ways of arguing and performing knowledge, and discovering imaginative ways to represent and circulate not just information but contested images of rhetorical agency in text.

Community literacy ends up speaking through many kinds of "texts"—from reflective essays to newsletters, booklets, flyers, brochures, newspapers, technical reports, proposals, policy documents, documentaries, digital storytelling, and multimedia productions. They can circulate by hand, in public meetings, to mailing lists, over e-mail, on the Web, and in academic and professional journals.

A rhetorically based collaborative community literacy *starts* in inquiry. And in most cases, this means an *intercultural inquiry* that must cross lines of difference—race, class, status, social background, age, education, or discourse. So I would like to end this story of community literacy in its beginning with the art of such inquiry by describing a small toolkit of strategies drawn from projects illustrated in this book.

Writing a Multivoiced Inquiry

The foundation for community-literacy writing is the multivoiced inquiry that can stand alone or be embedded in other kinds of text. In either case, you will want to do three major things.

Frame a Question

Inquiry starts in a sense of felt difficulty—of wondering, questioning, being perplexed—that leads to posing the problem, that is, trying to name the problem, explain the conflict between an A and a B, or explore the dissonance between the reality you see and what others assert it is or should be. Advocacy often starts with answers; inquiry starts with problems and questions and, what is even harder, with a focus on what you *don't know*, rather than what you do.

You can give shape to your problem-posing by writing a proposal for an inquiry. Start with a well-focused *problem/purpose statement* that describes the problem as you (currently) see it in both up-close and specific terms and in its larger context. Answer three questions: (1) What is the conflict/problem/question? (2) What is at stake? Why do we need to conduct an inquiry? What do we need to learn? and (3) What is the specific purpose and plan of your investigation? Think more specifically about methods and a timetable: how are you going to answer the questions you have posed?

Then see if your analysis can pass the *shared-problem test*. A first attempt to pose a problem normally reflects the writer's perspective (and often an untested assumption about the proper response). To draw others into a dialogue, you need to pose a shared problem—one that recognizes how the conflict or difficulty looks from the perspective of the various people you wish to address. Would others in the local public you want to engage describe the situation, conflict, or desired goals in this way? Can you reshape your statement to include their image of the problem?

Finally, use your proposal to sketch some rival hypotheses about what this inquiry *could* uncover. By predicting what you think you *might* discover, you are able to reflect later on how far your understanding has grown or changed.

Bring Multiple Voices to the Table

Now design a research plan that collects interpretations and analyses of your problem from *at least three different kinds of participants, sources, or perspectives*. Imagine your inquiry going on with others at a comfortable round table. As a college mentor, you might want to bring some voices past and present from books you have been reading (theorists, researchers, educators, novelists, journalists) as well as the voices of the people you mentor, their peers, the community, other college students, and, of course, your own voice—responding and trying to interpret and negotiate what you hear. Some will speak directly to your problem/question or maybe even to each other. Others might offer rival perspectives that reframe the whole question. Still others will require *you* to find the connections and draw inferences and insights from their words, because they are talking about a different but relevant topic.

Secondly, design your multivoiced inquiry to *collect at least three different kinds of data*. Look at the methods for inquiry below, and take advantage of the strikingly different kinds of knowledge you can get, for example, from library research versus observational notes, tapes of a collaborative planning session, rival readings, interviews, or transcripts of a public dialogue. Plan to collect at least three different kinds of data that will be the most revealing for what *you* want to learn.

Reflect Multiple Voices in Your Text

What form should the text itself take? A traditional academic paper—one that is focused on making and supporting claims or reporting the results of research—carries a great deal of credibility with many audiences. However, used alone, this genre can make it difficult to convey experiential insights, unresolved questions, or perspectives not well captured by formal prose. A multivoiced inquiry, on the other hand, can *design the text to reflect the shape of an inquiry as well as different forms knowledge takes.* Like any good piece of research and analysis, this approach requires you to be explicit and to support your ideas and inferences. But it also invites you to use techniques you know from creative or documentary writing, from visual and verbal document design, or multimedia to help readers move into an *attitude of inquiry with you.* Consider, for instance, how you could help them to experience your problem as a felt difficulty, to visualize a situation, or to hear the conflicting voices that are part of a good inquiry. Or, how could you help them listen to and take seriously texts not written in Standard Written English or voices that do not come from an elite or "educated" discourse (without turning into editors or mere sympathizers; see chapter 8)? In short, give yourself the freedom (and the real challenge) to *design* your final text to reflect the multiple voices you have collected and to draw readers into an intercultural inquiry or even a local public dialogue with you. Consider using the textual conventions of narrative, dialogue, poetry, drama, autobiography, or imaginative document design seen in the preceding chapters.

Because the format and structure of such texts may vary, here is a checklist for elements that readers will probably want to find somewhere in your text, especially if it is a more formal essay, report, or proposal.

Some Significant Areas for Inquiry

You may have noticed that each chapter of this book was organized around a significant issue or problem in community literacy from "How do communities function?" to "How is (or is?) the agency of marginalized people being represented?" These are "good problems" in the sense that they raise questions others share; they invite us into issues with rival interpretations, and our answers have consequences. But the problems we work with are the ones we define. In community literacy, you can expect to encounter challenges in at least four areas: in how communities work, in intercultural relationships, in difference in situated meaning, and in the work of local publics. Intercultural inquiry starts with trying to define the generative problem within a challenging situation. Below, I illustrate this approach to problem-

Fig. 10.1 Checklist for writing a multivoiced intercultural inquiry

_____ 1. Have I "named" a significant *shared* problem and situated it in its larger social (including cultural, historical, or political) context?

_____ 2. And have I "named" the question that guides this inquiry? Have I answered the readers' "so what?" question and made the purpose of this paper (and reason for reading it) clear. These two kinds of "naming" or conceptualizing an issue usually appear early in a text (as in a Problem/Purpose Statement) because they give the reader both a way to focus and a motivation to read on.

_____ 3. Have I drawn on the key concepts, arguments, or voices of published texts from my library research and/or course readings? That is, have I located this inquiry in a larger, public or academic discussion?

_____ 4. Have I brought other voices to the table from at least three different nonacademic, local, community, underrepresented, or silenced perspectives?

_____ 5. Have I allowed them to offer rival interpretations in response to important questions, such as: What is going on here? What is the problem? Why? Why does it matter? What does the topic of our inquiry (such as "literate achievement" or "family support" or "police-enforced curfew") *mean* in their *experience*? What are some options for responding this situation? What are some outcomes? In short, have I allowed them to enter this discussion as experts and analysts?

_____ 6. Have I used different kinds of data to create a multidimensional account of the knowledge, attitudes, experience, and insights of these various voices? Have I tapped their local and "situated knowledge"?

_____ 7. Have I stepped back to analyze these claims, responses, and dialogues in order to *interpret* what this *means*, as least as I understand the problem and question at this point in my inquiry. Have I done the hard work of trying to put this all together for myself and my reader?

_____ 8. Have I reflected on what I may have learned, on where I am in this ongoing process of inquiry, on how I or we might act in response, and on the next set of open questions that this work has raised?

_____ 9. Have I understood what Paulo Freire meant when he said,

To exist, humanly, is to *name* the world, to change it. Once named, the world in its turn reappears to the namers as a problem and requires of them a new *naming*. Men are not built in silence, but in word, in work, in action-reflection. (1989, p. 76)

posing with a set of examples in which different writers have moved beyond identifying a general concern to naming the source of conflict and/or posing specific questions. As the Risk and Stress project (chapter 2) illustrates, your grounded understanding of a "good" problem will develop when you move from describing an abstract issue to engaging in deliberative conversations with community partners about work, school, aspirations, and struggles.

Inquiry into a Community

In community literacy, one of the first questions an intercultural inquiry can pose is "How does a community, institution, or group *actually* function for both insiders and outsiders?" The answer may surprise you. Good places for inquiry are schools, community organizations, neighborhood gangs, social-service bureaucracies, urban clinics, women's shelters, support groups, writing groups in neighborhoods, prisons, churches, and/or extended "non-nuclear" families. Your problem definition, like the ones below, will point you down a path of inquiry.

Problems Writers Have Posed

I grew up assuming that non-traditional *families* were "broken" and left children without family support. But my mentees seem to talk about a "family" distributed around town in very different ways—ones that maybe we need to understand.

Poor women are often criticized for avoiding prompt medical care for themselves or their children—for being either ignorant or irresponsible. But women tell a different story about their reasons and experiences at *urban clinics*. What are the problems? What would help women take more responsibility for themselves and help medical staff become better intercultural communicators?

Inquiry into Relationships

This area for inquiry leads us to look at problems of power, privilege, responsibility, and interpretation. On the one hand, we need to understand the history and logic of how such relationships turn some people into experts or authorities and others into recipients or problems. On the other, we need to look closely at how specific relationships are actually working and why. What makes an institutional or personal relationship sustainable and/or balanced? How do college partners see their role, their struggles? How do community partners interpret the situation?

Problems Writers Have Posed

How can we best use literacy to support equality and social justice through mentoring? How do *programs and individual partners* choose among and balance competing images of mentoring?

When I first began to volunteer as a freshman, I thought of myself as a male, college-bound role model to the boys I tutored. Now I see why African American men can be more important to them as *role models*. So how do they see *our* intercultural relationship working?

Inquiry into Local, Situated Meanings

Our lives are shaped on all sides by social structures, practices, assumptions, or ideologies. To be shaped but not determined by them, it is important to recognize, analyze, critically interrogate, and evaluate the forces working around us and in our own thinking. One way to do this is with historical and theoretical analysis. For an intercultural inquiry, it is even more important to ask how these structures, practices, and assumptions actually play themselves out in experience—especially in the experience of people who are rarely asked for their interpretations. Conflicting situated meanings are often found in important social and institutional goals, in policies, and in everyday notions of performance.

Problems Writers Have Posed

The notion of literate *achievement* is often defined by assessment mandates, English-only policies, everyday notions of "correct" versus "Black" English, or in the value placed on academic essay writing. But what does literate achievement actually *mean in* practice if, for instance, you are not "school comfortable" but care about writing, if your learning disability means you must find alternative ways to succeed, if your goal is to *communicate* in an intercultural context, or if you are an expert in some valued, but non-elite literate practice from rap to reading racing forms?

Public, school, or workplace *policies*—such as a city curfew, or a suspension policy, or the rule of three late clock-ins and you're fired—have both literal and situated meanings. How does the meaning-in-context of a policy change depending on who (or what color) you are, on how you interpret motives (e.g., of police or school officials), or on how it plays out in everyday experience (e.g., if you must take three busses and manage childcare)? What are the local outcomes of such a policy and the situated meanings it holds for diverse stakeholders? Is there a better way to achieve its goals?

Employers say they value *responsibility taking* and *decision making*. But what does that really mean if you are an urban teenager in an unfamiliar, downtown job placement?

Inquiry into the Public Work of Local Publics

Local publics are created when people are drawn together by—and give their attention to—a shared concern through various forms of communication, including, most ideally, dialogue. The local publics of community literacy can form around issues like parental involvement in schools, environmental action, housing policies on campus, and summer employment for urban youth. Trying to understand how a given local public works (or how you can help create one) poses some challenging questions. How is the public called into being? Who is authorized to speak and be heard in this public? How do information and decisions "circulate" in this local public—face-to-face, word of mouth, e-mail, official documents, newsletters, papers, and/or the Internet? And what circulates in this public dialogue—ideas, arguments, advice? How about images, stories, identities, or even new models of dialogue or ways people interact with others?

Some Problems Writers Have Posed

When the new outside-management redesigned campus food service, it suddenly lost student customers yet never consulted the experienced (low-wage) service staff, who now fear losing their jobs. What are the *shared problems* a local public dialogue could consider?

Last semester, a well-designed service-learning course helped a local community group create brochures that encouraged parents to "take back" their neighborhood schools. The campaign bombed. Why? Another project tried to organize an intercultural discussion and writing group for recent immigrant and local parents. It too suffered. Why? How do the different stakeholders in these situations see the problem—and the options for creating a *sustainable* local public?

Methods for Intercultural Inquiry

Different kinds of data open the door to different ways people "know" something and the ways they represent such knowledge, experience, or attitudes to themselves or others. Each of the methods below has distinctive strengths and weaknesses for tapping this multimodal reservoir. An important part of doing intercultural inquiry is testing out which methods yield the most for your question. Some will be familiar; others you may want to investigate in more detail.[1]

Working with Texts

Review course readings for key concepts that speak to your issue. "Ask" the authors you have read to "say" how they would apply their insights or arguments to your situation; that is, draw inferences based on a careful reading of their arguments.

Conduct library research that uncovers theoretical discussions of the larger issue, more specific social and historical analysis, and more practical or local discussions of the problem, the situation, and possible responses. This means using not only Google-style links but database searches for work in journals and books.

Collect relevant artifacts or documents, such as locally produced texts, reports, or public information, that play a part in this situation. Use the tools of discourse analysis to analyze not only the content but also the underlying assumptions, the rhetorical structure, and the rhetorical agency.

Observations

Collect observational data of people in the process of doing something. One way is to keep a two-column observation/reflection journal. Write detailed notes of what happened and what people said in the left column as soon after the fact as possible. In the right column, put comments on context, reflections, and interpretation.

Another method is to audiotape or even videotape public performances, mentoring sessions, and group work or use such data from other sources or published research as a parallel to your own inquiry. (When taping non-public discussions or interviews, always ask permission, which may include written permission from the speaker, the parents of minors, or institutional review board for research. Use pseudonyms in written or oral discussion, and make sure identity can not be easily inferred, unless you have explicit permission to use real names (usually after you have shown the data or your writing to a participant).

Interviews

In all these cases, you will learn a great deal more, be less likely to misinterpret from your own biases, and be more persuasive with quoted evidence if you *tape* the interview, review or analyze it, and quote verbatim rather than speaking from unreliable memory or an approximate note. Again, always get permission, normally in writing. In my experience, community partners are happy to be taped, appreciate your desire to listen carefully to them, and even check from time to time to make sure the tape is working.

In general, start interviews with open-ended questions that do not "lead" your informants to specific answers. After they have been free to approach things in their own (maybe surprising) terms, then you can ask more specific questions that will speak to your interests and hypotheses. But be aware that these will also influence what the interviewee notices or tells you and may create what is called "an experimenter effect" in which they say what they think you expect or want to hear. On the other hand, one hallmark of an intercultural inquiry is that early in these interviews, you tell your partner about the question you are trying to understand and ask their help. That is, invite your interviewee to move from being a "subject" or "informant" to joining you in this *inquiry* into a *shared* problem as a *problem-solving partner.*

Use *cued recall* in which your interviewee looks with you at a text they have written, a group discussion, or a public event they were part of. Work in short (preplanned) segments, and ask them to interpret the text, tape, or video for you. Always start with open-ended questions, such as, What is happening here? What were you doing/thinking? What was the other person(s) doing/thinking? Why? Then you can go to specific questions.

Do a *critical incident interview* in which you ask your informant to recall and recreate a specific incident related to your question, such as a time when they experienced a sense of achievement as a writer or of a specific, difficult encounter with a doctor. The key to this technique is to avoid people's tendency to give you abstract or generalized, even canned responses by insisting first of all that they recall a specific, critical incident or event that they can locate in a time and place. Then ask for a detailed reconstruction of what happened, what people said or did, what happened in response, and the like. Only then invite them to go to more speculative comments on what they thought people were thinking, why they did that, or what the problem was.

An *intercultural interpretation* or *rhetorical reading interview* uses a text (such as a public document, an advertisement, or a description of someone in the informant's situation) to draw out interpretations. You can use different and multiple kinds of prompts. Ask your participant(s) to think aloud while reading and/or to read the text in segments, stopping at places you have marked to answer questions, such as, How do you interpret this text now? What do you predict will come next? Or ask more specific but possibly leading questions: How do you envision this writer? What do you think the writer was trying to do here (e.g., by using this example, rhetorical question, visual, or heading)? How do you think this connects to/helps us understand the issue we are investigating?

One special strength of a rhetorical reading is that it can not only help you understand someone's situated knowledge and reveal their interpretation of an event, person, argument, and so on, it can also let you compare the interpretations and knowledge of multiple, different readers.

Dialogues

Dialogues offer a special kind of information, because they are often focused on a specific issue and show what people think is important enough to think about or to share in a live situation.

Collaborative planning sessions are focused discussions between a writer and his or her planning partner. In collaborative planning, unlike a peer review or teacher/tutor conferences, it is the writer/planner who does most of the talking. The role of the supporter is to draw out the writer's best thinking by focusing attention on three important areas: (1) What is your key point or purpose? (2) How do you predict a reader will respond? and (3) What sorts of text conventions (from genres to formats to rhetorical techniques) might you use to support your purpose or reach this reader? Tapes of these sessions give writers insight into their own writing process and strategies. As a tool in an inquiry, they can also reveal the thinking behind the text and let you glimpse what writers are trying to do.

Another kind of collaborative planning is less about developing a text and more about developing a *supportive dialogue* that lets people explore issues in their own life. Here, some of the powerful questions can be, What are you going through? What are you up against? and How can I be with you? Being able to review a tape of such dialogues can be revealing to both the writer/participant and the supporter. They can also let both partners share the inquiry into broader questions a researcher might pose: What are the concerns this group is facing? How do teens and parents in this project see their situation differently? What kinds of things does such a dialogue achieve and for whom?

Some of the best insights into mentoring, intercultural relations, and learning come from e-mail or electronic bulletin-board *posts among mentors.* Responses in a threaded discussion can show an experience and its interpretation from different perspectives.

Local public dialogues take many face-to-face forms, from informal discussions in a meeting to small focus groups, to community-organizing events where everyone's comment gets recorded on the newsprint covering the walls, to structured town meetings where speakers line up for their three minutes at the microphone, to formal forums in which experts educate participants in the issues. Each has it advantages and limitations.

The local publics of community literacy (in community conversations and think tanks) attempt to support intercultural inquiry and the voices of the silenced. Some key methods that support such dialogue—and offer revealing data for your own inquiry—include:

- get the story-behind-the-story. Privilege the special perspective of the speaker, by valuing narrative and drawing out situated knowledge, which sees ideas and problems in context and in performance and includes motives, feelings, and outcomes.
- seek rival hypotheses. Replace adversarial argument with a collective search for multiple interpretations, predictions, and hypotheses, in which partners in a dialogue are expected to draw out rivals from one another and to rival their own ideas.
- explore options and outcomes. Go beyond yes/no decisions to seek multiple options, testing these options by playing out possible outcomes and subjecting imagined outcomes to the energetic and serious play of rivaling from different perspectives.
- make the discourse "rules" of this dialogic process playfully explicit. Prompt and facilitate an inquiry stance that may take people out of their familiar modes of discourse by supporting discussion with verbal prompts, such as, "What is the problem here?" or requesting what-if stories in the search of rival options.
- record the discussion. If you cannot transcribe it, code it from the tape or computer file, noting the location of rhetorical moves (e.g., rivals) or topics you were looking for, plus important or surprising events and your running commentary. This coding sheet allows you to review whole episodes, discern patterns, make comparisons, and reexamine and quote key places.
- design a way to document the ideas, arguments, insights, and agency that emerge in this local public. Work to represent the rhetorical agency of its diverse speakers in a way that dramatizes a model of public dialogue—one that respects the identities of marginalized speakers and demonstrates new, more just, caring, and creative forms of interaction.

Notes
References
Index

Notes

1. What Is Community Literacy?

1. A number of these newsletters are in the archive "The Community Literacy Center: A Snapshot History" available on Carnegie Mellon University's Intercultural Inquiry site, http://english.cmu.edu/research/inquiry/two.html.

2. In *Argument as Construction: A Framework and Method* (1992), Lorraine Higgins develops a constructivist theory of argument, focused on the process of case building within argument fields. What made this theoretical investigation unusual is that it was developed and tested in a project with returning women students at a local community college whose composing processes revealed a great deal about dealing with social and strategic constraints. ARGUE led to a series of projects with community partners, including landlords and tenants, community-planning groups, and police. The projects are detailed in chapter 2. Higgins's research with Brush into personal narrative and the welfare debate has continued to combine theory with practice (Higgins & Brush, 2006).

3. Educational writers typically distinguish among critical literacy (actions and tools for social analysis and change), cultural literacy (a knowledge of the codes and concepts that lets one fit in the elite status quo), academic literacy (an ability to do school-based analysis and argument in a given disciplinary style), and functional literacy (the basic skills of reading and writing required by the non-elite workplace and minimal civic life). Hull (1993) documents (and challenges) popular views of the basic or functional literacy that educators and policy makers assume American's low-wage workforce needs to acquire. Cushman, Kintgen, Kroll, and Rose's *Literacy: A Critical Sourcebook* (2001) offers a good overview of the wide-ranging debate around literacy and its definitions.

4. Shor's essay (1999) offers a broadly inclusive portrait of critical literacy that links the ideas of John Dewey, Lev S. Vygotsky, Paulo Freire, and Kenneth Burke, to data on social inequity in schooling and pedagogical experimentation by teachers around the country. As the most important voice in building a working-class network in composition studies and in bringing the work of Freire to American education, Shor's work models a combination of writing and organizing that grounds theory in live issues while foregrounding the work of everyday teachers.

Another body of critical literacy work not covered in Shor's essay is focused on local writing groups. It is exemplified in the community writing projects of Patricia Stock (1995) and David Schaafsma (1993), the Neighborhood Writing Alliance's *Journal of Ordinary Thought*, and Carol E. Heller's research (1997) with women writers in San Francisco's Tenderloin and Eli Goldblatt's New City Community Press (2007). Finally, digital storytelling projects, such as Glynda Hull and Michael James's DUSTY (Digital Underground Storytelling for Youth) (2003) and the Community House's STRUGGLE (Long, Peck, & Baskins, 2002), put new technology in the hands of urban children, who use multimedia to invent and screen the stories of their own lives in words, images, and music.

5. For good accounts of these different literate practices, see David Barton and Mary Hamilton's *Local Literacies* (1998), Patrick Finn's *Literacy with an Attitude*

(1999), Paul Willis's *Learning to Labor* (1977), Ellen Cushman's *The Struggle and the Tools* (1998), and Saul D. Alinsky's *Rules for Radicals* (1989).

6. Descriptions of STRUGGLE can be found in Long, Peck, and Baskins (2002); of DUSTY in Hull and James (2003). The *Journal of Ordinary People* is published by the Neighborhood Writing Alliance in Chicago.

7. Bellah, Madsen, Sullivan, Swidler, and Tipton (1985) describe this disintegration of a sense of civic participation in American life just as Habermas (1962/1989) bemoans the loss of an openly communicative public sphere.

8. In addition to Lorraine Higgins and Elenore Long, who became post-doctoral CLC directors, Maureen Mathison, David Fleming, Susan Lawrence, Patricia Wojan, Julia Deems, Jennifer Flach, and Gwen Gorzelsky were partners in research and mentoring.

9. Kurt Spellmeyer's *Arts of Living* (2003) offers a probing analysis of the limits of critical theory in his argument for reinventing the humanities as an art of grounded personal and social engagement.

10. Harkavy and Puckett (1991) give a historical account of these unequal relationships at Penn State University, University Park. But similar accounts of kiss-and-run research came up in a local dialogue with community leaders in Pittsburgh (Flower and Heath, 2000) and in the prevailing logics for such partnerships (Flower, 1997a).

11. Since then, a new journal has emerged (instigated in 1999 within the CCCC Special Interest Group on Service-Learning), entitled *Reflections: A Journal of Writing, Service-Learning, and Community Literacy,* followed in 2006 by another journal simply titled, *Community Literacy* (in which Higgins, Long, and Flower argue for a rhetorical model of community literacy).

12. The habit of defining a community as an entity has had problems. The warmly persuasive idea of "community," Joe Harris (1989) argues, is often no more than a sweeping, fuzzy, friendly notion defined by the presence of common beliefs, purposes, consensus, or perhaps no more than a common set of references or allusions (as in a discourse or an interpretive community) but without defining boundaries. Moreover, when it exists at a distant remove from actual experience—as a metacommunity or utopia—it is "oddly free of many of the tensions, discontinuities, and conflicts that go on every day in the classrooms and departments of a university" (p. 14) Academic discourse itself, he says, would be more accurately represented by the metaphor of a city—a place where struggle and change are not threats to coherence but part of its normal activity (p. 20). John Swales (1998) proposes a localized notion of a community by describing an academic research center as a *discourse forum,* yet here a common goal and purpose still unites the group. Like Harris, we want to imagine "a community without consensus" (1989, p. 19).

The problem of defining *community* arises for Michael Moore and John Warnock (2007), editors of *Community Literacy,* in framing a research design, as it did for the faculty and students of Jeffrey Grabill and Ellen Cushman's graduate class in defining their subject (Fero, et al., 2007). To anthropologist Anthony Cohen (1985), a community (unlike a social structure like a clan or neighborhood) is symbolically constructed by the way its members define, use, and share cultural symbols. Rhetorician Gerard Hauser (1999) describes the related notion of "public" in similar ways: publics, like public opinion, do not exist waiting to be found by marketing people but are formed by the shared activity of communication. So instead of looking for a place or group, we will focus on the communication and interaction that are pulling a particular community or a public into being, even as we observe it. The "community" we are describing is at once local and concrete, held together by a rhetorical symbolic choice to address its shared problems as a local public sphere characterized by tension and contradiction.

13. Hauser (1999) describes what he calls the "vernacular rhetoric" of informal deliberative publics. And as Susan Gilpin (2004) discovered, a rhetoric of local, public exploratory inquiry (versus advocacy) may even be going on in the midst of shampoos and haircuts. Her observational study of hair salons documents a style of spontaneous, nonargumentative dialogue on social issues, in which people relate issues to personal experiences and express values but remain open to other perspectives.

14. For example, in a study of collaborative student groups, Rebecca Burnett (1991) showed that structures that allowed conflict over substantive and procedural (rather than personal) issues produced more effective arguments and designs.

15. For descriptions of these counterpublics, see Fraser, 1990; Warner, 2005; and Black Public Sphere Collective, 1995.

16. Facing this same contradiction, Elenore Long justifies a decision to include the questionably "legitimate" public of Cintron's gangs in her study of community-literacy publics by noting that "in part, it's exclusion from a public sphere that forces marginalized people to develop their own 'guerrilla life' and 'tactics' in the first place" (2008, p.143). Moreover, in analyzing publics that defy formal institutions, drawing a continuum that leads to black girls punished for the sexual overtones of their "stepping" routines on school property, she argues that "the gutsy willfulness to lift the veil on a system's hidden hypocrisies is part of what makes the rhetorical force of a counterpublic so compelling" (2008, p.146).

17. Beyond the citations in the text, I want to note that arguments here are particularly indebted to stimulating work at the intersections of public rhetoric and justice. In particular, Jürgen Habermas's foundational and much-disputed image of the bourgeois public sphere, Nancy Fraser's astute analysis of its suppression of difference, Iris Young's philosophical argument for the justice of inclusion, Gerard Hauser's analysis of an alternative, networked, vernacular public, Patricia Roberts-Miller's support of deliberative democracy with an astute and balanced critique of how traditional models of public discourse suppress conflict and deliberation in the public and the classroom, extended by the historical work of Janet Atwill and Susan Jarrett in the roots of humanist education and rhetoric that silence difference, and in Michael Warner's bold model of circulating discourse and subversive counterpublics.

18. Spellmeyer goes on to argue that under the spell of specialization and instrumentalism, education no longer holds out "the promise of their full participation in the *res publica*; . . . [students] see themselves as quiescent actors in a play authored by Culture, or History, Art or Science" (1993, p. 58).

19. In *The Rhetoric of Literate Social Action: Mentors Negotiating Intercultural Images of Literacy*, Elenore Long's study of the semester-long discovery process and negotiation of college mentors turns up some revealing parallels between their assumptions and the academic debate over the nature of literacy and suggests the consequences different notions of literacy can have for our relationships with others. Long's insight shaped the training of mentors at the CLC and her later work as its director.

20. In *Learning to Rival: A Literate Practice for Intercultural Inquiry*, we observed college students struggling with the request to depart from the secure stance of thesis and support they had developed in high school, even when the assignment explicitly asked them to pose open questions and consider rival approaches to an issue that had no possibility of an easy answer. (Flower, Long, & Higgins, 2000). Like Spellmeyer (1993), we see the need to actively and explicitly help students learn this search for common ground. Paulo Freire (1970/1985) locates the difficulty not only as an intellectual challenge but as an ethical and relational one of choosing to be in dialogue.

2. Taking Literate Action

1. *Observation-based* theory building in rhetoric and writing research is a search for working theories that are grounded in the investigation of actual writers and speakers in specific contexts (Flower, 1989). As a theory-building process, it attempts to craft an explanatory account (not just an empirical "finding"), but one that is not merely logically coherent but also empirically based, that seeks rival interpretations, and is willing to be surprised and challenged by the unpredicted and often unpredictable data of experience. It presumes the constant interaction of cognition and social context but treats the nature of that interaction as an open question.

2. Ian Rawson's broader perspective on health is documented in his family story in Barry Paris's account of Gwen Mellon and Dr. Larimer Mellon, the founders the Albert Schweitzer Hospital in Haiti, in *Song of Haiti* (New York: Public Affairs, 2000).

3. This research is reviewed in *The Construction of Negotiated Meaning*, Flower (1994), and in chapter 4 of the current volume.

4. This argument for how inquiry can produce change is developed in chapters 6 and 9. In the current chapter, I draw a contrast between Habermas's (1962/1989) notion of a public sphere working through rational deliberation and Michael Warner's (2005) alternative account in which a public is in fact created by the "circulation" (and transmutation) or ideas.

5. Julia Deems designed *Rivaling about Risk: A Dialogue Tutorial* (1996) as an interactive HyperCard program in which CLC teens wrote and performed short video clips dramatizing risky encounters with peers. Users were invited to interpret the problem first in writing and then using their printouts in small groups and to propose rival responses, including those of adults, from a storekeeper to their grandmother.

Amanda Young created *What's Your Plan? Sexuality and Relationships: A Multimedia Dialogue/Tutorial* (1996) in Director software to support personal planning in a on- and off-line dialogue with young women, using community literacy strategies to make and print out an individualized plan. The program was used with a Planned Parenthood high school program and then became part of large research and pregnancy prevention project with Pittsburgh's Children's Hospital (A. J. Young, 2000). In "Patients as Partners; Patients as Problem Solvers" (2002), Young and Flower proposed a theoretical framework for collaborative health care communication illustrated with Young's observations in the ER study.

Lorraine Higgins took the design of ARGUE (described in chapter 1's Suspension project) to an urban free clinic to help women talk and work through their difficulties dealing with health care providers. Their written booklet, *Getting to Know You: A Dialogue for Community Health*, combined stories, rivals interpretations, and alternative endings. It revealed the source of some communication problems with doctors and was incorporated in a hospital residency training program (Higgins & Chalich, 1996).

6. *Teamwork* was produced by the CLC's Hands On Video production team, led by Donald Tucker and directed by Linda Flower. The text was written together with the teen actors. A transcript is available on the CLC archive Web site: http://english.cmu.edu/research/inquiry/two.html.

3. Images of Engagement in Composition Studies

1. For reviews of this history from different perspectives, see North (1987), Faigley (1992), Spellmeyer (1993), and Harris (1997).

2. *Defining the New Rhetorics*, edited by Enos and Brown (1993), reflects how the revival of rhetoric in fact took the form of creating multiple rhetorics.

3. Books like Jarratt's (1991b) *Rereading the Sophists: Classical Rhetoric Refigured* and Lunsford's (1995) *Reclaiming Rhetorica* revived rhetoric, while challenging traditional interpretations of it, by taking us back to the classical texts. Nevertheless, the vigorous study of rhetorical invention that marked the earlier "new rhetoric" movement (cf. the retrospective collections by Atwill and Lauer [2002] and Lauer, Young, and Liu [1994]) gave way to the study of language and text as linguistic and social objects.

4. Bakhtin (1986) describes these typified forms as "speech genres," which correspond to typical speech or communicative *situations* (rather than the vast range of possibilities within, say, academic discourse). And as Wertsch (1991, pp. 60–66) points out, these "ready-made" resources for performance are deeply dialogic (i.e., addressed to someone), making the speech genre of "formal instruction," for instance, strongly situated in classroom practice and its patterns of authority.

5. As Lester Faigley notes in his largely adulatory account of postmodernist thinking in English, *Fragments of Rationality*, the paradigm never came to grips with the problem of individual agency (1992, pp. 225–39).

6. Guides to this way of thinking have long existed in the differing examples set by writers like Shirley Brice Heath (1983; 1993; 1999) exploring ways with words in Appalachia and the language of identity-making and achievement in urban neighborhoods; by Mike Rose (1989) finding his way as a teacher in South Los Angeles; by Glenda Hull (1997) bringing the literacies and logic of low-wage workers into the discussion of management and national workforce policy; by Ira Shor (1987) bringing into print the vision of Paulo Freire and the voice of the working-class students and teachers in a far-flung network of projects and alliances, and by Kurt Spellmeyer (1993) seeing freshman writing as an introduction to a new humanities, based on *involvement* with the world.

Scholars, such as Ellen Cushman and Scott Lyons, conduct their research by immersing themselves in the rhetorical encounters between African American women and the welfare system and Native Americans and the Bureau of Indian Affairs (Cushman, 1999; Lyons, 2000). They then lead us into recognizing hidden forms of agency, envisioning the possibility of a collaborative rhetorical sovereignty, and accepting the role of teachers as public intellectuals. Elenore Long, Wayne Peck and Joyce Baskins (2002) allow us to see literacy as a tool of struggle as urban teens and caring adults work toward identity and understanding. Lorraine Higgins and

Lisa Brush (2006) show how women stigmatized by welfare establish an ethos in the face of a discrediting discourse and turn narrative into a strategy for public engagement.

7. The phrase *discovery and change* comes from the influential text by Young, Becker, and Pike (1970), whose legacy is traced in Maureen Goggin's *Inventing a Discipline* (2000). My own understanding of rhetoric and its focus on shared problems in this work is profoundly indebted to the work and example of Richard Young.

8. In a revealing comparative analysis of community literacy programs, Elenore Long (2008) documents the dominant images or metaphors different programs use to define themselves as well as the kinds of literacy and the methods of rhetorical invention they support. These choices allow her to examine the implications each stance has for local public discourse.

9. Berlin went so far as to argue that a problem-solving stance was a politically suspect way of thinking that made one the dupe of corporate capitalism. And, indeed, learning to name and analyze problems in this way is a highly transferable professional skill; it is the discourse of American management. In contrast to the more literary and/or critical style focused on problem "posing," problem "solving" calls for an action in response. Berlin had an important point (especially if one chooses to focus on quick-fix "solutions" instead of "solving"). But I believe he got the problem wrong. The ethical decision here has little to do with the genre of analysis and even less to do with the ubiquitous cognitive-literate act of defining and responding to problems (what Berlin was himself doing in his essay). What he should have targeted was the choices we make about which problems we attend to, how we define and analyze them, and what we do then. In particular, whose problem are we addressing and whose perspectives are not merely allowed but invited into the framing. This literate practice, I would argue, can be a powerful tool in the rhetoric of making a difference—the question will be teaching ourselves how to use it best. Berlin argued for (and modeled) an alternative discourse of deconstruction and critique in his own teaching and writing, preferring the rather flamboyant gestures of standing against something, in the community organizing style of Saul Alinsky—polarizing issues to spark debate (Alinsky, 1989).

If we have our eyes on change outside the classroom walls, we must also be cautious about misreading Paulo Freire's necessary emphasis on problem posing as a license to stop there. Complex social problems do not get "solved"—it is good to be suspicious of anyone who seems to think that. But, as Freire argues, they call for praxis, for action wedded to reflection (1970/1985). Problem solving requires us to go beyond critique—to respond where we cannot solve. We cannot choose to keep our hands clean by disdaining the hard work of building solutions—those invariably flawed and vulnerable to critique, but revisable actionable images of engagement.

10. *Cognitive* has come to mean many things in social cognitive comparisons. "Social" critiques of the cognitive perspective frequently reduce it to "cognitivism," in which thinking is reduced to "the manipulation of 'information' ('facts') using general ('logical') rules and principles [and to computer-like information processing] based on its form/structure, not its meaning" (Gee, 2000). The metaphors of "information processing" clearly inform the Hayes and Flower cognitive model (1980), which did indeed have little to say about society or culture. On the other hand, a companion paper in the same 1980 volume on "The Dynamics of Composing: Making Plans

and Juggling Constraints" (Flower & Hayes, 1980), shows how, from the beginning, cognitive *rhetoric* uses the "think aloud" methods and modeling metaphors of cognitive psychology to investigate *people thinking*. These thinkers were certainly not dependent on formal rules of logic; instead, they were actively constructing meaning—juggling the demands of discourse and affect as well as ideas. Perhaps the really critical and enduring distinction between these two perspectives in rhetoric and composition is the chosen unit of analysis: social research looks closely at textual, social, and cultural patterns and conventions; cognitive research is focused on people thinking with, within (and at times against) those structures.

11. The picture that emerged from this planning research is elaborated in Flower, "Construction of Purpose" (1988) and Flower, Schriver, Carey, Haas, & Hayes, "Planning in Writing: The Cognition of a Constructive Process" (1992).

12. See Dell Hymes and John Gumperz's influential 1972 collection of ethnographies of communication.

13. This attempt to respond to larger patterns of marginalization and injustice within local situations can be seen by comparing Mark's problem analysis with those of later projects, such as the one on city curfew (see chapter 8). Here the problem is raised not only as face-to-face police encounters but also in terms of city policy, simmering racism in the suburbs, and the history of civil rights action.

14. The notion of a social cognitive literate *practice*, developed by Scribner and Cole (1981) in their landmark research on literacy, has figured in the subsequent development of activity theory and its focus on situated purposeful action. See Chaiklin and Lave's (1993) excellent introduction to activity research in education and psychology and Bazerman and Russell's 2002 collection of emerging activity theory work in writing and literacy.

15. A note on method in social cognitive inquiry: The critical problem is obviously defining one's unit of analysis. If a researcher wants to understand how a profoundly integrated and interactive cognitive and social act is working—that is, to go beyond what can be postulated in theory and to make one's hypothesis more fully accountable to experience—what phenomenon or object should be put in focal attention? As Wertsch (1991) argues, both Mikhail Bakhtin and Lev S. Vygotsky made a radical break with other formalist research by defining their unit of analysis as mediated action and "individual(s)-operating-with-mediational-means" (pp. 12, 96, 120). Activity theory, which is examined in chapter 6, develops that insight into the systematic framework of an activity system.

Our search for better ways to study the "activity" postulated in this social cognitive theorizing led us to look at collaborative planning episodes—sessions in which writers were dealing with an emphatically social cognitive moment in writing. Tapes and transcripts of these writer-controlled sessions became not only a source of formal research data but also a tool that teachers, teacher researchers, and students used to explore writing strategies and thinking as well as to improve a given text (see Flower, 1994, chapters 5 and 6 for more detail on these methods and chapter 8 for what they revealed in the hands of students; Flower, Wallace, Norris, & Burnett, 1994, for its use by teacher researchers).

16. By this, I mean interpreters who have access to data, not just fleeting memories. The experiments with collaborative-planning data mentioned above taught us two important things: first, writers with access to this data have privileged insight into the

complex orchestration of ideas and assignments, emotions, decisions, conversations, and éclaircissements that uniquely shaped their learning and writing. Do not get me wrong; researchers bring a necessary and different conceptual lens to interpreting such data, but we fool ourselves if we think our methods or theory will allow us to also infer the "situated knowledge" of others. An intercultural rhetoric of engagement requires even more collaborative ways of eliciting and listening to that sort of knowledge. Secondly, data from a writer's planning and collaborative sessions with a partner gave us a vivid insight into what we called "the logic of learners"—and a new way to see the hidden forms of rhetorical agency (see Flower, 1994, chapter 7).

17. In another study that compared university and community-college freshmen, David L. Wallace (1996) found that the predictor of success was not the student's institution but the amount of specifically rhetorical planning the writer did.

18. Although this study described in *Learning to Rival* (Flower, Long, & Higgins, 2000) focused on how students learn a literate practice valued in multiple disciplines, we felt that the real significance was in its value for intercultural inquiry—in how one learns to support such thinking, seek out its hidden logics, and share the knowledge it constructs.

19. This argument is worked out in *The Construction of Negotiated Meaning: A Social Cognitive Theory of Writing* (Flower, 1994, chapters 2 and 3).

20. A word on rethinking. The methodological and theoretical evolution of this social cognitive theory of negotiated meaning making was a kind of rethinking sparked in part by opposing paradigms. It was responding to both a rising awareness of social forces throughout educational research and to the critiques of the cognitive paradigm in writing. Rethinking comes from critiques that point out limitations and blindsides, that disagree with the goals or premises of a theory, and that worry about (or much better, actually offer evidence of) its outcomes. However, the adversarial stance so admired in literary and cultural critique and the assumption that productive rethinking is the result of deconstruction rather than construction are overrated. They encourage writers to operate on a model of conflict, competition, resistance, or capitulation within a marketplace of ideas. By contrast, the image of negotiated meaning making emerging in my research offers a different model in which rethinking can be guided by a strongly held set of goals, a personal insight, or a burning question, which draws the writer into an inquiry that attempts to embrace difference as a source of more complex understanding.

4. Who Am I? What Am I Doing Here?

1. An earlier version of this discussion appeared in Flower (1997a) "Partners in Inquiry: A Logic for Community Outreach."

2. Thomas Deans's (2000) excellent study of this new movement grounds the search for "writing partnerships" in composition in both Freire and Dewey and carefully sketches the logics that separate projects along his three-part taxonomy: writing about, writing for, and writing with the community.

3. In 1982, for example, the pool of marriageable (employed) men (ages sixteen to seventeen, based on a ratio of men to women) was 13% for blacks (but nearly 40% for whites). In the age twenty to twenty-four group, it was still under 50% (Wilson, 1987, pp. 84–86).

4. Dewey and Freire have offered the most important theoretical foundations for service-learning. Yet, as Tom Deans's (2007) richly developed comparisons of

Dewey, Rorty, and Freire detail, Freire's emphasis on a critical revelation of social reality, on unpacking myths and comprehending power, takes education beyond Dewey's preparation for civic participation into a more intercultural and political social action. West, who shares this critical temperament with Freire, speaks even more explicitly to what I would call the pedagogy of the privileged and, as discussed in chapter 8, what it can mean to be a partner in inquiry with others.

5. In 1995, my colleagues and I began a series of studies documenting what we called the "hybrid discourse" of community literacy as it appeared in the text and talk of urban teenagers, in public community conversations, in the writing of college mentors, and in dialogue within a community think tank (described in Peck, Flower, & Higgins, 1995; Flower, 1996a, 1996b, 2002a, 2002b). In these contexts, a hybrid discourse is not just a theorized ideal, linguistic artifact, or an expressive act a teacher accepts. It is a shared way of talking, thinking, and writing that must be constructed and nurtured, lost and regained—with difficulty and persistence. These studies described the difficulty with which these hybrid discourses were constructed and the ways they seemed to pull everyone who participated in them out of their comfort zone, yet, in the end, were able to create some distinctive ways of understanding and addressing issues. However, our studies, unlike the argument of *Alt Dis* discussed below, suggest that the problem here isn't merely accepting the idea of mixed or *alternative* ways with words; the problem is how do you (given your particular location) discover, support, and/or teach a truly *generative* alternative.

6. I want to be clear: My point is about the concluding discourse move Fox uses to interpret her activist stance. I read her discussion itself as a strong example of someone bent on constructing a situated and negotiated working theory.

7. The evidence for the large role that conflict and negotiation play here is based on electronic bulletin-board posts and audiotaped self-interviews Long identified as "conflict episodes" with a high level of interrater reliability.

8. For an extended discussion of mentors' wrestling with working theories of their own roles and identity, see Flower, 1996a.

9. Jon's college class, "Rhetoric of Making a Difference," helped organize the Community Think Tank on "Healthcare: The Dilemma of Teamwork, Time, and Turnover" with the management and staff of Lemington, a local African American nursing home. Background on the Carnegie Mellon Community Think Tank and the *Findings* from this project can be found on www.cmu.edu/thinktank, and some of the results are discussed in chapter 9.

5. *Images of Empowerment*

1. Identity-making and empowerment have been vividly portrayed in diverse contexts, from Caroline Heller's *Until We Are Strong Together*(1997) about women writers in San Francisco's Tenderloin district, to the social performers in Heath and McLaughlin's *Identity and Inner-City Youth*, (1993), to the hip hop writers and Chicano/Chicana scholars in Kells, Balester, and Villanueva's *Latino/a Discourses* (2004), to the urban students in McComiskey and Ryan's *City Comp* (2003).

2. Joseph Harris questions whether revealing one's self in a writing class ("the whole unflinching truth about themselves") to an authority figure is really empowering (1997, p. 43). In his alternative, students explore not just their personal but also their intellectual experience. In the place of expressing an authentic self, a writer comes to see how, as an intellectual, he or she uses discourses and texts "as a kind

of performance, a working through of the various roles and possibilities that her language and situation offer her" (pp. 35–36).

3. See Waterman (1997, pp. 7–9). Advocates of service-learning in the tradition of John Dewey often justify it as an ideal form of experientially based liberal education—for the service giver. Other important overviews are in Adler-Kassner, Crooks, & Watters (1997), Deans, 2000, and new journals, such as, *Reflections: A Journal of Writing, Service Learning, and Community Literacy* and *Community Literacy.*

4. The difficulty of achieving "collaborative design and empowerment" within community organizations (Grabill, 2001, p. 58) finds its parallel in accounts of students attempting to work with and for them (Deans, 2000, pp. 53–84; Bacon & Deans, 1997).

5. The New Literacy Group, associated with the work of Brian Street (2001) and James Gee, Glynda Hull, and Colin Lankshear (1996), combines detailed analyses of language and literacy use with critical analyses of discourse and power. David Barton and Mary Hamilton's *Local Literacies* (1998) gives an intensive look at reading and writing in one community in Lancaster, England. Glynda Hull's study of high-performance workplaces documents electronics workers resisting corporate notions of scripted empowerment. An excellent overview of this research is found in Hull and Schultz (2002, pp. 11–31).

6. Ira Shor's source book for liberatory teaching, *Freire for the Classroom* (1987), is remarkable not just for its multiple models of how to scaffold analysis and dialogue but also for its examples of "classroom" writing that leads students to larger public dialogues, such as the letters of victimized Bahamian women published in the local paper to their men (pp. 100–101).

7. For most writers in this collection, empowerment is synonymous with forging an identity. Yet the notion of Latino (or is it Chicano, Tejano, Mexicano, Hispanic?) identity is a site of contradictions, as is the literate practice an educator uses to scaffold identity making. In the literature at large, educational empowerment can range from supporting a literary Chicano/a voice, to a critical, historical ethnic consciousness, to a hip-hop rhymer. Less discussed are the critical choices we as educators make. Can we focus on just one of these practices and hope the others will tag along? Can you have a transcultural identity without *also* cultivating critical awareness, without a public voice?

8. In a disagreement with Kenneth Bruffee, Kurt Spellmeyer (1993) argues that "dialogical" can't simply mean peer dialogue or peer conversation. Rather, he would plunge students into a demanding, written "'conversation' between convention and experience"—that is between intellectual traditions, scholarly knowledge, and disciplinary thinking, on the one hand, and local knowledge, personal experience, and the learner's own life world on the other (pp. 32, 5–59).

9. This account is drawn from "Literate Action," Flower, 1996a, pp. 257–60.

10. By *negotiated* I mean he is attending to the real and metaphorical "voices" embedded in tradition and personal experience, in language and convention, as well as in personal goals and intuitions. Rising to awareness of problems, options, and rivals within his own thinking, he chooses to embrace (rather than avoid) these generative conflicts and work toward a provisional but actionable meaning—a working theory of how to empower his mentee.

This account of negotiated meaning grows out of research with college writers and collaborators, responding to the often-unnoticed stream of conflicting voices that echo throughout the writing process (Flower, 1994, chap. 5). It has parallels to the classroom inquiry Dennis Lynch, Diana George, and Marilyn Cooper describe, when students must "negotiate" not only "conflicts of knowledge" and "conflicts of positioning and power" but also the internal conflicts of reformulating their own position, understanding, and even identity as they enter "unexpected alliances" and "new relations with others" (1997, pp. 66, 69).

6. Intercultural Inquiry and the Transformation of Service

1. An earlier version of this chapter appeared in *College English*, 65(2), (2002): 181–201.

2. The term *guerrilla service* is borrowed from Joe Mertz, who worked with me as codirector of the Carnegie Mellon Center for University Outreach. In "Computer Science in the Community," Mertz and Kathy Schroerlucke describe the changes in course design and student thinking it took for computer science students to partner with community groups not as "superhacker" experts but as consultants supporting the learning of community partners.

3. This account is based on Jean Lave's fine overview of "The Practice of Learning" (1993, cf. p. 17) and Yrjö Engeström's excellent introduction to activity analysis in "Developmental Studies of Work as a Testbench of Activity Theory" (1993) in *Understanding Practice*, one of the best, early overviews of activity analysis across disciplines.

4. Although not the focus of this paper, intercultural inquiry can also lead to more direct social action. An in-depth activity analysis of a Community Think Tank (Flower, 2002b) shows how this literate practice can work as a mediating tool for change. For an overview of the Think Tank process and *Findings*, see www.cmu.edu/thinktank.

5. The context was a course called Community Literacy and Intercultural Interpretation, which combined mentoring at Pittsburgh's Community Literacy Center with an inquiry into "the networks of support and images of identity" on which urban youth draw. These student inquiries became part of an ongoing dialogue published on the Intercultural Inquiry Web site, http://english.cmu.edu/research/inquiry/two.html. Research methods for this sort of inquiry are discussed in chapter 10 of the current volume.

6. These phrases, borrowed from Schutz and Gere (based on the work of Hannah Arendt and Maxine Green) lets them connect service-learning to the larger disciplinary history of public rhetoric.

7. In practice, such a stance means being alive to the diverse ways people represent their knowing, moving across multiple kinds of discourse and sources of data. In these projects, students are asked to use at least three kinds of data: from published research, theory, archives and texts; from observations; and from texts, dialogues, and interviews, including their own bulletin-board exchanges and reflections. Although personal reflection typically plays a key role in service-learning, intercultural inquiry asks students to base that reflection on the rich data of observation.

8. The full texts of Scott's "5 O'clock World" and Anne's paper are published on the Intercultural Inquiry website at http://english.cmu.edu/research/inquiry/two.html. His is under the Culture of Work projects; hers is under Other Inquiry projects.

9. Students used this text-based rival-reading strategy to initiate a dialogue with their teenage mentees and to initiate themselves through this manageable step into

the process of structured inquiry. Flach's (1999) classroom study documents how the process of sharing these rival readings of student-selected passages often led partners into "mutually constructed situated meanings" and into revealing interpretations and dialogues based on "trying to understand another person's reality" (pp. 178–79).

10. Readers of the manuscript of this article raised an important question about the fate of deep political differences within an inquiry. This is an open question, but I was able to document one such charged experience. It was ignited at the CLC by a fifteen-minute workshop on revising, based on my "impeccably grounded" linguistic knowledge and my personal value for and politically engaged recognition of Black English. The surprising mixture of incredulity and resistance to this as a "racist" concept (from mentors, teens, and leaders) posed some teacherly and ethical dilemmas (described in Flower, 1996b). In this case, I believe it was reframing the issue (including my own supposed expertise) into the subject of an intercultural inquiry that turned this suddenly polarized and mutually perplexing debate into a mutual learning experience.

11. I owe special thanks for good advice on the earlier version of this chapter to Tom Deans, Joseph Harris, Shirley Brice Heath, Lorraine Higgins, Andrea Lunsford, and Tim Flower, to readers Karen Paley and Susanmarie Harrington, and to an anonymous reviewer.

7. *The Search for Situated Knowledge*

1. Spelling and punctuation of the teen-authored excerpts throughout follows the original published text.

2. As seen in chapters 2 and 3, writers appropriated this strategy for various ends. The minority college students (whom we also followed in the Learning to Rival project) used the stance less flexibly as they tried to enter an academic conversation. At the same time, they used it to wrestle not only with the meaning of discourse features, such as evidence and authority but also with issues of race and identity as writers.

3. Just as writing can move among different external sign systems (language, drawing, equations), our thinking works with multiple modes of internal representation as well. The differences become acutely apparent when we must turn a visual, affective, or kinesthetic representation, for instance, into language or a gist, standard prose, or coherent argument. The implications of these multiple representations are elaborated on and then updated in Flower and Hayes (1984) and Flower (1994), pp. 85–107.

4. This distinction does not make a mentalist claim that ignores the role of embodied representations—in artifacts, bodies, and actions—but focuses us on the tacit character of this aspect of cognition.

5. An important source of an individual's situated knowledge is likely to be the shared schemas described in cognitive research and the patterns of ideology described in literary theory. However, reducing our account of this phenomenon to those levels of generality would lose sight of its multiple sources, its richly detailed, often individualized content, and its unpredictable influence on interpretation.

6. The phrase *situated knowledge* is often used in feminist philosophy of science and educational psychology to make a broader epistemological claim—that all knowing is ultimately a situated hypothesis. I am using it in a more local sense here to describe a form of representation that we can distinguish from alternative forms of cognition and communication.

7. Coogan's argument draws on the materialist rhetoric of Michael McGee, who, not unlike Dewey, argues that "concepts (such as liberty or equality) are adjectival, meaningful only in attachment to a concrete political practice" (McGee, qtd. in Coogan, 2002, pp. 294–95). Public discussion relies on "a vocabulary of concepts that function as guides, warrants, reasons, or excuses for behavior or belief" (McGee, qtd. in Coogan, 2002, p. 280). The problem is in knowing what those locally embedded concepts *mean* to a particular group of people in a given place and time. Coogan argues for an understanding of the concepts that shape public thought based on the study of the political practice in which they gained currency. He has gone on to develop a program of community/university collaboration, first in Chicago then Richmond, Virginia, that is a model of inquiry, collaboration, and student engagement based on grounded rhetorical research (cf. also Coogan, 2005). His studies and the ones offered here also show how a cognitive and a materialist rhetoric can help us examine two sides of the same coin.

8. In a study of knowledge building within an intercultural community think tank (another form of these problem-solving dialogues), I argued that the think tank's unique strength may be its ability to re-represent or translate policies and decisions from propositions into more dynamic *inter*cultural "activities" in the sense proposed by Engeström (1993) and other activity analysts (Flower, 2002b).

9. Just as a problem only exists as a problem *for someone,* the understandings transformed by cross talk must take shape in the minds of individuals in response to their needs. But these understandings will take their meaning in the actions people take, as members of families, communities, and institutions—whether it is as a single mother, a voting councilperson, or college student entering professional life.

10. However, as Teun van Dijk (1993) has shown, the ostensibly balanced, elite discourses of the academy and the media often enact domination and racism with a variety of indirect moves.

8. Taking Rhetorical Agency

1. A detailed account of this event is found in Flower, Long, and Higgins, *Learning to Rival* (2000), pp. 277–84.

2. After some discussion, the Writers (as the teen participants were always called) had decided to design their document as a sort of newspaper. As a matter of policy, the CLC normally published texts, after joint editing sessions, as the writer wrote them. It was this session time Raymond missed.

3. One of the most grounded accounts of individualism in the popular imagination is found in Bellah, Madsen, Sullivan, Swidler, and Tipton's extended case studies in *Habits of the Heart* (1985). The authors document how America's conflicting traditions of individualism and community play out in the experience of growing up, marriage, and work.

4. Kurt Spellmeyer describes the strong choice: "On the one hand, Progressive Era educators took for granted the Cartesian autonomy of the subject, a subject fully aware of its motives and guided in action by reason, . . . [remaining] steadfastly oblivious to the real conditions" of social lives that are subject to forces beyond our control. Others, in an effort to escape the charge of a naïve or sentimental image of the self or who are persuaded cultural theory's determinism, "rewrite the story of the individual as a footnote to knowledge or tradition or social systems on the grand

scale" (1993, p. 31). In David Bartholomae's (1985) milder version of this rewriting, the goal of basic writers is to appropriate and be appropriated by academic discourse.

5. Mowitt sums up Smith's conclusion in words that pile one qualification atop another, "Smith appears willing to identify agency with the general preconditions that make the theoretical articulation of the critique of the subject possible" (1988, p. xii).

6. This ironic image of the critic, as the only agent left standing within the critique of agency, turns up in rhetorical theory. As Michael Leff describes this move, "Again the reader is active; the text is inert. From this perspective, of course, the rhetor ceases to function as a significant agent, but the ideology of agency remains. Instead of the *orator perfectus*, we have the master reader, the *lector perfectus*" (1993, p 298).

7. Gaonkar himself theorizes that the theoretical/interpretive stance of contemporary rhetoric must abandon the "ideology of human agency" central to the productive/performative stance of classical rhetoric. My alternative argument for embedded agency is, however, illustrated by Gaonkar's own critical practice in this provocative essay. In Gaonkar's own case study, as commentator Michael Leff notes, "Agency becomes a matter of the circulation of influence, something that remains fluid as one positioned subject engages the work of another, altering the work while being altered by it" (1993, p. 299).

8. The method of rhetorical reading used here, based on Haas and Flower (1988), combines thinking aloud with a series of prompts asking, "How do you interpret the text now?" that reveal at least a part of the changing and increasingly complex representation the reader is constructing.

9. In a classroom context, Wallace and Ewald (2000) show how encouraging what they call "interpretive agency" (a joint search for understanding with students) supports the kind of *mutuality* valued in Deweyan, Marxist, and feminist pedagogies.

10. James Wertsch's *Voices of the Mind* (1991) offers a richly complex introduction to the notion of mediated action. Some accounts in composition, such as Martin Nystrand, Stuart Greene, and Jeffrey Wiemelt's (1993) useful history, create a dichotomy between a rhetorical, constructivist account of writing and a dialogic one. However, I find it more useful to seek an integrated account in which individual, purposive writers, rhetors, and agents operate within an unavoidably, intensely dialogic process. Moreover, it is one in which expertise and impact are often tied to one's awareness of that dialogic reality.

11. The convergence on *performance* and *relations* I mention was most clearly suggested to me in a set of thirty-nine position papers responding to the troubled question, "How ought we to understand the concept of rhetorical agency?" The space for these particular acts of rhetorical agency was an invitational Alliance of Rhetoric Societies Conference—a sort of think tank on the future of rhetoric held in 2003 in Evanston, Illinois. Though hardly a place to expect agreement, this discussion was actively wrestling with postmodern critiques of the ideology of agency and rhetoric's necessity to name the ground for social action. Scholars giving particular presence to this idea in various guises include Janet Atwill, Jerry Blitefield, Dan Brouwer, Celeste Condit, Rene Dube, Cheryl Geisler, Carl Herndl, Nan Johnson, John Lucaites, and Susan Wells.

12. This is not to discount all the other often-unrecognized forces that shape an act of embedded agency but to highlight the choice to respond to some of them.

13. In this social cognitive theory of negotiated meaning, rhetorical agents construct meaning around contested matters of significance. The forces that would shape meaning are both external (material, social, or cultural pressures) and internal voices in the writer's own mind (goals, values, assumptions, strategies, habits of mind, discourses, and ideologies). And these forces are often in tension, even conflict. However, in this account, the writer is neither the controller nor simply the victim of such forces. The writer is—at times—an actor at the center of a negotiation, actively attempting to construct a meaning out of it. The central aspect of this process is what I have described as "rising to negotiated meaning making"—that is, attending at some level of awareness to competing and conflicting voices and attempting acknowledge and deal with, rather avoid this complexity (Flower, 1994).

14. The Learning to Rival study of which this is a part describes some personally significant interpretive choices made by both college students and CLC teens—and how their decisions and acts of interpretive agency were obscured to the eyes of teachers and mentors when the writers' choices included failing to follow expected conventions (Flower, Long, and Higgins, 2000).

15. Elenore Long, David Fleming, and I compared the teens' argument to a newsletter circulated by the university at the same time in which the warning about drugs was marked by its scientific tone, tables, and logical, statistical, and probabilistic arguments. In choosing to dramatize possibilities with a performative and dialogic style, Fleming wrote, "The writers in this project evidenced a low estimation of the transactive power of facts and probabilities" (2000, p. 271).

16. These counter traditions in rhetoric help explain how some of the practices we prize in community literacy (from the rivaling strategy to linking critical reflection with public dialogue to giving explicit standing to marginalized people and literate practices) operate in other, larger forums. For example, Janet Atwill's *Rhetoric Reclaimed: Aristotle and the Liberal Arts Tradition* (1998) traces the tradition of social and political intervention identified with "Protagoras's political *technē* and Isocrates' *logōn technē* and preserved, in a somewhat modified form, in Aristotle's Rhetoric" (p. 1). Jarratt's *Rereading the Sophists: Classical Rhetoric Refigured* (1991) traces the antifoundational, self-consciously interpretive stance of the Sophists, who sought knowledge by embracing rather than routing out *dissoi logoi*—the presence of contradictory propositions. "The sophist found it both impossible and unnecessary to determine any single Truth about appearances; more important is negotiating useful courses of action for groups of people given their varying perceptions about the world" (p. 50). Gerard Hauser's *Vernacular Voices: The Rhetoric of Publics and Public Spheres* (1999), concerned with contemporary rhetoric and public deliberation, challenges Habermas's image of a unitary public sphere and the story of its loss. In Hauser's theoretical account, deliberation is carried on by *plural local* publics, organized as a network of discursive arenas "in which strangers develop and express public opinions. . . . These dialogizing interactions are our continuous means to form shared meaning; discover new cultural, political, and social possibilities; and shape an understanding of our common interests" (pp. 11–12).

17. Aristotle is often interpreted as supporting the superiority of dialectic (philosophic logic) over rhetoric's art built on techne, but Atwill argues that what he in fact asserted is that techne's mode of rhetoric is simply different—"a distinct model of knowledge, with its own boundaries, methods, and assumptions" (1998, p. 100).

18. Writing to technical communicators who are preparing students for civic engagement, Rude describes the process of delivery "by multiple media, by multiple voices over time" that it takes to shift policy (2004, p. 283).

9. Affirming a Contested Agency

1. As Higgins, Long, and Flower (2006) argue, this knowledge isn't necessarily cut off from formal public knowledge. For instance, a tenant may be fluent with many public institutions' forms, regulations, and procedures. But it is also the case that marginalized people often have something to say about institutional discourse that isn't usually part of collective social knowledge; moreover, they know something about the gaps between the professed intent of specific public policies, on the one hand, and how they play out in live experience, on the other.

2. For an introduction to the Think Tank methods and PDFs of its Findings and related research, see www.cmu.edu/thinktank. For an analysis of Think Tanks as a knowledge-building process, see Flower, 2002b.

3. The text in figures 9.2 and 9.3 come from the Think Tank's published *Findings*. Before the group session, participants also received a short briefing book with this same format including the scenario, the prompt questions, and some sample responses that we used to jump-start the discussion.

4. In a study of the CLC's Landlords and Tenants project, Higgins, Flower, and Deems (1996) compare these discussions to the dynamics of standard community meetings, and Flower and Deems (2002) track the way conflict leads to action in the absence of consensus.

5. The academic contribution is from J. Kirschenman and K. Neckerman (1991, pp. 203–31).

6. This insistence on workable options is one of the most difficult goals for participants to remain focused on (i.e., one constantly in need of reminder). But it is also what allowed the Think Tanks to create what I have described as a distinctive form of "working knowledge" (see Flower, 2002).

7. As Elenore Long (2008) points out, the term *local* functions with a load of implications. In rhetorical scholarship, it denotes an alternative, nonformal space. Observational studies populate these spaces with ordinary people, speaking an unprivileged vernacular, identified with the consequences of opening such a discursive space. Implicit in the term, Long argues, is the assumption that a more just public policy will take into account local values and practices.

8. Although I am speaking to the work of academics here, I can't overemphasize the absolutely central role of nonacademic partners who have the credibility to draw a wide network of community people into this local public. At one point in the history of the Think Tank, I was director of Carnegie Mellon's Center for University Outreach, which gave me a somewhat larger entrée into civic and professional circles, but the fresh insights and persuasive impact of these sessions depended more on the community participants, CBO workers, neighborhood opinion makers, church members, welfare-to-work employees, nurses aides, and teenagers with learning disabilities who asserted their rhetorical agency. The significance of our academic engagement rests on *their* contributions.

9. An analysis of an extended negotiation that rivaled and qualified the positions of an academic, manager, and union member is developed in "Intercultural Inquiry and Knowledge Building," Flower, 2002b.

10. Intercultural Inquiry: A Brief Guide

1. A good way to develop your own tool kit for inquiry is to reread these chapters and the studies cited, not just for claims but also to *mine* them for their methods. For discussions of specific observational methods see Coogan, 2006b; Cushman, 1998; Engeström, 1993; Flower, 1997b, 1998, 2002b; Greene and Higgins, 1994. The Carnegie Mellon Think Tank Web site, www.cmu.edu/thinktank, documents a variety of techniques for inquiry and dialogue. At my institution, rhetorical investigation and think-tank development became an explicitly structured process and a course unit. As an alternative to standard techniques of library research and survey data, it allowed writing majors to fulfill a department research requirement.

References

Adler-Kassner, L., Crooks, R., & Watters, A. (Eds.). (1997). *Writing the community: Concepts and models for service-learning in composition* (Vol. 1). Washington, DC: American Association for Higher Education.

Alinsky, S. D. (1989). *Rules for radicals: A practical primer for realistic radicals.* New York: Vintage Books.

Alliance of Rhetoric Societies. (2003, September). *Position papers regarding agency.* Paper presented at the meeting of the Alliance of Rhetoric Societies, Evanston, IL.

Anzaldúa, G. (1987). *Borderlands/la frontera: The new mestiza.* San Francisco: Spinster/Aunt Lute Books.

Applebee, A. N. (1986). Problems in process approaches: Toward a reconceptualization of process instruction. In A. R. Petrosky and D. Bartholomae (Eds.), *The teaching of writing* (pp. 95–113). Chicago: National Society for the Study of Education.

Ashby, A. (1996, Fall). The story-behind-the-story strategy might make the curfew safer for teens and cops. In *Raising the curtain on curfew.* [Booklet]. Pittsburgh, PA: Community Literacy Center. Retrieved December 3, 2007, from Carnegie Mellon Web site: http://english.cmu.edu/research/inquiry/two.html.

Atwill, J. (1998). *Rhetoric reclaimed: Aristotle and the liberal arts tradition.* Ithaca, NY: Cornell UP.

Atwill, J., & Lauer, J. (Eds.). (2002). *Perspectives on rhetorical invention.* Knoxville: U of Tennessee P.

Bacon, N., & Deans, T. (1997). Community service and composition: Annotated bibliography. In L. Adler-Kassner, R. Crooks, & A. Watters (Eds.), *Writing the community: Concepts and models for service-learning in composition* (Vol. l, pp. 181–91). Washington, DC: American Association for Higher Education.

Bakhtin, M. M. (1981). *The dialogic imagination: Four essays by M. M. Bakhtin* (C. Emerson & M. Holquist, Trans.). Austin: U of Texas P.

Bakhtin, M. M. (1986). *Speech genres and other late essays* (V. W. McGee, Trans.). Austin: U of Texas P.

Balester, V. M. (1993). *Cultural divide: A study of African-American college-level writers.* Portsmouth, NH: Boynton/Cook.

Bartholomae, D. (1985). Inventing the university. In M. Rose (Ed.), *When a writer can't write: Studies in writer's block and other composing-process problems* (pp. 134–65). New York: Guilford Press.

Barton, D., & Hamilton, M. (1998). *Local literacies: Reading and writing in one community.* New York: Routledge.

Bazerman, C., & Russell, D. (Eds.). (2002). *Writing selves/writing societies: Research from activity perspectives.* Fort Collins, CO: WAC Clearing House and Mind Culture, and Activity. Retrieved December 3, 2007, from Colorado State University Web site: http://wac.colostate.edu/books/selves_societies/.

Belenky, M. F., Bond, L. A., & Weinstock, J. S. (1997). *A tradition that has no name: Nurturing the development of people, families, and communities.* New York: Basic Books.

Bellah, R., Madsen, R., Sullivan, W., Swidler, A., & Tipton, S. (1985). *Habits of the heart: Individualism and commitment in American life.* Berkeley: U of California P.

Benson, L., & Harkavy, I. (1991). Progressing beyond the welfare state. *Universities and Community Schools (University of Pennsylvania)*, 2(1&2), 2–28.

Berlin, J. (1988). Rhetoric and ideology in the writing class. *College English, 50*(5), 477–94.

Bizzell, P. (1982). Cognition, convention, and certainty: What we need to know about writing. *Pre/Text, 3*, 213–44.

Bizzell, P. (1992). *Academic discourse and critical consciousness*. Pittsburgh, PA: U of Pittsburgh P.

Bizzell, P. (2002). The intellectual work of "mixed" forms of academic discourses. In C. Schoeder, H. Fox, & P. Bizzell (Eds.), *Alt dis: Alternative discourses and the academy* (pp. 1–10). Portsmouth, NH: Boynton/Cook.

Black Public Sphere Collective. (1995). *The black public sphere*. Chicago: U of Chicago P.

Borg, M. J. (1987). *Jesus: A new vision: Spirit, culture, and the life of discipleship*. San Francisco: Harper & Row.

Boyd, F. (1996, Fall). Bad experiences after hours. In *Raising the curtain on curfew*. [Booklet]. Pittsburgh, PA: Community Literacy Center. Retrieved December 3, 2007, from Carnegie Mellon Web site: http://english.cmu.edu/research/inquiry/two.html.

Boydston, J. A. (Ed.). (1988). *John Dewey: The later works, 1925–1953* (Vol. 4: 1929). Carbondale: Southern Illinois UP.

Brown, S. G. (2000). *Words in the wilderness: Critical literacy in the borderlands*. Albany: State U of New York P.

Brueggemann, Walter. (1978). *The prophetic imagination*. Decatur, GA: Fortress Press.

Buber, M. (1958). *I and thou*. New York: Charles Scribner's Sons.

Burke, K. (1950). *A rhetoric of motives*. Englewood Cliffs, NJ: Prentice Hall.

Burnett, R. E. (1991). *Conflict in the collaborative planning of coauthors: How substantive conflict, representation of task, and dominance relate to high-quality documents*. Unpublished doctoral dissertation, Carnegie Mellon University, Pittsburgh, PA.

Canagarajah, A. S. (1997). Safe houses in the contact zone: Coping strategies of African-American students in the academy. *College Composition and Communication, 48*(1), 173–96.

Carter, M. (1990). The idea of expertise: An exploration of cognitive and social dimensions of writing. *College Composition and Communication, 41*(3), 265–86.

Chai, G., Clark, A., Gilbert, A., Knittel, E., Milhelic, J., Schwartz, C., et al. (1999). *Campus campaign*. Unpublished manuscript, Carnegie Mellon University.

Chaiklin, S., & Lave, J. (Eds.). (1993). *Understanding practice: Perspectives on activity and context*. Cambridge, England: Cambridge UP.

Cintron, R. (1997). *Angels' town: Chero ways, gang life, and rhetorics of the everyday*. Boston: Beacon Press.

Cohen, A. P. (1985). *The symbolic construction of community*. New York: Routledge.

Coles, R. (1993). *The call of service: A witness to idealism*. New York: Houghton Mifflin.

Coles, W. E. (1978). *The Plural I*. New York: Holt, Rinehart, & Winston.

Coogan, D. (2002). Public rhetoric and public safety at the Chicago Transit Authority: Three approaches to accident analysis. *Journal of Business and Technical Communication, 16*(3), 227–305.

Coogan, D. (2005). Counterpublics in public housing: Rethinking the politics of service. *College English, 67*(5), 461–82.

Coogan, D. (2006a). Community literacy as civic dialogue. *Community Literacy, 1*(1), 95–108.

Coogan, D. (2006b). Service learning and social change: The case for materialist rhetoric. *College Composition and Communication, 57*(4), 667–93.

Cooper, D., & Fretz, E. (2006). The service-learning writing project: Re-writing the humanities through service-learning and public work. *Reflections, 5*(1), 133–52.

Cooper, D., & Julier, L. (1995). *Writing in the public interest: Service-learning and the writing classroom.* East Lansing: Writing Center of Michigan State University.

Cushman, E. (1996). Rhetorician as an agent of social change. *College Composition and Communication, 47*(1), 7–28.

Cushman, E. (1998). *The struggle and the tools: Oral and literate strategies in an inner-city community.* Albany: State U of New York P.

Cushman, E. (1999). Opinion: The public intellectual, service learning, and activist research. *College English, 61*(3), 328–36.

Cushman, E. (2003). Beyond specialization: The public intellectual, outreach, and rhetoric education. In J. Petraglia & D. Bahri (Eds.), *The realms of rhetoric* (pp. 171–85). Albany: State U of New York P.

Cushman, E. (2006). Toward a praxis of new media. *Reflections, 5*(1&2), 111–32.

Cushman, E., Kintgen, E., Kroll, B., & Rose, M. (Eds.). (2001). *Literacy: A critical sourcebook.* Boston: Bedford/St. Martin's.

Deans, T. (1999, Fall). Service-learning in two keys: Paulo Freire's critical pedagogy in relation to John Dewey's pragmatism. *Michigan Journal of Community Service Learning, 6*, 15–29.

Deans, T. (2000). *Writing partnerships: Service-learning in composition.* Urbana, IL: National Council of Teachers of English.

Deans, T. (2007). Writing pragmatically: John Dewey's philosophy of education, Richard Rorty's social hope, and service-learning in composition. Manuscript in preparation.

Deems, J., & Flower, L. (1996). Rivaling about Risk: A Dialogue Tutorial. [Interactive hypercard program]. Pittsburgh, PA: Community Literacy Center.

Delpit, L. D. (1986). Skills and other dilemmas of a progressive black educator. *Harvard Educational Review, 56*(4), 379–85.

Delpit, L. D. (1988). The silenced dialogue: Power and pedagogy in educating other people's children. *Harvard Educational Review, 58*(3), 280–98.

Dewey, J. (1964). The nature of aims. In R. Archambault (Ed.), *John Dewey on education* (pp. 70–80). Chicago: U of Chicago P. (Reprinted from *Human Nature and Conduct*, Henry Holt, 1922).

Dewey, J. (1966). *Democracy and education: An introduction to the philosophy of education.* New York: Free Press. (Original work published 1916).

Dewey, J. (1988). *The quest for certainty.* In J. A. Boydston (Ed.), *John Dewey: The later works, 1925–1953* (Vol. 4: 1929). Carbondale: Southern Illinois UP. (Original work published 1929).

Dickens, C. (1950). *David Copperfield.* New York: Modern Library. (Original work published 1849).

Dobrin, S. (1997). Race and the public intellectual: A conversation with Michael Eric Dyson. *JAC, 17*(2), 7–28.

Dobrin, S. (2002). The problem with writing (about) "alternative" discourse. In C. Schoeder, H. Fox, & P. Bizzell (Eds.), *Alt dis: Alternative discourses and the academy* (pp. 45–56). Portsmouth, NH: Boynton/Cook.

DuBois, W. E. B. (1961). *Souls of black folk.* New York: Fawcett. (Original work published 1903).

Engeström, Y. (1993). Developmental studies of work as a testbench of activity theory: The case of primary care medical practice. In S. Chaiklin & J. Lave (Eds.), *Understanding practice: Perspectives on activity and context* (pp. 64–103). Cambridge, England: Cambridge University Press.

Engeström, Y. (1997). Coordination, cooperation, and communication in the courts: Expansive transitions in legal work. In M. Cole, Y. Engeström, and O. Vasquez (Eds.), *Mind, culture, and activity: Seminal papers from the Laboratory of Comparative Human Cognition* (pp. 369–85). Cambridge: Cambridge UP.

Engeström, Y. (1999). Activity theory and individual and social transformation. In Y. Engeström, R. Miettinen, and R.-L. Punamäki (Eds.), *Perspectives on activity theory* (pp. 19–38). Cambridge, England: Cambridge UP.

Enos, T., and Brown, S. C. (Eds.). (1993). *Defining the new rhetorics.* Sage series in written communication. Newbury Park, CA, Sage.

Faber, B. (2002). *Community action and organizational change.* Carbondale: Southern Illinois UP.

Faigley, L. (1992). *Fragments of rationality: Postmodernity and the subject of composition.* Pittsburgh, PA: U of Pittsburgh P.

Farrell, T. (1991). Practicing the arts of rhetoric: Tradition and invention. *Philosophy and Rhetoric, 24,* 183–212.

Fero, M., Ridolfo, J., Chrobak, J. M., Duinen, D. V. V., Wirtz, J., Cushman, E., & Grabill, G. T. (2007). A reflection on teaching and learning in a community literacies graduate course. *Community Literacy, 1*(2), 81–93.

Finn, P. J. (1999). *Literacy with an attitude: Educating working-class children in their own self-interest.* Albany: State U of New York P.

Flach, J. (1999). *Making a difference with difference: A study of mutual situated meaning making construction through strategic intercultural interpretation and inquiry.* Unpublished doctoral dissertation, Carnegie Mellon University, Pittsburgh, PA.

Flanagan, J. C. (1954). The critical incident. *Psychological Bulletin, 51*(4), 327–58.

Flower, L. (1979). Writer-based prose: A cognitive basis for problems in writing. *College English, 41*(1), 19–37.

Flower, L. (1988). The construction of purpose in writing and reading. *College English, 50*(5), 528–50.

Flower, L. (1989). Cognition, context, and theory building. *College Composition and Communication, 40*(3), 282–311.

Flower, L. (1993). Cognitive rhetoric: Inquiry into the art of inquiry. In T. Enos & S. C. Brown (Eds.), *Defining the new rhetorics* (Vol. 7, pp. 171–90). Newbury Park, CA: Sage.

Flower, L. (1994). *The construction of negotiated meaning: A social cognitive theory of writing.* Carbondale: Southern Illinois UP.

Flower, L. (1996a). Literate action. In L. Z. Bloom, D. A. Daiker, & E. M. White (Eds.), *Composition in the twenty-first century: Crisis and change* (pp. 249–60). Carbondale: Southern Illinois UP.

Flower, L. (1996b). Negotiating the meaning of difference. *Written Communication, 13*(1), 44–92.

Flower, L. (1997a). Partners in inquiry: A logic for community outreach. In L. Adler-Kassner, R. Crooks, & A. Watters (Eds.), *Writing the community: Concepts and models for service-learning composition* (pp. 95–117). Washington, DC: American Association for Higher Education.

Flower, L. (1997b). Observation-based theory building. In G. A. Olson & T. W. Taylor (Eds.), *Publishing in rhetoric and composition* (pp. 163–85). Albany: State U of New York P.

Flower, L. (1998). *Problem-solving strategies for writing in college and community.* Fort Worth, TX: Harcourt Brace College.

Flower, L. (2002a). Intercultural inquiry and the transformation of service. *College English, 65*(2), 181–201.

Flower, L. (2002b). Intercultural knowledge building: The literate action of a community think tank. In C. B. D. Russell (Ed.), *Writing selves/writing societies: Research from activity perspectives* (pp. 239–79). Fort Collins, CO: WAC Clearinghouse & Mind, Culture, and Activity. Available from http://wac.colostate.edu/books/selves_societies/.

Flower, L. (2003). Talking across difference: Intercultural rhetoric and the search for situated knowledge. *College Composition and Communication, 55*(1), 38–68.

Flower, L., & Deems, J. (2002). Conflict in community collaboration. In J. M. Atwill & J. Lauer (Eds.), *Perspectives on rhetorical invention* (pp. 96–130). Knoxville: U of Tennessee P.

Flower, L., & Flach, J. (1996). *Working partners: An urban youth project on risk, stress, and respect.* Pittsburgh, PA: Community Literacy Center and Carnegie Mellon University. Retrieved December 3, 2007, from Carnegie Mellon Web site: http://english.cmu.edu/research/inquiry/five.html. Reprinted in Flower, 1998.

Flower, L., & Hayes, J. R. (1980). The dynamics of composing: Making plans and juggling constraints. In L. Gregg & E. Steinberg (Eds.), *Cognitive processes in writing: An interdisciplinary approach* (pp. 31–50). Hillsdale, NJ: Erlbaum.

Flower, L., & Hayes, J. R. (1981). A cognitive process theory of writing. *College Composition and Communication, 32*(1), 365–87.

Flower, L., & Hayes, J. R. (1984). Images, plans, and prose: The representation of meaning in writing. *Written Communication, 1*(1), 120–60.

Flower, L., & Heath, S. B. (2000). Drawing on the local: Collaboration and community expertise [Special issue: Service learning]. *Language and learning across the disciplines, 4*(3), 43–55.

Flower, L., Long, E., & Higgins, L. (2000). *Learning to rival: A literate practice for intercultural inquiry.* Mahwah, NJ: Erlbaum.

Flower, L., Schriver, K. A., Carey, L., Haas, C., & Hayes, J. R. (1992). Planning in writing: The cognition of a constructive process. In S. P. Witte, N. Nakadate, & R. D. Cherry (Eds.), *A rhetoric of doing: Essays on written discourse in honor of James L. Kinneavy* (pp. 181–243). Carbondale: Southern Illinois UP.

Flower, L., Stein, V., Ackerman, J., Kantz, M. J., McCormick, K., & Peck, W. C. (1990). *Reading-to-write: Exploring a cognitive and social process.* New York: Oxford UP.

Flower, L., Wallace, D. L., Norris, L., & Burnett, R. E. (Eds.). (1994). *Making thinking visible: Writing, collaborative planning, and classroom inquiry.* Urbana, IL: National Council of Teachers of English.

Foucault, M. (1977). What is an author? (D. F. Bouchard & S. Simon, Trans.). In D. F. Bouchard (Ed.), *Language, counter-memory, practice* (pp. 124–27). Ithaca, NY: Cornell UP.

Fox, H. (2002). Being an ally. In C. Schoeder, H. Fox, & P. Bizzell (Eds.), *Alt dis: Alternative discourses and the academy* (pp. 57–68). Portsmouth, NH: Boynton/Cook.

Fraser, N. (1990). Rethinking the public sphere: A contribution to the critique of actually existing democracy. *Social Text, 25/26*, 58–60.

Freire, P. (1985). *Pedagogy of the oppressed* (M. B. Ramos, Trans.). New York: Continuum. (Original work published in 1970).

Gabor, C. (2006). Ethics and expectations: Developing a workable balance between academic goals and ethical behavior. *Reflections, 5*(1&2), 27–48.

Gaonkar, D. (1993). The idea of rhetoric in the rhetoric of science. *Southern Communication Journal, 58*(4), 258–95.

Gates, H. L. J. (1988). *The signifying monkey: A theory of Afro-American literary criticism.* New York: Oxford UP.

Gates, H. L. J. (1991). Critical Fanonism. *Critical Inquiry, 17*, 457–70.

Gee, J. P. (1989). Literacy, discourse, and linguistics: Introduction. *Journal of Education, 171*(1), 5–17.

Gee, J. P. (2000). The new literacy studies: From 'socially situated' to the work of the social. In D. Barton, M. Hamilton & R. Ivanic (Eds.), *Situated literacies: Reading and writing in context* (pp. 180–96). New York: Routledge.

Gee, J. P., Hull, G. A., & Lankshear, C. (1996). *The new work order: Behind the language of the new capitalism.* Boulder, CO: Westview Press.

Geertz, C. (1983). *Local knowledge: Further essays in interpretive anthropology.* New York: Basic Books.

George, D. (2002). The word on the street. *Reflections, 2*(2), 5–18.

Gilligan, C. (1993). *In a different voice: Psychological theory and women's development.* Cambridge, MA: Harvard UP. (Original work published 1982).

Gilpin, S. (2004). *Heuretic engagement: Everyday talk about social issues.* Unpublished doctoral dissertation, Carnegie Mellon University, Pittsburgh, PA.

Gilyard, K. (1991). *Voices of the self: A study of language competence.* Detroit, MI: Wayne State UP.

Goggin, M. D. (Ed.). (2000). *Inventing a discipline: Rhetoric scholarship in honor of Richard E. Young.* Urbana, IL: National Council of Teachers of English.

Goldblatt, E. (1994). Van rides in the dark: Literacy as involvement in a college literacy practicum. *Journal for Peace and Justice Studies, 6*(1), 77–94.

Goldblatt, E. (2005). Alinsky's reveille: A community-organizing model of neighborhood-based literacy projects. *College English, 67*(3), 274–95.

Goldblatt, E. (2007). *Because we live here: Sponsoring literacy beyond the curriculum.* Cresskill, N.J.: Hampton P.

Grabill, J. T. (2001). *Community literacy programs and the politics of change.* Albany: State U of New York P.

Grabill, J. T., & Simmons, W. M. (1998). Toward a critical rhetoric of risk communication: Producing citizens and the role of technical communication. *Technical Communication Quarterly, 7*(4), 415–41.

Greene, R. (2002). Rhetorical pedagogy as a postal system: Circulating subjects through Michael Warner's "Publics and counterpublics." *Quarterly Journal of Speech, 88*(4), 434–43.

Greene, S., & Higgins, L. (1994). "Once upon a time": The use of retrospective accounts in building theory in composition. In P. Smagorinsky (Ed.), *Speaking about writing: Reflections on research methodology* (Vol. 8, pp. 115–40). Thousand Oaks, CA: Sage.

Grossberg, L. (1986, Summer). On postmodernism and articulation: An interview with Stuart Hall. *Journal of Communication Inquiry, 10*(2), 45–60.

Gudykunst, W. (1983). *Intercultural communication theory: Current perspectives.* Beverly Hills, CA: Sage.

Gudykunst, W., & Kim, Y. (1997). *Communicating with strangers: An approach to intercultural communication.* New York: McGraw-Hill.

Gutman, A., & Thompson, D. (2004). *Why deliberative democracy.* Princeton, NJ: Princeton UP.

Haas, C., & Flower, L. (1988). Rhetorical reading strategies and the construction of meaning. *College Composition & Communication, 39*(2), 167–83.

Habermas, J. (1984). *A theory of communication action* (T. McCarthy, Trans., Vol. 1). Boston: Beacon Press. (Original work published 1981).

Habermas, J. (1989). *The structural transformation of the public sphere: An inquiry into a category of bourgeois society* (T. Burger with F. Lawrence, Trans.). Cambridge, MA: MIT Press. (Original work published 1962).

Haraway, D. (1991). *Simians, cyborgs, and women: The reinvention of nature.* New York: Routledge.

Harkavy, I., & Puckett, J. L. (1991). Toward effective university-public school partnerships: An analysis of a contemporary model. *Teachers College Record, 92*(4), 556–81.

Harris, J. (1989). The idea of community in the study of writing. *College Composition and Communication, 40*, 11–22.

Harris, J. (1992). The other reader. *JAC, 12*, 121–38.

Harris, J. (1997). *A teaching subject: Composition since 1966.* Upper Saddle River, NJ: Prentice-Hall.

Hauser, G. (1999). *Vernacular voices: The rhetoric of publics and public spheres.* Columbia: U of South Carolina P.

Hauser, G., & Grim, A. (Eds.). (2004). *Rhetorical democracy: Discursive practices of civic engagement.* Mahwah, NJ: Erlbaum.

Hayes, J. R., & Flower, L. (1980). Identifying the organization of writing processes. In L. Gregg & E. R. Steinberg (Eds.), *Cognitive processing in writing: An interdisciplinary approach* (pp. 3–30). Hillsdale, NJ: Erlbaum.

Heath, S. B. (1983). *Ways with words: Language, life, and work in communities.* Cambridge: Cambridge UP.

Heath, S. B., & McLaughlin, M. W. (Eds.). (1993). *Identity & inner-city youth: Beyond ethnicity and gender.* New York: Teachers College, Columbia University.

Heath, S. B., & Smyth, L. (1999). *ArtShow: Youth and community development.* Washington, DC: Partners for Livable Communities.

Heller, C. E. (1997). *Until we are strong together: Women writers in the tenderloin.* New York: Teachers College, Columbia University.

Herndl, C. (2004). The legacy of critique and the promise of practice. *Journal of Professional and Technical Communication, 18*, 3–8.

Herzberg, B. (1994). Community service and critical teaching. *College Composition and Communication, 45*, 307–19.

Herzberg, B. (2000). Service learning and public discourse. *JAC, 20*(2), 391–405.

Higgins, L. (1992). *Argument as construction: A framework and method.* Unpublished doctoral dissertation, Carnegie Mellon University, Pittsburgh, PA.

Higgins, L., & Brush, L. (2006). Personal experience narrative and public debate: Writing the wrongs of welfare. *College Composition and Communication, 57,* 694–729.

Higgins, L., & Chalich, T. (Eds.). (1996). *Getting to know you: A dialogue for community health. Discussion points for women and their health care providers.* Pittsburgh, Pa: Community Literacy Center and Rainbow Health Clinic. Retrieved December 3, 2007, from Carnegie Mellon Web site: http://english.cmu.edu/research/inquiry/five.html.

Higgins, L., Flower, L., & Deems, J. (1996). *Collaboration and community action: Landlords and tenants.* Unpublished manuscript, Pittsburgh, PA.

Higgins, L., Long, E., & Flower, L. (2006). Community literacy: A rhetorical model of personal and public inquiry. *Community Literacy, 1*(1), 9–43.

hooks, b. (1989). *Talking back: Thinking feminist, thinking black.* Boston, MA: South End Press.

Howard, M. (1992, Fall). Communication breakdown: "Whassup with suspension?" The real scoop. In *Raising the curtain on curfew* (p. 2). [Booklet]. Pittsburgh, PA: Community Literacy Center. Retrieved December 3, 2007, from Carnegie Mellon Web site: http://english.cmu.edu/research/inquiry/two.html.

Howard, M. (1993, Fall). A usual day in Wilkinsburg. In *Community Literacy* (pp. 1, 3). [Booklet]. Pittsburgh, PA: Community Literacy Center. Retrieved December 3, 2007, from Carnegie Mellon Web site: http://english.cmu.edu/research/inquiry/two.html.

Hull, G. A. (1993). Hearing other voices: A critical assessment of popular views on literacy and work. *Harvard Educational Review, 61*(1), 21–49.

Hull, G. A. (Ed.). (1997). *Changing work, changing workers: Critical perspectives on language, literacy, and skills.* Albany: State U of New York P.

Hull, G. A. (2003). Youth culture and digital media: New literacies for new times. *Research in teaching, 38*(2), 229–33.

Hull, G. A., & James, M. A. (2007). Geographies of hope: A study of urban landscape and a university-community collaborative. In P. O'Neill (Ed.), *Blurring boundaries: Developing writers, researchers, and teachers: A tribute to William L. Smith* (pp. 255–89). Cresskill, NJ: Hampton Press.

Hull, G. A., & Katz, M.-L. (2006 August). Crafting an agentive self: Case studies of digital storytelling. *Research in Teaching of English, 41*(1), 43–82.

Hull, G. A., & Rose, M. (1989, April). Rethinking remediation: Towards a social-cognitive understanding of problematic reading and writing. *Written Communication, 6*(2), 139–54.

Hull, G. A., & Schultz, K. (2001, Winter). Literacy and learning out of school: A review of theory and research. *Review of Educational Research, 71*(4), 575–611.

Hull, G. A., & Schultz, K. (2002). *School's out! Bridging out-of-school literacies with classroom practice.* New York: Teachers College Press.

Hymes, D., & Gumperz, J. (Eds.). (1972). *Directions in sociolinguistics: The ethnography of communication.* New York: Holt, Rinehart, and Winston.

Intercultural Inquiry Website. (1999). Carnegie Mellon University, Pittsburgh, PA.

Available on Carnegie Mellon Web site: http://english.cmu.edu/research/inquiry/default.html.

James, W. (1967). What pragmatism means. In J. J. McDermott (Ed.), *The writings of William James: A comprehensive edition* (pp. 376–90). New York: Random House. (Original work published 1907).

Jarratt, S. C. (1991a). Feminism and composition: The case for conflict. In P. Harkin & J. Schilb (Eds.), *Contending with words: Composition and rhetoric in a postmodern age* (pp. 105–23). New York: Modern Language Association of America.

Jarratt, S. C. (1991b). *Rereading the Sophists: Classical rhetoric refigured.* Carbondale: Southern Illinois UP.

Johnson, C. (1992). *Tina: A portrait of literate awareness.* Unpublished manuscript, Carnegie Mellon University, Pittsburgh, PA. Retrieved December 3, 2007, from Carnegie Mellon Web site: http://english.cmu.edu/research/inquiry.

Jury, M. (1997). Widening the narrowed paths of applied communication: Thinking a curriculum big enough for students. In G. A. Hull (Ed.), *Changing work, changing workers: Critical perspectives on language, literacy, and skills* (pp. 214–45). Albany: State U of New York P.

Kates, S. (2001). *Activist rhetorics and American higher education 1885–1937.* Carbondale: Southern Illinois UP.

Keith, N. Z. (1997). Doing service projects in urban settings. In A. Waterman (Ed.), *Service learning: Applications from the research* (pp. 127–49). Mahwah, NJ: Erlbaum.

Kells, M. H., Balester, V., & Villanueva, V. (Eds.). (2004). *Latino/a discourses: On language, identity, and literacy education.* Portsmouth, NH: Boyton/Cook, Heinemann.

Kendall, J. C., & Associates. (1990). *Combining service and learning: A resource book for community and public service.* (Vol. 1). Raleigh, NC: National Society for Internships and Experiential Education.

Kirsch, G., Maor, F., Massey, L., Nickoson-Massey, L., & Sheridan-Rabideau, M. (Eds.). (2003). *Feminism and composition: A critical sourcebook.* Boston: Bedford/St. Martin's.

Kirschenman, J., & Neckerman, K. (1991). 'We'd love to hire them, but . . . ': The meaning of race for employers. In C. Jencks & P. Peters (Eds.), *The urban underclass* (pp. 203–31). Washington, DC: Brookings Institute.

Kotlowitz, A. (1991). *There are no children here.* New York: Doubleday.

Labov, W. (1972). *Language in the inner city: Studies in the Black English vernacular.* Philadelphia: U of Pennsylvania P.

Lauer, J., Young, R. E., & Liu, Y. (Eds.). (1994). *Landmark essays in rhetorical invention.* Davis, CA: Hermagoras Press.

Lave, J. (1993). The practice of learning. In S. Chaiklin & J. Lave (Eds.), *Understanding practice: Perspectives on activity and context* (pp. 3–32). Cambridge, England: Cambridge UP.

Lawrence, S. (1996). "Reading others' realities: Double-sided discourse moves." Unpublished manuscript, Carnegie Mellon University, Pittsburgh, PA.

Lee, C. D. (1993). *Signifying as a scaffold for literary interpretation: The pedagogical implications of an African American discourse genre.* Urbana, IL: National Council of Teachers of English.

Leff, M. (1993). The idea of rhetoric as interpretive practice: A humanist's response to Gaonkar. *Southern Communication Journal, 58*(4), 296–300.

Lerner, M., & West, C. (1996). *Jews & blacks: A dialogue on race, religion, and culture in America*. New York: Plume/Penguin.

Lipscomb, D. (1995). Sojourner Truth: A practical public discourse. In A. Lunsford (Ed.), *Reclaiming rhetorica: Women in the rhetorical tradition* (pp. 227–45). Pittsburgh: U of Pittsburgh P.

Logan, S. W. (1999). *"We are coming": The persuasive discourse of nineteenth-century black women*. Carbondale: Southern Illinois UP.

Long, E. (1994). *The rhetoric of literate social action: Mentors negotiating intercultural images of literacy*. Unpublished doctoral dissertation, Carnegie Mellon University, Pittsburgh, PA.

Long, E. (2000). The rhetoric of social action: College mentors inventing the discipline. In M. D. Goggin (Ed.), *Inventing a discipline: Rhetoric scholarship in honor of Richard E. Young* (pp. 289–318). Urbana, IL: National Council of Teachers of English.

Long, E. (2008). *Community literacy and the rhetoric of local publics*. West Lafayette, IN: Parlor Press.

Long, E., Fleming, D., & Flower, L. (2000). Rivaling at the CLC: The logic of a strategic process. In L. Flower, E. Long, & L. Higgins (Eds.), *Learning to rival: A literate practice for intercultural inquiry* (pp. 255–76). Mahwah, NJ: Erlbaum.

Long, E., Peck, W., & Baskins, J. (2002). STRUGGLE: A literate practice supporting life-project planning. In G. A. Hull & K. Schultz (Eds.), *School's out! Bridging out-of-school literacies with classroom practice* (pp. 131–61). New York: Teachers College Press.

Lunsford, A. (Ed.). (1995). *Reclaiming rhetorica: Women in the rhetorical tradition*. Pittsburgh, PA: U of Pittsburgh P.

Lunsford, A. (1998). Toward a mestiza rhetoric: Gloria Anzaldúa on composition and postcoloniality. *JAC, 18*(1), 1–27.

Lyle, S. (1994, Fall). A wake up call for adults. *Listen up! Teen stress*. [Booklet]. Pittsburgh, PA: Community Literacy Center. Retrieved December 3, 2007, from Carnegie Mellon Web site: http://english.cmu.edu/research/inquiry/two.html.

Lynch, D. A., George, D., & Cooper, M. M. (1997, February). Moments of argument: Agonistic inquiry and confrontational cooperation. *College Composition and Communication, 48*(1), 61–85.

Lyons, S. R. (2000, February). Rhetorical sovereignty: What do American Indians want from writing? *College Composition and Communication, 51*(3), 447–68.

Lyons, S. R. (2000, December). Review of *Words in the Wilderness*. *College Composition and Communication, 52*(2), 306–8.

Macrorie, K. (1970). *Uptaught*. New York: Hayden Book.

Mathieu, P. (2005). *Tactics of hope: The public turn in English composition*. Portsmouth, NH: Boyton/Cook, Heinemann.

McComiskey, B., & Ryan, C. (Eds.). (2003). *City comp: Identities, spaces, practices*. Albany: State U of New York P.

McGee, M. (1990). Text, context, and the fragmentation of contemporary culture. *Western Journal of Speech Communication, 54*, 274–89.

McKerrow, R. (1989). Critical rhetoric: Theory and praxis. *Communication Monographs, 56*, 91–111.

McKnight, J. (1995). *The careless society: Community and its counterfeits*. New York: Basic Books.

McLaughlin, M. W., Irby, M. A., & Langman, J. (1994). *Urban sanctuaries: Neighborhood organizations in the lives and futures of inner-city youth.* San Francisco: Jossey-Bass.

Mertz, J., & Schroerlucke, K. (1998). *Computer science in the community.* Pittsburgh, PA: Carnegie Mellon Center for University Outreach.

Miller, T. P. (2003). Changing the Subject. In J. Petraglia & D. Bahri (Eds.), *The realms of rhetoric* (pp. 73–89). Albany: State U of New York P.

Minter, D. W., Gere, A. R., & Keller-Cohen, D. (1995). Learning literacies. *College English, 57*(6), 669–87.

Moneyhun, C. (1996). *Stories out of school: Literacies of the academy, the community, and the home.* Unpublished doctoral dissertation, University of Arizona, Tucson.

Moore, M., & Warnock, J. (2007). Note from the editors. *Community Literacy, 1*(2), 9–11.

Moss, B. (2003). *A community text arises: A literate text and a literacy tradition in African-American churches.* Cresskill, NJ: Hampton Press.

Mowitt, J. (1988). Foreword. The Resistance in Theory. In P. Smith (Ed.), *Discerning the subject* (pp. ix–xxiv). Minneapolis: U of Minnesota P.

Musgrove, R. (1992, Summer). A teenager that needs help but don't know how to face it. In *Let's talk about sex drugs* (pp. 10–12). [Booklet]. Pittsburgh, PA: Community Literacy Center. Retrieved December 3, 2007, from Carnegie Mellon Web site: http://english.cmu.edu/research/inquiry/two.html.

Niebuhr, H. R. (1963). *The responsible self: An essay in Christian moral philosophy.* New York: Harper & Row.

North, S. M. (1987). *The making of knowledge in composition: Portrait of an emerging field.* Upper Montclair, NJ: Boynton/Cook.

Nystrand, M., Greene, S., & Wiemelt, J. (1993, July). Where did composition studies come from? An intellectual history. *Written Communication, 10*(3), 267–333.

Ogbu, J. U. (1992 November). Understanding cultural diversity and learning. *Educational Researcher, 21*(8), 5–14.

Paris, B. (2000). *Songs of Haiti: The lives of Dr. Larimer and Gwen Mellon at the Albert Schweitzer Hospital of Deschapelles.* New York: PublicAffairs.

Parks, S. (1999). *Class politics: The movement for the students' right to their own language.* Urbana, IL: National Council of Teachers of English.

Peck, W. C. (1991). *Community advocacy: Composing for action.* Unpublished doctoral dissertation, Carnegie Mellon University, Pittsburgh, PA.

Peck, W. C., Flower, L., & Higgins, L. (1995). Community literacy. *College Composition and Communication, 46*(2), 199–222.

Pincus, T., & Callahan, L. (1994). Associations of low formal education level and poor health status: Behavioral, in addition to demographic and medical, explanations? *Journal of Clinical Epidemiology, 47*, 355–61.

Pough, G. D. (2002, February). Empowering rhetoric: Black students writing Black Panthers. *College Composition and Communication, 53*(3), 466–86.

Poulakos, J. (1983). Toward a sophistic definition of rhetoric. *Philosophy and Rhetoric, 16*, 35–48.

Pratt, M. L. (1991). Arts of the contact zone. In *Profession 91* (pp. 33–40). New York: Modern Language Association of America.

Prendergast, C. (1998, September). Race: The absent presence in composition studies. *College Composition and Communication, 50*(1), 36–53.

Prior, P. (1997). Literate activity and disciplinarity: The heterogeneous (re)production of American studies around a graduate seminar. *Mind, Culture, and Activity, 4*(4), 275–95.

Roberts-Miller, P. (2004). *Deliberate conflict: Argument, political theory, and composition classes.* Carbondale: Southern Illinois UP.

Robinson, J. (1990). *Conversations on the written word.* Portsmouth, NH: Boynton/ Cook.

Rose, M. (1989). *Lives on the boundary: The struggles and achievements of America's underprepared.* New York: Free Press.

Rousculp, T. (2006). When the community writes. *Reflections, 5*(1–2), 67–88.

Royster, J. J. (1995). To call a thing by its true name: The rhetoric of Ida B. Wells. In A. Lunsford (Ed.), *Reclaiming rhetorica: Women in the rhetorical tradition* (pp. 167–84). Pittsburgh, PA: U of Pittsburgh P.

Royster, J. J. (1996, February). When the first voice you hear is not your own. *College Composition and Communication, 47*(1), 29–40.

Rude, C. (2004). Toward an expanded concept of rhetorical delivery: The uses of reports in public policy debates. *Technical Communication Quarterly, 13*(3), 271–88.

Schaafsma, D. (1993). *Eating on the street: Teaching literacy in a multicultural society.* Pittsburgh, PA: U of Pittsburgh P.

Schutz, A., & Gere, A. R. (1998, February). Service learning and English studies: Rethinking "public" service. *College English, 60*(2), 129–49.

Scribner, S., & Cole, M. (1981). *The psychology of literacy.* Cambridge, MA: Harvard UP.

Serow, R. (1997). Research and evaluation on service-learning: The case for holistic assessment. In A. Waterman (Ed.), *Service-learning: Applications from the research.* Mahwah, NJ: Erlbaum.

Shor, I. (Ed.). (1987). *Freire for the classroom: A sourcebook for liberatory teaching.* Portsmouth, NH: Boynton/Cook.

Shor, I. (1999). What is critical literacy? In I. Shore & C. Pari (Eds.), *Critical literacy in action* (pp. 1–30). Portsmouth, NH: Boynton/Cook.

Shor, I., & Pari, C. (Eds.). (1999). *Critical literacy in action: Writing words, changing worlds.* Portsmouth, NH: Boynton/Cook.

Simmons, W. M., & Grabill, J. (2007). Toward a civic rhetoric for technologically and scientifically complex places: Invention, performance, and participation. *College Composition and Communication, 58*(3), 419–48.

Smith, P. (1988). *Discerning the subject.* Minneapolis: U of Minnesota P.

Spellmeyer, K. (1993). *Common ground: Dialogue, understanding and the teaching of composition.* Englewood Cliffs, NJ: Prentice-Hall.

Spellmeyer, K. (2003). *Arts of living: Reinventing the humanities for the twenty-first century.* Albany: State U of New York P.

Spivak, G. (1988). Can the subaltern speak? In C. Nelson & L. Grossberg (Eds.), *Marxism and the interpretation of culture* (pp. 271–313). Urbana: U of Illinois P.

Stack, C. (1974). *All our kin: Strategies for survival in a black community.* New York: Harper & Row.

Stock, P. (1995). *The dialogic curriculum: Teaching and learning in a multicultural society.* Portsmouth, NH: Boynton/Cook–Heinemann.

Street, B. (2001). Literacy 'events' and literacy 'practices': Theory and practice in the 'New Literacy Studies.' In K. Jones & M. Martin-Jones (Eds.), *Multilingual literacies: Comparative perspectives on research and practice*. Amsterdam: John Benjamins.

Stringer, E. T. (1996). *Action research: A handbook for practitioners*. Thousand Oaks, CA: Sage.

Sullivan, P., & Porter, J. E. (1997). *Opening spaces: Writing technologies and critical research practices*. Greenwich, CT: Ablex.

Swales, J. M. (1998). *Other floors, other voices: A textography of a small university building*. Mahwah, NJ: Erlbaum.

Swan, S. (2002). Rhetoric, service, and social justice. *Written Communication, 19*(1), 76–108.

Taylor, C. (1985a). *Human agency and language: Philosophical papers* (Vol. 1). New York: Cambridge UP.

Taylor, C. (1985b). *Philosophy and the human sciences: Philosophical papers* (Vol. 2). New York: Cambridge UP.

Trimbur, J. (1989, October). Consensus and difference in collaborative learning. *College English, 51*(6), 602–16.

Trimbur, J. (2000). Composition and the circulation of writing. *College Composition and Communication, 52*(2), 188–219.

van Dijk, T. A. (1993). *Elite discourse and racism* (Vol. 6). Newbury Park, CA: Sage.

van Slyck, P. (1997). Repositioning ourselves in the contact zone. *College English, 59*, 149–70.

Villanueva, V. J. (1993). *Bootstraps: From an American academic of color*. Urbana, IL: National Council of Teachers of English.

Villanueva, V. J. (1997, Spring). Maybe a colony: And still another critique of the comp community. *JAC, 17*(2), 183–90.

Virgil, J. D. (1992). Gangs, social control, and ethnicity: Ways to redirect. In S. B. Heath & M. W. McLaughlin (Eds.), *Identity and inner-city youth: Beyond ethnicity and gender* (pp. 94–119). New York: Teachers College Press.

Wallace, D. L. (1996, May). From intentions to text: Articulating initial intentions for writing. *Research in the Teaching of English, 30*(2), 182–219.

Wallace, D., & Ewald, H. (2000). *Mutuality in the rhetoric and composition classroom*. Carbondale: Southern Illinois UP.

Warner, M. (2005). *Publics and counterpublics*. New York: Zone Books.

Waterman, A. S. (Ed.). (1997). *Service-learning: Applications from the research*. Mahwah, NJ: Erlbaum.

Watters, A., & Ford, M. (1995). *A guide for change: Resources for implementing community service writing*. New York: McGraw-Hill.

Weisser, C. (2002). *Moving beyond academic discourse: Composition studies and the public sphere*. Carbondale: Southern Illinois UP.

Wells, S. (1996, October). Rogue cops and health care: What do we want from public writing? *College Composition and Communication, 47*(3), 325–41.

Wertsch, J. V. (1991). *Voices of the mind: A sociocultural approach to mediated action*. Cambridge, MA: Harvard UP.

West, C. (1989). *The American evasion of philosophy: A genealogy of pragmatism*. Madison: U of Wisconsin P.

West, C. (1993). *Keeping faith: Philosophy and race in America*. New York: Routledge.

West, C. (1994). *Race matters*. New York: Vintage Books.

William T. Grant Foundation Commission on Work, Family, and Citizenship. (1988). *The forgotten half: Pathways to success for America's youth and young families*. Washington, DC: Author.

Willis, P. (1977). *Learning to labor: How working class kids get working class jobs*. Westmead, England: Saxon House.

Wilson, W. J. (1987). *The truly disadvantaged: The inner city, the underclass, and public policy*. Chicago: U of Chicago P.

Young, A. J. (1999). What's Your Plan? (Director 7.0.2) [Computer interactive multimedia software]. Pittsburgh, PA: Carnegie Mellon.

Young, A. J. (2000, May). *Patients as problem solvers: Toward a rhetoric of agency in healthcare*. Unpublished dissertation, Carnegie Mellon, Pittsburgh, PA.

Young, A. J., & Flower, L. (2002). Patients as partners: Patients as problem solvers. *Health Communication, 14*(1), 69–97.

Young, I. M. (1996). Communication and the other: Beyond deliberative democracy. In S. Benhabib (Ed.), *Democracy and difference: Contesting the boundaries of the political* (pp. 120–35). Princeton, NJ: Princeton UP.

Young, I. M. (1997). Difference as a resource for democratic communication. In J. Bohman & W. Regh (Eds.), *Deliberative democracy: Essays on reason and politics* (pp. 383–406). Cambridge, MA: MIT Press.

Young, R. E., Becker, A. L., & Pike, K. L. (1970). *Rhetoric: Discovery and change*. New York: Harcourt, Brace, & World.

Zlotkowski, E. (1996, January/February). A new voice at the table? Linking service-learning and the academy. *Change, 28*(1), 21–27.

Index

Italicized page numbers indicate figures.

Linda Flower is a professor of rhetoric at Carnegie Mellon University. Her previous books include *Problem Solving Strategies for Writing in College and Community* and *The Construction of Negotiated Meaning*, on social cognitive processes in writing, and *Learning to Rival*, on intercultural inquiry. She received the NCTE Braddock Award in 1987 and 1989 and the AERA Steve Witte Award in 2007.